UNDERSTANDING THE ARCHAEOLOGICAL RECORD

This book explores the diverse understandings of the archaeological record from historical and contemporary perspectives while also serving as a guide to reassessing current views. Gavin Lucas argues that archaeological theory has become too fragmented and disconnected from the particular nature of archaeological evidence. The book examines three ways of understanding the archaeological record – as historical sources, through formation theory, and as material culture – then reveals ways to connect these three domains through a reconsideration of archaeological entities and archaeological practice. Ultimately, Lucas calls for a rethinking of the nature of the archaeological record and the kind of history and narratives written from it.

GAVIN LUCAS is Associate Professor in the Department of Archaeology at the University of Iceland. He is the author of three books, *Critical Approaches to Fieldwork* (2001), *An Archaeology of Colonial Identity* (2004), and *The Archaeology of Time* (2005). He is also the editor of several volumes, including *Hofstaðir: Excavations of a Viking Age Feasting Hall* (2009), *Archaeologies of the Contemporary Past* (with Victor Buchli, 2001), and *Interpreting Archaeology* (with Ian Hodder, Michael Shanks, Alexandra Alexandri, Victor Buchli, John Carmen, and Jonathan Last, 1995).

T0381683

UNDERSTANDING THE ARCHAEOLOGICAL RECORD

Gavin Lucas

UNIVERSITY OF ICELAND

CAMBRIDGE
UNIVERSITY PRESS

CAMBRIDGE
UNIVERSITY PRESS

32 Avenue of the Americas, New York NY 10013-2473, USA

Cambridge University Press is part of the University of Cambridge.

It furthers the University's mission by disseminating knowledge in the pursuit of
education, learning and research at the highest international levels of excellence.

www.cambridge.org
Information on this title: www.cambridge.org/9780521279697

First published 2012

A catalogue record for this publication is available from the British Library

Library of Congress Cataloguing in Publication data

Lucas, Gavin, 1965–
Understanding the archaeological record / Gavin Lucas.
p.   cm.
Includes bibliographical references and index.
ISBN 978-1-107-01026-0 (hardback) – ISBN 978-0-521-27969-7 (paperback)
1. Archaeology – Philosophy.   2. Archaeology – Methodology.
3. History – Sources.   4. Ontology.   5. Antiquities.
6. Material culture.   7. Social archaeology.   I. Title.
CC72.L83   2012
930.1–dc23   2011033628

ISBN 978-1-107-01026-0 Hardback
ISBN 978-0-521-27969-7 Paperback

For Elín, Marteinn, and Benjamín

CONTENTS

ILLUSTRATIONS

ix

TABLES

PREFACE

This is one of those books that had a long gestation. It began primarily as an attempt to develop some of the themes explored in the last chapter of my book *Critical Approaches to Fieldwork* (Lucas 2001a; see also Lucas 2001b), in which I looked at the idea of archaeology as a materializing practice. These ideas were most immediately developed in the context of seminars I gave, first at the Department of Archaeology at Manchester University in 2002 and then at the Center for Archaeology at Stanford University in 2004. Much of this work has been used extensively in Chapter 6. I first started to write a book on this theme during a sabbatical break in Portugal in 2005, but it simply did not work. In the same year, however, I published a book called *The Archaeology of Time* (Lucas 2005), and the chapter I wrote on the archaeological record was instrumental in taking me in a new direction. Discussions on the subject with Tim Murray during this period were particularly influential (see e.g. Lucas 2007b), and these ultimately led me to develop the concept of a book on the archaeological record, but connecting it to my earlier interest in materiality. My sabbatical in the fall of 2008 took me back to Stanford, where I began work on the new manuscript in earnest. Over the next few years of writing the book, interrupted inevitably by other tasks, I also wrote and published a number of shorter articles in which I explored and rehearsed many of the themes addressed in this book, especially the rather complex ideas presented in Chapter 5 (e.g. Lucas 2007a, 2008, 2010b, 2010c).

Given all this, many people need to be thanked: the University of Iceland, for the time in which to write this book; the Archaeology Center at Stanford University, for hosting my sabbatical as a visiting scholar in 2008, especially Ian Hodder, Lynn Meskell, Michael Shanks, and Barbara Voss; Tim Murray, for his inspirational conversations on the archaeological record; Oscar Aldred, Tim Webmoor, Chris Witmore, and Tom Yarrow, for our various conversations on themes related to the ideas in this book; Astrid Daxböck, Natascha Mehler, and Aline Wacke, for help with the German references to archaeological source criticism discussed in Chapter 2 and especially Astrid for her translations. I particularly thank those who read draft versions of chapters for this book and offered valuable and critical comments in many key places: Victor Buchli, Steve Roskams, Michael Shott, Tim Webmoor, Chris Witmore, and Alison Wylie, as well as four anonymous reviewers. I am also very grateful to Beatrice Rehl of Cambridge University Press, who has managed the book from proposal to publication; Peggy Rote of Aptara, Inc., who supervised the production process; and Katherine Faydash, who edited the manuscript. My brother, Mark Lucas, kindly drew the cartoon that is reproduced in Figure 1. Finally and most important of all, I thank my partner, Elín, for her unflagging support over what has been a very protracted process. To her and our two boys this book is dedicated.

·•·1·•·

The Trouble with Theory

The New Interpretive Dilemma

EVERY ONCE IN A WHILE, archaeological theory gets a bashing. In the 1980s, in the wake of nearly two decades of new archaeology and its progeny, many started to believe that archaeological theory had devolved into methodology for its own sake. James Moore and Arthur Keene, editors of a 1983 volume which attempted to reappraise the role and status of archaeological method, were critical of the way archaeology had borrowed methods and models from outside the discipline with little thought about whether they were actually viable with the aims of archaeology (Moore & Keene 1983: xiv). They were also especially critical of the way methodology, best exemplified through the growth of middle-range theory, had become increasingly detached from a theoretical base. Two decades later, Michael Shanks launched another major criticism of the direction postprocessualism was heading, in the way it was all too easily drawing on the writings of major French poststructuralists without proper concern for the way it connected to archaeology. 'Where is the archaeology?' he asked (Shanks 1990: 294). Whereas processualism was borrowing methods without thought to theory, postprocessualism seemed to be borrowing theory without thought to method. It appears, then, that the potential for a schism between theory and method has been a recurrent concern within archaeology, at least since theory became an explicit subfield of archaeological discourse in the 1960s, if not earlier. Such concerns are still with us today.

In a recent polemical piece for the journal *Archaeological Dialogues*, Matthew Johnson suggested that there was a real disjuncture between theory and practice – between what we say in theoretical papers and what we do in practice (Johnson 2006: 118). He identified various forms of this lack of correspondence, but the one he singled out was the undertheorization of the link between overt theory on the one hand and other elements of archaeological thought and practice on the other hand (ibid.: 120). Johnson took two examples to explore this, agency theory and phenomenology, which he argued revealed opposing trends. Thus, in the first case, practical applications were argued to be resistant to agency theory because basic archaeological concepts like culture, phase, and type worked against any easy incorporation of the theory. In the second case, it was the opposite problem – the uptake of phenomenology found an all-too-receptive audience in British archaeology because of its strong fieldwork tradition, such that adopting the theory of phenomenology was largely a question of terminological change without any substance behind it. Although one might disagree with Johnson's diagnosis in these particular cases (see, for example, the responses which follow the paper), no doubt most of us can relate to his general point: sometimes a theoretical approach just does not work with archaeological data, and sometimes a theory is so vague that it can work on any data.

Johnson's point can perhaps be restated as the hazards faced by any archaeological interpretation: vacuity and incommensurability. One could even see this as the contemporary version of the interpretive dilemma which plagued archaeologists in the 1970s and 1980s (DeBoer & Lathrap 1979; Wylie 1989). That dilemma, one may recall, invoked the opposition between a safe, yet dull description of the archaeological record (artifact physics) and a more speculative, yet exciting interpretation. It was based on a certain naive view of the relation between theory and data which has since been superseded (e.g. Wylie 1992b), a relation in which the entire burden rested on the role of evidence. The current dilemma – if one can call it that without sounding overly pessimistic about archaeological theory – is also based on the relation between theory and data (the updated postpositivist version), but here the burden falls squarely on theory. It is no longer a question of whether the evidence supports the theory: does the theory work in the context of the evidence? The classic symptom of this malaise is the case study, as when an empirical piece of research which is intended to illustrate a theoretical argument fails; the contemporary literature abounds with such instances, and no doubt we would not be hard pressed to find examples in which the case study simply does not live up to expectations raised in the theoretical part.

Admittedly, the difference between these versions of the interpretive dilemma is subtle, and in fact the opposition between theory and data, though still meaningful at one level (see e.g. Hodder & Hutson 2003), needs to be rethought. Indeed as Tomášková suggests in her reply to Johnson, theory is a practice too, and she alludes to other divisions of labour within archaeology, such as that between fieldwork and laboratory work (Tomášková 2006: 166). Turning this back onto the updated version of the interpretive dilemma, we might say that the hazards of vacuity and incommensurability arise not so much because of a lack of correspondence between theory and practice and/or data but because of a disjuncture between the metaphysical assumptions of different practices or discourses. In a way, the change might also be characterized in terms of a shift from a correspondence between theory and data to the coherence between different statements. In short, the current interpretive dilemma is not an epistemological one, as that framed in the 1970s and 1980s, but an ontological one, insofar as the metaphysical assumptions framing different discourses often remain unexamined. Does the reality posited in archaeological discourse about agency theory bear any correspondence to the reality posited through excavation or through artifact analysis?

This, in essence, is what this book is about. I want to ask, What is the ontological relationship between 'methodological' concepts like stratigraphy and typology on the one hand and current 'theoretical' notions like materiality and agency on the other hand? However, in approaching this question, a difficulty emerges: although our methodological concepts are relatively few and stable, the theoretical ones are diverse and ever changing. This difference in a way expresses one of the main reasons one can still talk about methodological and theoretical concepts as distinct, even though the former are of course theoretical, whereas the latter are operational – hence the inverted commas around them. Yet my point is that to attempt an analysis of the connections between these two discourses would be a massive undertaking because of the pace of change and variety in theoretical practice – too massive for any single book or perhaps author. As an alternative, I could just select some theories, as Johnson did, for comparison – but even that seems daunting, as well as somewhat arbitrary. Instead, what I wish to do is explore this problem in terms of a very confined and specific discourse: the nature of the archaeological record.

One could describe this as an attempt to rewrite middle-range theory but from an ontological rather than an epistemological position. Binford's original conception of middle-range theory was to build epistemic links between what we observe in the archaeological record and our explanations of the past processes which created that record. It was his solution to the original interpretive dilemma. In this book, in accordance with the updated version of that dilemma, I thus want to explore the ontological links between our practical engagements with the archaeological record and the interpretations we produce. However, I would not insist on adopting a terminology developed during a very different period of archaeological thought – no doubt advocates of the Binfordian middle-range theory would dislike my appropriation of this term as much as those who think middle-range theory is an implausible fantasy of processualism. We can call it what we like, so long as the objectives are clear, and I hope they will become so as the course of this book unfolds. Nonetheless, to give the reader some sense of direction, I want to briefly outline the structure of the argument that is presented in this book.

In approaching the question of the archaeological record, I have tacitly divided the book into two parts. The first part (Chapters 2–4) treats what I call the received view of the archaeological record – that is, how it is currently depicted and its historical background. I find taking a historical perspective extremely useful, not only for enabling a better grasp of concepts and practices which inform what we do today but also for the pedagogical value of those concepts and practices in argumentation and debate. It is also a necessary corrective to an academic amnesia that often accompanies more theoretical texts. The chapters of the first part thus each treat a different conception of the archaeological record, which though related, are essentially distinct. The second part (Chapters 5–6) then presents a reassessment of the concept of the archaeological record and attempts to respond to the

fragmentation of the concept presented in the first part – to ontologic-
ally suture what I see as critical ruptures between different domains of
the archaeological record. Fundamentally, one could characterize such
ruptures in terms of a broad schism between the archaeological record
as something which is given (e.g. remains of the past) and something
which is constituted by archaeologists (e.g. the archive). It is, if you
like, an attempt to steer between a naive empiricism and social constructivism, yet to do this requires shifting from an epistemological to
an ontological and operational perspective on the issue.

In this respect, the approach taken in this book bears some similarity to the work of the anthropologist-historian Michel-Rolph Trouillot
(Trouillot 1995). Trouillot accepts the doubling of history as both past
events and present narratives, and rather than get caught up in dichotomous thinking (e.g. past as real versus past as constructed), he focuses
on history as a continuum, identified through four moments. These
moments are the generation of documents, the collation of documents
into an archive, the retrieval of facts from documents, and the construction of historical narrative. For Trouillot, focusing on these moments is
critical to understanding the intersection of power and knowledge and
how silences are created in history; to locate and contest such silences,
historians need to adopt strategies which focus on these key moments.
It is easy to see how the archaeological record can also be considered
along these lines, and indeed Alison Wylie has explicitly connected
Trouillot's division of four moments in the production of history to
comparable moments in archaeology (Wylie 2008). In the same way –
but with a less political agenda – in this book I explore archaeology as a
continuum by examining the nature of the archaeological operation and
archaeological entities deployed in our narratives. For me, the concept
of the archaeological record is an obvious starting point insofar as it
connects and encapsulates the duality of archaeology as process (what
we do) and as remains (the past). By way of an introduction, then, I
begin with an obvious question: what is the archaeological record?

What Is the Archaeological Record?

A CONVENTIONAL WAY to answer the question 'What is the archaeological record?' would be to turn to some standard dictionary and quote
the definitions therein of 'archaeology' and 'record' – or even better to

go to their etymological roots, in this instance, to Greek and Latin, respectively. We all know about archaeology ('the study of ancient things', from the Greek), but the etymology of the word 'record' may be less familiar. Although originally from Latin ('to remember'), it more directly comes to us through Old French, meaning 'testimony committed to writing'; however, since the 1890s, it came increasingly to cover other recording modes in relation to the new technologies. I am not terribly fond of dictionary definitions or etymologies, although I admit such recourse can be (and most often is) a rhetorical move to legitimize a certain approach, a fact no less true in my instance. Thus, one of the reasons I focus on the term 'archaeological record' is precisely because it connotes an ambiguity about the nature of archaeological evidence – as something which is its own testimony, an autoarchive (the fossil), as well as something which archaeologists testify to in the archive they produce (the text). Although superficially similar, this bears no resemblance to Patrik's distinction of the physical and textual models of the archaeological record discussed later in this section (Patrik 1985). 'Record' thus evokes something of the semiautonomous nature of modern recording devices such as tapes and cameras, as well as the primacy of human agency in the production of written testimony. Nonetheless, I am aware that the term may still be problematic for some (see e.g. Barrett 1988, 2006; Edgeworth 2003: 5–6).

Perhaps more important than etymology, though, is the context and timing of a word coming into common parlance; the recurrent use of the term 'archaeological record' may have originally come to archaeology via geology and palaeontology, although in the nineteenth and early twentieth centuries, a variety of terms, including both 'source' and 'record', was used interchangeably (see e.g. Newton 1851). Indeed, the transference of more broadly literary or textual concepts to characterize all histories from the earth, including archaeology, was common practice in the nineteenth century. Referring to material remains – whether fossils, rocks, or artifacts – as documents, archives, testimonies, records, and sources was a standard device, and one which remains with us today. However, the first persistent reference I find to the term 'archaeological record' is by Childe (1956a), but I freely admit this is not based on any systematic search on my part – although it would not surprise me if the 1950s was when the term first became more common, like the associated term 'material culture' (Childe 1956a;

Table 1. *Patrik's Five Meanings of the Archaeological Record*

1	Past objects and events (e.g. systemic context)
2	Material deposits (e.g. layers, stratigraphy)
3	Material remains (e.g. objects, assemblages)
4	Archaeological sample (e.g. excavated area, retrieved finds)
5	Archaeological record (e.g. archives, publications)

Source: Patrik (1985).

see Chapter 4). Whatever the origins of the term, however, it is clear that it encapsulates more than one meaning, and this is where I really focus my attention.

The various meanings of the term 'archaeological record' were made very clear in Linda Patrik's seminal article on the subject, published a quarter of a century ago (Patrik 1985). In the beginning of her paper, Patrik identified five different meanings used by archaeologists (Patrik 1985: 29–30; see also Table 1). The first is the material context in which past events and/or processes occurred – in short, what is variously called the ethnographic past or the systemic context. The second and third meanings refer, respectively, to the material deposits and material remains left behind by these past processes; the fourth concerns the part of these remains recovered by archaeology (i.e. the sample), and the fifth, the record archaeologists themselves create of these remains (e.g. archives, reports). It is a pity that Patrik ignores the last two meanings in her paper; nowhere does she discuss the role of the archaeologist in the constitution of the archaeological record, but rather she focuses her attention on the first three meanings. Moreover, her distinction of the physical and textual models conflates the differences among these three meanings, which I think actually aids the confusion surrounding the concept – a confusion she acknowledges at the end of the paper.

The physical model, according to Patrik, asserts that there is a causal and physical connection between past events or processes and the record itself – the prototype being the fossil record. The textual model, in contrast, asserts that the record encodes information about the past – the prototype being a historical document. Patrik's paper was an extremely balanced and considered piece insofar as it was a review of the then-current theoretical positions; indeed it was an attempt to create a bridge

of understanding between the rifts of processualism and postprocessualism. However, it did not really offer a constructive or different view
on the archaeological record. Her concluding call for a synthesis of
the two models has largely been ignored, yet it revealed an interesting
schism in the concept itself:

> *Perhaps the two models apply to different levels of archaeological*
> *evidence: the physical model seems more appropriate for*
> *archaeological remains, and the textual model for the original*
> *material artifacts, in use and as deposits. They should be*
> *synthesized by treating one as the temporal, causal consequence of*
> *the other.*
>
> (Patrik 1985: 55)

What seems accurate about this observation is the distinction between
two levels of evidence, which might be better characterized as two
ontological conceptions of the archaeological record: one which treats
it as comparable to a contemporary material context, yet one from
another time, and the other which treats it as fundamentally historical.
In other words, it is the difference between the archaeological record
as synonymous with material culture on the one hand and the archaeological record as a set of remains or residues on the other hand. What
is misleading about this observation however, is the ascription of the
textual and physical models to these respective ontological representations. I would argue that both the textual and the physical models
of Patrik's scheme are in fact examples of the same ontology, one
which sees the archaeological record in terms of material culture in
a past 'present', and that there is in fact no model in contemporary
archaeology which adequately covers the second ontology – a historical ontology of residues. This is the key theme of the second part of
this book.

Despite offering a possible reconciliation between the models, a
deeper sense of misgiving emerges from Patrik's paper, and her final
paragraph questions whether the concept of the archaeological record
is at all useful – she asks us to consider whether 'archaeological evidence may not form any kind of record at all' (Patrik 1985: 56). Indeed,
subsequent reflections on Patrik's paper tended to reject either of her
models as a suitable way of understanding the archaeological record.

John Barrett's answer to Patrik's concluding suggestion was quite emphatic in its assertion that the concept of record was inadequate and preferred the use of the term 'evidence' (Barrett 1988, 2006). For Barrett, the problem with the term 'record' is that it encourages us to see material remains as representations of past events rather than evidence of the material conditions structuring and structured by people. I have a lot of sympathy with Barrett's position, but as I have already articulated, I think the concept of record can be thought of in more complex ways (see also Thomas 1996: 55–64). Indeed, the problem is not really about the utility of the concept of record but rather about the recognition of the ontological constitution of archaeological remains qua remains, not as something else, such as material culture. This is especially ironic, as in the following year, Patrik published another paper on just this aspect, but from an art historical perspective; her paper titled 'The Aesthetic Experience of Ruins' is probably unknown to most archaeologists (Patrik is a philosopher, not an archaeologist), but it addressed the importance of the fragmentary and incomplete nature of antique art to its aesthetic appreciation (Patrik 1986). It would have been interesting if she had considered the fragmentary nature of the archaeological record in relation to its status as historical evidence; indeed, the notion of incompleteness is something which takes on great significance in Chapter 2. However, the immediate point I wish to emphasize is that, in articulating these two models, Patrik felt the need at the end to invoke her original five meanings of the archaeological record – or rather the first three. Yet it is the full list which is important, because it clearly shows that the concept of the archaeological record can – and perhaps ought to – entail both the physical remains themselves and the work archaeologists perform on them to constitute them as archaeological evidence. This is a theme that is central to this book and consequently results in a very different view to the one that Patrik gave in her otherwise stimulating paper.

I begin by redrawing up Patrik's original list and condensing it to just three meanings, which also form the basis of the following three chapters (Table 2). The first refers to the archaeological record as composed principally of material culture or the human material environment. In short, this is the archaeological record conceived of as material culture or artifacts, in the broadest sense of the term (see the next section) and is equivalent to Patrik's first meaning. The second meaning

Table 2. *Three Meanings of the Archaeological Record as Used in This Book Compared to Patrik's Scheme*

Patrik's Fivefold Division	Threefold Division Used in This Book
Past objects and events	Artifacts and material culture (Chapter 4)
Material deposits	Residues and formation theory (Chapter 3)
Material remains	
Archaeological sample	Sources and fieldwork (Chapter 2)
Archaeological record	

refers to the archaeological record as the remains or traces of a past material environment, and here I discuss both her second and her third meaning in terms of an oppositional tension – between deposits and assemblages in relation to formation theory. The third and final meaning refers to the archaeological record as something we encounter and construct in the present, and once again, the tension here is between Patrik's fourth and fifth meanings. I want to elaborate on each of these in a little more detail before I treat them more fully in their respective chapters.

Artifacts

When we think about the objects that archaeologists deal with – their immediate object of study – a central notion is that of the artifact. 'Artifact' can mean just small and/or portable objects made and used by humans, although the term is also more generally employed to cover any material object or construction, such as a pit or a building. Textbooks, however, are also quick to point out that the archaeological record is composed not just of artifacts but also of a variety of non-human objects, such as seeds, bones, and soils, which are commonly called ecofacts (for a typical example of such a discussion, see Renfrew & Bahn 1996: 45–6). However, the distinction of ecofacts from artifacts is a little spurious – seeds and bones have in many cases been used by humans and even modified (i.e. domesticated), and more generally, almost all such remains have been influenced by or are associated with human action in one way or another; otherwise, archaeologists would not be interested in them. Indeed, the artifact-ecofact distinction is really a manifestation of a deeper culture-nature dichotomy which has been under constant critique for decades. Nonetheless, there is a clear sense in which humans occupy the key position here in defining the limits of archaeological stuff; archaeologists do not dig for dinosaurs – despite what a portion of the misinformed public might believe. Notwithstanding the fuzziness of this boundary of the human, there are places and times where humans simply do not exist and, therefore, neither does the archaeological record. We can call the objects in these places and times *nature* if we like, but given how loaded that word is, it might be better to rethink our terminology.

Extending the concept of the archaeological record to include ecofacts does, however, raise the issue of the historical contingency of which objects fall under its umbrella. Certainly, in the nineteenth century, many archaeologists did retrieve what we would call ecofacts today, such as animal bones and seeds. But equally, the range and diversity of such ecofacts have undoubtedly increased, especially since the 1950s, under the influence of environmental research in archaeology, not to mention ecofacts becoming a more integrated and standard part of retrieval policies. Yet although some parts of the archaeological record have expanded, others have conceptually contracted, especially the catholic attitude of the antiquarian, whereby effectively anything and everything relating to the past fell within the domain of archaeology, including folklore and manuscripts as well as church buildings and Roman pottery. However, despite the historically contingent nature of which objects fall under the term 'archaeological record', in contemporary terms the overwhelming connotation is that one is dealing with physical things but things connected in some way to human activity. 'Artifacts' is one word used to describe these things, and another phrase is 'material culture', although neither quite captures the full diversity of objects studied today, probably because they are essentially nineteenth-century constructs. One gets a sense of this in the recent move away from discussing material culture in favour of the more open term 'materiality', which captures something of this tension between physical matter and human behaviour.

Residues

However, even in contemporary terms, not everyone would agree with equating the archaeological record with material culture but would prefer to add the temporal qualifier: *past* material culture. Archaeologists used to ignore all objects which postdated medieval times, but since the latter half of the twentieth century, the chronological limits of the discipline have been pushing ever closer to the present, and for many, there is no chronological boundary any more. Despite this, many might implicitly still draw a line between archaeological and non-archaeological material culture based on some random distance from the present, usually connected to a spurious argument about having access to better sources (e.g. documents). I do not need to rehearse the fallacy of such arguments here (see e.g. Lucas 2004). For some, artifacts become archaeological only if they are more than a century or more old; for others, yesterday's garbage is archaeology (Rathje & Murphy 2001). In effect, this makes archaeology almost synonymous with material culture studies, irrespective of time and place.

This broad definition has some merits insofar as it is extremely difficult to draw a line between conventional archaeological objects and more contemporary objects – aside from the obvious fact that all archaeological stuff is contemporary in one sense. Yet even under this definition, for some there is still a distinguishing feature of the archaeological record which would not place all contemporary material culture under its purview; this distinction is not about age or time elapsed or even accessibility to other sources but about whether or not the material in question is part of an active, living context. In short, what makes objects archaeological is that they are *dead*. Of course the problem with this view is, What constitutes a dead context? Is yesterday's garbage dead? It has certainly been ejected from one context (the household), but it has also entered another (the garbage disposal system). What about when it gets to the landfill? Are landfills dead contexts? And when the landfill is closed – is it dead then? And in what sense is it dead, if biological and chemical processes are still operative? It is no doubt a fuzzy boundary, but much like the one circumscribing the limits of the human, it is also an important one which should not be forgotten. It is also one which forms the basis of the second meaning of the archaeological record: residues.

Hence, besides the use of the terms 'artifact' or 'material culture' to denote the archaeological record, another set of terms with quite different meanings have been widely used since the birth of archaeology in the nineteenth century, and even earlier. The family of terms such as 'remains,' 'relics,' 'fragments,' 'traces,' 'vestiges', and 'residues' has been employed throughout the history of archaeology but has rarely received much, if any, explicit theoretical discussion, until the mid-twentieth century, when the first systematic work on formation theory started to appear. This took a number of different approaches, which are described in more detail in Chapter 3, but it is sufficient here to point out a distinction between, on the one hand, a strand which was influenced by environmental and geoarchaeological research, which focused on deposit formation, and on the other hand, an approach using actualistic studies to model the short-term transformations of objects as they move from the living to the dead context. The key conceptual device for this meaning of the archaeological record is a distinction articulated in numerous ways, but most familiarly by Binford's terms of statics and dynamics or Schiffer's systemic and archaeological context (Binford 1977; Schiffer 1972). Yet these divisions are somewhat problematic, as I have already pointed out: when does a context become static or archaeological? In a sense, no context is static, it is just dynamic in a different way, and one of these different ways is, of course, through archaeological intervention. This brings us to the third and final meaning of the archaeological record: sources.

Sources

The archaeological record, as human-related material residues, is also constituted as having a particular epistemological function as source material or evidence, facts or data; such residues may have other meanings for contemporary society and operate in other fields and practices, such the antiquities and art market, but for archaeologists it is their status as sources that defines them as archaeological, as opposed to something else (e.g. the aesthetic). This is not to say that such fields are entirely separate – archaeology was, after all, born in part in conjunction with art history, and the links between archaeology and art have been recently revisited in the context of modern art (e.g. Renfrew 2003). The same is true more generally of the wide and diverse range of meanings that such objects or residues have in popular culture and notions of heritage (e.g. Holtorf 2005, 2007). Without downplaying the important connections between archaeology and popular or 'high' culture – or indeed non-Western perspectives on heritage and the past – what concerns me here is the peculiarly archaeological perception of such objects as sources.

As such, one of the primary issues surrounding sources has been their representivity; how much can or do they tell us about the past? The basis here is the recognition that the archaeological record is a contemporary phenomenon, yet also one which derives from the past; the question is thus also of survival or of the persistence of the past into the present. Here again, the historical links between archaeology and art history are important to recognize. Aesthetic theories of the nature of ruins and fragments would have influenced a tacit archaeological sensibility, and it is useful to reflect on what Robert Ginsberg has defined as two opposing theories of the ruin: the romantic and the classical (Ginsberg 2004: 315–34). Romanticism sees the ruin as a remnant of an irrecoverable past, a unity which is forever lost – it focuses on loss and melancholy. Classicism, in contrast, sees the ruin as evidence of continuity with the past and the possibility of reconstitution of a former unity in the imagination – it focuses on the glory of the original unity and the possibilities it offers to the imagination. These opposing perspectives have been seen to permeate more generally throughout the humanist disciplines, such as philology, law, and history (Vismann 2001; on monumental, antiquarian, and critical history, see Nietzsche 1957). Vismann has suggested that where Renaissance scholars used the metaphor of fragments to evoke a lost unity, nineteenth-century historians considered the fragments real links to the past, source material for the construction of histories. It is thus the reconstitution of a former whole from fragments which determines much of the definition of the archaeological record as sources, and why the notion of incompleteness plays such a critical role in methodological and analytical procedures (e.g. Anglophone sampling theory and German source criticism).

Absent Presences

THE ISSUE OF INCOMPLETENESS raised in the previous section might actually be considered a manifestation of a more general property which affects all three facets of the archaeological record: absence. The idea that something is missing, a gap, pervades not only the notion of source but also residues and material culture. In the case of residues the property is self-evident – some diminution of the original, some loss which is inflected by a much more temporal quality than in the case of incompleteness: that of ephemerality or durability. In the case of material culture, the absence is subtler; it is not so much about the ephemeral as the intangible or immaterial: the mental, the unobservable, or those aspects of objects which seem to have only a ghostly presence. The diverse connotations of absence have been recently addressed by several authors from different fields, many of which connect with the absences I invoke here (see papers in Bille, Hastrup, & Sørensen 2010). I suggest that perhaps each of these archaeological absences is in fact mutually reinforcing by virtue of the fact that each facet of the archaeological record is kept distinct. In other words, the very fragmentation and separation of the concept of the archaeological record into three different discourses, which rarely impinge on one another, actually creates the problem of absence felt in each. The only way to deal with such absences is to reconnect the domains, which is the intention of the later chapters of this book.

The idea of the archaeological record being somehow haunted by absence is expressed perhaps most succinctly in the scepticism often felt around archaeological narratives – how archaeologists manage to weave often-monumental accounts of the past from just a few scraps (Figure 1). The flip side of this scepticism is the phenomenon of the time capsule, a trend which began in 1936; current estimates put the

Carruthers - come quickly! I think I have found evidence that the ideological infrastructure of the Wösschlangen culture may have concealed an antagonistic pluralism, resulting in the construction of a third gender!

Figure 1. Archaeological alchemy; or, how archaeologists spin stories from scraps (drawing by Mark Lucas).

number of time capsules at more than ten thousand worldwide, 80 percent of which have or will be forgotten long before their due opening date (Jarvis 2003). Such deposits can be viewed as an implicit lack of confidence in the traces we leave of ourselves to future generations and their ability to read these traces. The irony is, of course, that such deliberate testaments are often very poor records of what we are, much worse than archaeological remains (Jarvis 2003). It should also be noted that such scepticism is just as often matched by wonder and awe at the skills deployed by archaeologists, and this is no doubt how most of us would prefer to see it. Yet this ambivalence towards what archaeology claims to be able to do, whether expressed as scepticism or as wonderment, balances on this issue of absence – the ability of the archaeologist to see what others cannot. This pervades our work at all levels; I was recently excavating some building foundations and a historian expressed her doubt over the very existence of what I took to be self-evident. She simply could not see the building. This of course is a common-enough event, and one most students go through as they learn to see layers and features on-site. But exactly the same kind of transformations are at play throughout the whole archaeological process – learning to 'see' pottery types, to read graphs, to understand the complex networks that are involved in constructing archaeological narratives. By the time we become proficient, so much of the process has become black boxed (i.e. assumed or taken for granted) so that what to us seems self-evident, to outsiders seems magical. And magic, as we all know, can be taken either as a sleight of hand (the sceptic) or as the product of special powers (the believer).

The only way to begin to dispel this ambivalence is to try to open out these black boxes, to unravel the process of our work, a point argued for some time ago by Joan Gero and a central tenet of researchers working in the sociology of scientific knowledge and science and technology studies (see Gero 1995; see also Edgeworth 2003; Witmore 2004; Yarrow 2003, 2006, 2008). Such studies play an important role in this book, especially in Chapter 6. However, in themselves, they do not directly resolve the problem of absence as it is articulated in archaeological discourse; the only way to achieve that is to rethink the conceptualization of the archaeological record, and in such a way that it conjoins what are currently three, fragmented discourses about that record: fieldwork, formation theory, and material culture studies.

I suggest that the concept of materialization is a useful way to conjoin these domains and, at the same time, to avoid the whole issue of absence. Materialization is a process, it is never completed, always fluid; this does not rid us of the concept of absence, but it does disarm it, removing its negative connotations, because it suggests that it is a very condition of presence itself. Now all three facets of the archaeological record can be viewed in terms of a process of materialization. In the case of material culture, the key issue is about materialization and how objects come into being in the first instance. In the case of formation theory, it is about the dematerializing processes that affect objects and transforms artifacts into residues. Finally, in the case of fieldwork, we can think of the archaeological process as itself, a (re)materializing process, bringing old objects back into circulation but in very different ways from when they were made and used before deposition. The archaeological record, then, as a unity, is all about the tension between (re)materialization and dematerialization.

This characterization is admittedly a little crude, but it serves as a preliminary sketch of the intentions of this book. The new interpretive dilemma which opened this chapter is in many ways a product of theoretical fragmentation; this is not the same as theoretical plurality. I am certainly not arguing for homogeneity or a grand unified archaeological theory. Rather that, over the past half century, as theoretical discourse has expanded in ever-larger and more diverse ways, the connections among all the components of the archaeological process have come under threat of being severed. The distance between those scraps we unearth and the monumental narratives we construct has become so great, and often so black boxed, that it is no wonder that our interpretations sometimes appear either vacuous or disconnected to the data, as Johnson observed. My aim in this book is to try to begin to reconnect these components through the lens of one concept: the archaeological record.

—◦—2—◦—

The Total Record

I N THIS CHAPTER, my focus is on the archaeological record as it is
encountered by archaeologists in the present and how it is constituted as historical evidence in the form of archaeological archives.
Indeed, the term 'archaeological record' can refer both to what archaeologists find in the ground and to their notes, drawings, or photographs
produced in the course of fieldwork. Such records or archives – not the
actual remains themselves – in many ways form the principal basis of
interpretation (Lucas 2001b: 44). This is not to deny the interpretive element in producing such archives, but rather to emphasize that
archaeologists work on texts and documents as much as objects and
deposits in their work. The issue of how these two aspects of the archaeological record – as given and as produced – are related is addressed
in Chapter 6; my primary concern in this chapter is examining how
both these aspects of the archaeological record have been problemat-
ized through the idea of incompleteness, hence the title of this chapter.
The concept of the total record has various meanings; on the one hand,
it can refer to a contemporary sense of an objective and complete representation of what lies in or on the ground. This has perhaps always been
a fiction, but a useful one nonetheless in certain circumstances, as I discuss later in this chapter. But other meanings are implied by the concept
of a total record, even if this particular term has not necessarily been
used. Thus, I argue that from the late nineteenth and early twentieth

centuries, the problem of incompleteness was chiefly linked to acquiring as full or complete collections of material as possible, a goal enshrined in the concept of the corpus. Incomplete collections were the bane of proper interpretation. During the twentieth century, this concept gradually migrated so that incompleteness increasingly came to apply to the nature of the archaeological remains vis-à-vis the past rather than to archaeological practices of collecting. Issues of preservation and representivity became paramount through the Central European tradition of source criticism or Anglo-American sampling theory.

Thus, we have at least three different ways to understand a total – or incomplete – record: in terms of representation, preservation, and retrieval. In the past two decades, archaeology has developed an interest in theorizing fieldwork and practice, yet the issue of incompleteness remains ambiguous. Certainly the idea of a total record as representation has more or less been rejected, but anxieties still abound about archive production. Moreover, these different meanings of incompleteness are rarely discussed together, with the exception perhaps of sampling theory and its notion of information entropy as we pass from preservation to retrieval to representation. In this chapter, I explore the historical roots and connections among these three aspects of the archaeological record through the lens of the twinned notions of incompleteness and the total record.

Defining the Archaeological Record in the Nineteenth Century

ARCHAEOLOGISTS AND ANTIQUARIANS did not regularly use the term 'record' to describe the nature of their evidence or material until well into the twentieth century, although it did occur (e.g. Newton 1851: 1). More commonly, a diverse collection of words such as 'antiquities', 'relics', 'vestiges', and 'remains' were employed. What all these words share in common, of course, is a notion of the archaeological record as something from the past but in the present. Indeed, a more general connection between a broad spectrum of historical evidence which included folklore, documents, language, art, and archaeological remains came through a specific view of history as inherited, that is, seeing the present in descendant terms or, conversely, the past in ancestral terms. It is easy to dismiss such catholic approaches to the past as unsystematic and to relegate them to a prescientific era of antiquarianism, but there was a clear consistency in such views which is captured in the dominant terms, listed already, used to describe antiquarian sources. Those terms quite emphatically recognize the contemporary nature of the archaeological and historical record: that it exists in the present even if it references the past. The German historian Gustav Droysen made this very clear in his key work on historical method:

> *The data for historical investigation are not past things, for these have disappeared, but things which are still present here and now, whether recollections of what was done, or remnants of things that have existed and, of events that have occurred.*

> *(Droysen 1897: 11)*

Included among these remnants was a type of historical source which also existed in the present, yet in a different way – sources which became known as survivals. These referred to practices, customs, and words but also to material elements like design motifs and parts of clothing, which clearly derived from an earlier period in history, and although they were still in use in the present, their usefulness or significance was not self-evident – in fact they seemed to be somewhat anachronistic, temporally out of place. However, the term 'survival' was adopted only in the later nineteenth century, and before that, other terms were used, including 'antiquities'. In short, the image one gleans from early archaeological and antiquarian views is that a whole jumble of material was seen as constituting the archaeological record, and it was only over the course of the late nineteenth and early twentieth centuries that our modern concept of it emerged. In this section, I explore these early conceptions of the archaeological record as remains or relics and draw out their discontinuities with the concepts of sources and survivals as they relate to the emerging separation of archaeology from history and ethnology, respectively.

Archaeology, History, and the Accidental Record

Without doubt, one of the most important characterizations of the archaeological record in the early nineteenth century was its eclectic nature.

One has to bear in mind that during most of the nineteenth century, European archaeologists chiefly focused on historical periods (Roman or classical and medieval), not prehistory (as the term did not exist until later that century), and their sources included not only artifacts from the earth but standing structures, documents, and antiques. Charles Thomas Newton, one of the most distinguished British archaeologists of the mid-nineteenth century, described this ecumenical approach in his paper 'On the Study of Archaeology', whose purpose and function was

> [T]o collect, to classify, and to interpret all the evidence of man's history not already incorporated in Printed Literature... This evidence, the subject matter of Archaeology, has been handed down to us, partly in spoken language, in manners, and in customs, partly in written documents and manuscript literature, partly in remains of architecture, painting, and sculpture, and of the subordinate decorative and useful arts.
>
> (Newton 1851: 2)

Of Newton's classification of the sources into three branches – the oral, the written, and the monumental – only the latter includes what we today would normally consider within the field of archaeology. Similarly, Churchill Babington, in his *Introductory Lecture on Archaeology* to the University of Cambridge in 1865 described archaeology as 'the science of teaching history by its monuments' (Babington 1865: 3), although in 'monuments', Babington included original manuscripts and inscriptions. However, such views as Newton's did not go uncontested even at the time, as alluded to by William Thomson (1867: 85), the archbishop of York, in his inaugural address to the annual meeting of the Royal Archaeological Institute:

> Archaeology is a science of the remote past; but this general description would include ethnology, the history of languages and the study of ancient written records or palaeography. Archaeology, according to one authority, should be content to separate herself from all these tempting subjects and to confine herself to the study of the works of human skill which indicate the growth and social condition of man.

Thomas Wright also made a clear separation between literary and monumental antiquities or relics, with the former being the materials of historians and the latter of archaeologists – a distinction he traces to France (Wright 1866: 64–7).

Yet it was this ecumenical approach to sources that, in part, made archaeologists, historians, and antiquarians indistinguishable at that time, a division which fully emerged only with the development of prehistoric archaeology, from the 1860s, and the professionalization of history, from the 1870s (Levine 1986). Indeed, the very distinction made by Wright can be considered part of a strategy to secure archaeology as an independent science in the context of this wider scramble towards professionalization and scholarly status. Thus, ironically and yet predictably, perhaps, the legacy of this connection remains clearer in history than in archaeology; although archaeologists may cite texts and other sources as useful to the archaeologist, there is a clear sense that these are not part of the archaeological record. A call by Dymond in the 1970s to revive this nineteenth-century view of the archaeological record to what he called a total archaeology has been more or less ignored, even if in practice historical archaeologists do make heavy use of a variety of sources (Dymond 1974). In contrast, historians typically cite archaeological remains as a subcategory of primary historical sources (e.g. Elton 1967: 89; Brundage 2008: 19). Such a perception has recently been restrengthened in the wake of a new interest in material culture by historians, among others, an interest originally connected to the issue of consumption and consumer revolutions (for a recent review, see Trentmann 2009; see also Auslander et al. 2009). However, it is important here to distinguish the historian's interest in material culture (archaeological or otherwise) from the use of material culture as sources; historians can study material culture through texts – they do not need to go to the things themselves. Nonetheless, many do, and increasingly so, perhaps largely as a consequence of this new interest in materiality (see e.g. Harvey 2009).

This inclusion of material culture as a subcategory of historical evidence may be because of a much older legacy of the impact of antiquarian methods on history, which effectively introduced source criticism into the humanities through the study of coins, inscriptions, statues, and charters (Momigliano 1950). Indeed, the distinction between literary and nonliterary evidence can be traced back to the late seventeenth century, when the study of numismatics, epigraphy, diplomatics, and iconography provided one solution to the increasing scepticism felt over ancient texts as sources of history. However, although nonliterary evidence might have been argued to provide a more reliable source, ultimately it was the methods used to interpret such sources that were paramount, being subsequently adopted by philologists and those studying ancient texts (Momigliano 1950; see also Schnapp 1996). In German classical studies (*Altertunswissenschaft*) both aspects were considered part of a common field of study, even if there was an acknowledged hierarchy between textual and nontextual sources. Indeed, they were often seen as two complementary aspects of philology: *Sachphilologie*, or *Realphilologie* (philology of objects/material culture), and *Wortphilologie* (linguistic philology) – a connection later taken up by Eduard Gerhard in his manifesto for monumental philology (see next section; Marchand 1996: 40–3). In the early nineteenth century, the Berlin professor August Böckh was emphatic in his promotion of *Sachphilologie* and his more general stance on the necessity of incorporating all aspects of a past culture or people to achieve a proper understanding, and he was particularly influential to the subsequent generation of scholars, including Gustav Droysen and Ernst Curtius (Marchand 1996: 43).

The question of reliability in relation to sources, however, remained a key issue well into the nineteenth century, when the distinction between antiquarian and philological sources was more explicitly mapped onto another distinction: that between accidental and intentional sources. One of the clearest expressions of this view was given by Gustav Droysen. In his *Outline of the Principles of History* (*Grundisse der Historik*), he distinguishes three types of historical record: remains, sources, and monuments:

> *Historical material is partly what is still immediately present, hailing from the times which we are seeking to understand (Remains), partly whatever ideas human beings have obtained of those times, and transmitted to be remembered (Sources), partly things wherein both these forms of material are combined (Monuments).*
>
> (Droysen 1897: 18)

His concept of remains includes not only artifacts or material culture but also customs or folklore and literature, whereas sources refers to any preserved record of past events and monuments are remains which were left as intentional records (i.e. remains as sources; ibid.: 19–20). Droysen's categorization may appear strange to our contemporary ways of thinking, but at its base lies a key distinction: between accidental and intentional records, remains being the former, sources and monuments being the latter. Droysen's scheme was later systemized in more detail by Ernst Bernheim (1899), who used the terms 'remains' (*Überrest*) and 'tradition' (*Tradition*) for the same basic opposition. However, for Droysen, it was the unintended or accidental type of historical sources (remains) that was paramount, because the very absence of intention enabled them to act as proofs, independent of historical writing (see Vismann 2001: 201–2). Remains do not lie, because remains had no intention of saying anything in the first place; that very quality makes them the most valuable historical source and has echoes in our contemporary valuation of forensic evidence over witness testimony.

Droysen's argument was taken up in the early twentieth century by Marc Bloch (1954: 60), who in his discussion of historical method from the 1940s, talked of intended and unintended sources. Like Droysen, Bloch suggested that it was the unintended source that was increasingly of greater importance to historians: 'there can be no doubt that, in the course of its development, historical research has gradually been led to place more confidence in the second category of evidence, in the evidence of witnesses in spite of themselves' (ibid.: 61). Archaeological remains were seen as falling clearly within this group, alongside a host of documentary sources from the Egyptian *Book of the Dead* to papal bulls, whereas memoirs, historical narratives, and chronicles belong to the former category of intended records. However, one could argue that many material remains are intended records – a prehistoric burial mound or monument could be considered a form of recording (i.e. commemorating) a particular person or event; indeed, the ambiguity of the phrase 'intention to record' is open to many different interpretations. It is precisely that feature which was captured in Droysen's original tripartite scheme, which included the hybrid concept of monuments, yet has been elided by Bloch.

R. G. Collingwood can be viewed as occupying a similar position to Bloch, although rather than articulate the issue in terms of intended and unintended sources, Collingwood draws a distinction between evidence and testimony (Collingwood 1946: 249–82). For Collingwood, the point is to treat documents as evidence, not as testimony, which results in effectively suspending the question of the content of documents and rather focusing simply on the fact that a document was made (ibid.: 275). Collingwood's method is the famous question-and-answer approach, which he draws out in a long analogy with detective work. Couse has helpfully traced the use of Collingwood's method in archaeology, specifically his work on Hadrian's Wall, and shows how important archaeological remains were in underpinning the preference Collingwood gave to what Couse calls circumstantial or indirect evidence, compared with testimony or direct evidence (Couse 1990).

Both Bloch and Collingwood are in many ways closer to Droysen than either might have acknowledged, although Droysen's original primary distinction between remains and sources was transected by another distinction which has subsequently overshadowed it, namely the opposition between things and texts. This latter distinction was made very clear in the seminal work on historical method by Charles-Victor Langlois and Charles Seignobos at the end of the nineteenth century. In their *Introduction to the Study of History*, they talk about the historical record in terms of documents, where documents are defined as traces of past events (Langlois & Seignobos [1898] 1925; see also Elton 1967: 88, where sources are defined as 'physical survivals from the events to be studied'). However, Langlois and Seignobos importantly divide such documents or traces into two forms: material traces (i.e. artifact or monument) and psychological traces (i.e. oral or written testimony; Langlois and Seignobos 1925: 65). As with most historians who talk about their sources this way, they then proceed to effectively ignore the former and focus solely on the latter in their discussion of historical method. Yet it is precisely this elevation of testimony in historical method that tells of the break between archaeology and history. Even so, many archaeologists refer to the record as a document (e.g. Childe 1956b: 9; Leroi-Gourhan 1950: 2; Barker 1982: 12) and, in doing so, highlight the testimonial quality of material remains. Simultaneously, however, it also renders them as secondary status compared to texts.

This last point in particular was the focus of much discussion in historical archaeology, particularly post-medieval, post-Reformation, and post-Columbian archaeology (to give it a few of the many epithets under which it has been discussed), which became a new field only in the 1960s (e.g. Andrén 1998; Moreland 2001). As in the similar debates that emerged in the late nineteenth century between literary and monumental sources (or tradition and remains in the German tradition), the distinction between things and texts was partly strategic and enabled those archaeologists working in the traditional territory of historians to justify their autonomy. However, such debates have overshadowed Droysen's more conciliatory concept of remains, which elevated the accidental quality of historical sources – whether material or textual.

Something of Droysen's original vision of historical method has been recently revived by the Italian microhistorian Carlo Ginzburg. For Ginzburg what counts in historical sources – whether in documents or in artifacts – is the involuntary component, which constitutes them primarily as clues rather than testimony. What Ginzburg implies is that, to read any historical source, one needs to bracket off the overt intentionality or meaning in its production as testimony or record to get at something deeper. In his paper 'Clues: Roots of an Evidential Paradigm' (Ginzburg 1990), Ginzburg sees the roots of this method in art history, particularly in the work of Giovanni Morelli, who during the 1870s developed a technique for attributing works to painters by focusing on trivial details which revealed unconscious traits of the individual, as opposed to learnt style. Such methods were of course taken up in classical archaeology in the analysis of painted ceramics, especially through the work of Furtwängler and Hartwig and later Beazeley (Walter 2008). It was 'a method of interpretation based on discarded information, marginal data, considered in some way significant' (ibid.: 101). Ginzburg sees such evidential analysis as a basic part of human interpretation a 'venatic deduction', which has been used by hunters following tracks or by diviners reading entrails since the dawn of history (ibid.: 103). Such a method, he argues, has been sidelined or even suppressed by the dominant paradigm of science, which works on generalizations and abstractions rather than connections between concrete observations. Yet the notion of evidence as clues, signs, or traces is displayed in numerous sciences, not just history, but palaeontology and archaeology as well, and is perhaps most evident, Ginzburg suggests, in medicine through its methods of diagnosis and prognosis (ibid.: 116–18).

In a way, Ginzburg's argument realigns Droysen's division between the voluntary and involuntary so that it refers not to the sources in themselves but rather to our reading of them – a point also recognized by both Bloch and Collingwood. It is through the intentionality of the historian that a text speaks, not through the intention of its writer; indeed, as Bloch originally put it, one reads a text in spite of what the author intended. In this way, material evidence and texts can share the same epistemological status. It is thus interesting that Ginzburg links his method of historical interpretation to the semiotic turn in the social and human sciences, because around the same time, many archaeologists were of course espousing the same about material culture, but from the opposite perspective. While Ginzburg argued that texts could be read as clues or traces, many archaeologists were arguing that material traces could be read as texts (e.g. Hodder 1982a, 1989a; Tilley 1990; Preucel & Bauer 2001). However, this is to digress; the relevant point here concerns the nature of an unintended or accidental record as opposed to an intended one, and it is with historians such as Droysen, Collingwood, Bloch, and Ginzburg that the archaeological and historical records are most closely aligned, as opposed to a view which emphasizes the distinction between objects and documents, things and texts.

However, although archaeologists do sometimes draw distinctions between the accidental and intentional nature of the archaeological record, this has never – as far as I am aware – been the subject of any extended discussion, except in the German tradition of source criticism, which I take up in more detail later in this chapter. In terms of Anglo-American traditions, this issue has never been a major point of discussion; Stuart Piggott once made passing reference to the nature of archaeological sources as unconscious evidence, clearly referencing this distinction but nothing more (Piggott 1966: 14–15). Archaeologists also often talk about accidental loss versus intentional deposition, in the case of finds, for example (e.g. Schiffer 1987, although Schiffer does not explicitly use this opposition), but it hardly plays a substantial role in contemporary formation theory (see Chapter 3). In contrast, the German tradition makes much more out of this. Heinrich Härke has drawn on the conventional distinction between Tradition (intentional) and Remains (accidental) in his discussion of burial data, using the terms 'intentional data' and 'functional data' to define this distinction (Härke 1993, 1997). The most detailed and extensive treatment, however, can be found in the recent work of Manfried Eggert (e.g. see Eggert 2001). I discuss Eggert's approach in more detail here, but it is important to note that he also draws heavily on Droysen in characterizing this distinction between accidental and intentional records. Such perspectives had also filtered into Scandinavian archaeology; thus, Carl-Axel Moberg once discussed the similarities between objects in terms of the accidental and intended (Moberg 1981: 3–4), whereas Anders Andrén adopted the distinction in relation to deposits and structures (Andrén 1985: 9–11).

However, it seems there is often some confusion here about how this distinction between the accidental and intentional apply, at least outside the German tradition (but see Härke 1997: 24); although one might talk of intentional deposits, this does not mean they are intentional records – that is, deposits intended to record an event or person. Robert Munro, writing in the early twentieth century, recognized this fact very explicitly in relation to the residual nature of the archaeological record: 'Owing to various causes, archaeological remains are both scanty and fragmentary – for it is no part of nature's programme to preserve ancient relics for the purpose of instructing archaeologists' (Munro 1905: 8–9). The issue of who the remains were intended as a record for is not really relevant – chronicles were not written with future historians in mind any more than a burial mound was built with future archaeologists in mind. But in both cases, one could argue that there was an intention to record (i.e. preserve for posterity) – in the one case, a series of key events, in the other, a particular person. Both, no doubt, were primarily targeted at contemporaries and immediate descendants. But the important thing is the intention to record. The archaeological record is full of intentions – intentions to build a house, to throw away a broken pot, to make a new pot – but these do not constitute intentions to record. As such, most of the archaeological record is accidental rather than intentional, in the sense discussed here. Indeed, it can be very difficult to identify intentions to record, as they will always be expressed alongside other intentions (e.g. to say good-bye to a loved one). Indeed, how do we understand an intention to record as opposed to one to merely communicate? Is commemoration really a form of recording similar to annals writing? Should we or can we distinguish between acts which intend to recall the past in the present from acts which intend to record the present for the future? One might contrast a memorial with a time capsule here. Are the two records in the same way? If not, then it reduces even further our potential examples of archaeological remains as intended records.

It is clear that such complexities did not preoccupy nineteenth-century archaeologists, even if Droysen clearly acknowledged such through his middle or hybrid term of the 'monument'. Archaeological remains (alongside other antiquities, such as survivals) constituted an accidental record because the process of transmission from past to present was accidental and not intentional. It is thus through the general notion of the accidental record that this distinction became important to archaeology – especially in historical and classical archaeology – because it offered a way of freeing archaeology from its alliance with art history. By stressing the importance of the accidental nature of historical sources, archaeologists had an inbuilt justification for collecting and recovering not just the best and most beautiful artifacts, works of 'art', but all the ugly or mundane fragments, detritus, and rubbish. Schmidt draws on Rudolf Virchow's reports to the Berlin Society for Anthropology, Ethnology and Prehistory in the early 1870s to show how excavations of a recent rubbish dump, originally hoped to be prehistoric, were not simply dismissed but used as a parable of the importance of such mundane objects to understanding the past (Schmidt 2002). Schmidt argues that such a perception marked an important turning point in German archaeology away from art history to archaeology and was in fact preceded by similar developments in German classical archaeology decades earlier (see next section).

Archaeology, Ethnography, and Survivals

The catholic approach to historical sources discussed in the previous section revolved around not just written documents and objects but also living customs and language; Droysen's concept of remains explicitly included such, as did Newton's understanding of what constituted archaeological evidence. But unlike ancient documents, manuscripts, inscriptions, or artifacts, the status of customs or folklore was decidedly different, and when used as a historical source, they became known as survivals. Unlike relics, survivals were still a part of contemporary society, active and in use – yet at the same time, such use was seen as irrational or pointless. Indeed, it was precisely this quality which gave them value as historical sources, because when seen as survivals from an earlier, different context (where they did make sense and serve a purpose), they offered vital clues to understanding the development of culture. The concept of survival largely derives from nineteenth-century ethnology, although it was also common in biology at the same time, where Darwin called attention to what he called rudimentary organs, as clues to a species evolution – 'the stump of a tail in tailless breeds, – or the vestige of an ear in earless breeds' (Darwin [1859] 1968: 431). Such rudimentary organs, or what later became more commonly known as vestigial organs after Robert Wiedersheim's book on human anatomy, were the biological counterpart of ethnological survivals (Wiedersheim 1895).

Unlike in biology, however, survivals in ethnology played a much more central role in understanding the past, especially through the work of Edward Tylor (Tylor 1913; see also Rivers 1913; Lowie 1918; Hodgen 1931). The concept of survivals can actually be traced back at least to the eighteenth century, when it formed a common topic of antiquarian interest among the middle and upper classes in Britain, whose subjects were the lower, especially rural, classes or peasantry (Stocking 1987: 54). Such survivals – revealingly called antiquities – were predominantly superstitions or beliefs reported in the *Gentleman's Magazine* or volumes such as Bourne's *Antiquitates Vulgares* (1725) or Brand's *Observations on the Popular Antiquities of Great Britain* (1777). It was W. J. Thoms, however, who coined the word 'survival' in 1846 from his observations on folklore published in the *Athenaeum* and *Notes and Queries* (Daniel 1975: 184–5). Such work was highly influential for Edward Tylor, who saw survivals as analogous to relics or artifacts – clues to the earlier history or stages of humankind – and they became a central and dominating part of the first volume of his major work, *Primitive Culture* ([1871] 1913). Tylor defined survivals thus:

> These are processes, customs, opinions, and so forth, which have been carried on by force of habit into a new state of society different from that in which they had their original home, and they thus remain as proofs and examples of an older condition of culture out of which a newer has been evolved.
>
> (Tylor 1913: 16)

For Tylor, archaeology and the study of folklore were thus twinned, one studying relics and the other survivals, although Tylor's focus lay more with folklore and survivals (Hodgen 1931). Indeed, though complementary, Tylor considered relics or vestiges as very different from survivals – the former being no longer part of a living culture, as already stated. In this, he was clearly trying to make a distinction which earlier scholars had not thought relevant, insofar as the term 'antiquities' was used to refer to both ancient customs surviving in the present and ancient objects unearthed from the ground. It is, however, important to underline the fact that the distinction between relics and survivals was not a distinction between material and nonmaterial elements; for although the concept of survivals largely referred to practices, beliefs, or words, it was also used with material culture, by Tylor and especially in the work of Otis J. Mason in North America (Tylor 1913: 17–18; Mason 1902; Daniel 1975: 185). Mason's study of inventions is a good example, as he attempts to trace the evolution of technology and material customs using survivals – among other lines of evidence – as a methodological tool. As an example, he quotes the presence of various material survivals in late-nineteenth-century Iceland:

> *In the more remote parts of Iceland, many articles of bone and stone are still in use, which in more accessible districts, have been replaced by metal or earthenware. Mr. Anderson saw a wheelbarrow with a stone wheel, a steelyard with a stone weight, a hammer with a stone head, and a net with bone sinkers. At the same farm a quern was in use, also horn stirrups, harness fastenings of bone, to say nothing of bone pins and bone dice.*
>
> (Mason 1902: 29)

Iceland became a very popular source of ethnographic data in the late nineteenth and early twentieth centuries which was primarily used to interpret ancient Nordic and Germanic culture, which is just one of many examples of this kind of research conducted at that time.

Another tradition, however, made a rather different connection between relics and contemporary practices. In the same year that Newton wrote his 'Study of Archaeology', the German archaeologist Eduard Gerhard ([1850] 2004) argued in his sixteen 'archaeological theses' that archaeology be viewed as a branch of philology – monumental philology, as he called it, to distinguish it from textual and/or literary philology (Gerhard [1850] 2004). Gerhard was in fact echoing a common link in German philology between material and textual sources (*Sach-* and *Wortphilologie*; see previous section) and was in many ways simply adding his voice to a growing call to make the study of things on a par with texts (Marchand 1996: 41). Gerhard's intention, like Virchow later, was to pull archaeology away from its association with art criticism as established by Wincklemann and to bring it closer to historical and philological research (Schnapp 2004; Marchand 1996: 41). Since the seventeenth century, philologists had been interested in tracing the connections between modern languages; such comparative philology, or what today is called historical linguistics, led in the eighteenth century to the notion of an Indo-European protolanguage (Blench 2006: 53–4; see also Renfrew 1987). The basic goal was to view languages in terms of family groups, or phyla, to establish relationships in the form of a family tree; one of the corollaries of this was the idea that former, extinct languages must have once existed from which modern languages descended – hence Indo-European as a kind of proto- or ur-language. Such approaches continued into the nineteenth century in various forms, including Pictet's version of linguistic palaeontology (Pictet 1859–63). The same idea was used in another branch of philology, textual criticism, which is especially linked to the work of the nineteenth-century German scholar Karl Lachmann, who developed it in the context of biblical and classical literature. Lachmann's method involved reconstructing standard or critical editions by producing a stemma (family tree or genealogy) of how a text becomes corrupted over time. By looking for similarities and differences between the different extant versions of the same text, Lachmann produced an archetypal text which was claimed to be as close to the original as possible, purged of transmission errors and additions. The archetype thus became the critical edition (Cerquiglini 1999; McGann 1983).

It is important to recognize that comparative philology dealt with living languages in a very different way to Tylor's concept of survivals. In philology and textual criticism, there is a genealogical interpretation based on classification – similarities between languages or texts are perceived in terms of relatedness, and from that, one can minimally establish historical connections between languages or texts and, more contentiously, infer or reconstruct ancient or archetypal languages and/or texts. Indeed, such an approach was also later adopted in the German culture historical approach in archaeology, especially by Oswald Menghin, who adapted Schmidt and Graebner's concept of primary culture cycles (archetypal cultures reconstructed from contemporary culture groups) and claimed that such could be detected in the archaeological record (Childe 1956a: 54–5; Trigger 2006: 219; Kohl & Pérez Gollán 2002). The similarities on which such reconstructions were based can be considered survivals, but in a very different sense to that used by Tylor; 'survival' in this context simply means the persistence of a trait in a living context – whether it is useful or meaningful or not. Indeed, this is how Maine used the term in his study *Ancient Law* (1861), where his influences are clearly from the German school of comparative philology rather than the British antiquarian tradition (Stocking 1987: 127). At the extreme, the term 'survival' was also used for whole groups of people, although this was uncommon; for example, Sollas refers to Australian Aborigines as survivals from Mousterian times in his book *Ancient Hunters and their Modern Representatives* (Sollas 1911: 162), and although this work in general is renowned for the way it sees contemporary peoples as survivals of different Palaeolithic periods, he does not use the term 'survival' except in this one instance.

The distinctions between remains and sources in the context of history, and between relics and survivals in the context of ethnology, reveal how the modern concept of the archaeological record emerged from a more common, even if heterogeneous, conception of historical evidence. Terms such as 'antiquities', 'vestiges', and 'remains' were often used interchangeably for ancient objects and modern customs, prehistoric bones, and medieval manuscripts during the eighteenth and early nineteenth centuries. The gradual emergence of our contemporary notion of the archaeological record was constituted through the increasing need to dissect this heterogeneous field and develop methods or approaches appropriate to each component. However, it was not until well into the twentieth century that such a separation had finally congealed. Despite a growing recognition of the different qualities of accidental material remains from intentional testimony, or objects from dead contexts as opposed to objects and customs in living

contexts, there was still a strong sense that these all constituted historical evidence, which should be integrated. Tylor drew on both survivals
and relics, whereas Collingwood employed material remains and written sources. In the following section, I explore in more detail the ideas
associated with archaeological evidence in relation to interpretation
during this period of the late nineteenth and early twentieth centuries.
Specifically, I suggest that precisely because of an inherited sense of
the common nature of this heterogeneous field of remains as fragmentary residues (whether relics, survivals, or sources), the predominant
concern – at least for archaeologists – was the problem of incompleteness. However, it was not incompleteness in the sense of what had
preserved or survived, but rather incompleteness of what had been
collected.

The Complete Collection: Archaeological Heuristics

EXPLICIT WORKS ON HISTORICAL SOURCES and methods, such as that
by Langlois and Seignobos mentioned already, were appearing precisely at the time when history was concerned with establishing for
itself a rigorous and distinct methodology (Iggers 1997); the authors
of *Introduction to the Study of History* characterized earlier attempts
as 'superficial, insipid, unreadable, sometimes ridiculous' (Langlois and
Seignobos 1925: 5). This may have been hyperbole, for they incorporated earlier ideas, especially from German scholars, notably those of
heuristics (recovery and collection of sources) and diplomatics (source
criticism). The development of source criticism (*quellenkritik*) in history
is particularly associated with the University of Berlin in Germany during the early nineteenth century, through the work of Barthold Niebuhr
and Leopold van Ranke, but it was only after the 1850s in Germany,
and then the 1870s in other European countries and North America,
that interest in a systematic method became a key concern – alongside
the professionalization of the discipline (Iggers 1997: 27). It is no coincidence that such professionalization of history – and archaeology –
coincided with the emergence of a heightened sense of nationalism in
Europe, and I do not need to – or indeed have the time to – rehearse
the manifold connections between nation-states and the construction

of official pasts (see e.g. Kohl & Fawcett 1995; for the specific case of Germany, see also papers in Härke 2002), suffice it to say, the very professionalization of disciplines and their concurrent concern for methodology clearly lent greater weight and authority to any statements about the past.

As already mentioned, the ideas of source criticism can be traced back to antiquarian studies in the sixteenth century in the fields of numismatics, epigraphy, diplomatics, and iconography, and their subsequent migration into philology during the seventeenth century (Momigliano 1950). Many of the more specific components of what later became historical source criticism derived, however, from related developments in jurisprudence (Franklin 1977). European medieval law was based on the Julian codification of Roman law – the *corpus juris*. During the sixteenth century, scholars started to treat this law philologically; that is, they attempted to reconstruct its original form and meaning from the incomplete texts that survived, rather than to write commentaries or exegeses, as had been the norm. The key to this approach was the development of source criticism. The new methods were sketched by Melchior Cano and François Baudouin in the early sixteenth century – it was Baudouin particularly who linked the study of law to history and raised the problem that sources were a mixture of fact and fiction, and he argued for the need to distinguish different types of fiction (e.g. outright lies from accidental errors). Baudouin compared historical sources to court testimonies and argued that they could be subject to the same principles of critique. He also outlined two principles for collecting sources: first, that despite the fact that much has been lost, by collating all available sources, one can still reconstruct the former whole; and second, sources need not be confined to intended historical narratives but ought to include all kinds of written documents (Franklin 1977: 133–4). To complete this revolution, Jean Bodin added the final element of source criticism: the role of the author and how the author's own position can colour a narrative text. It was Bodin who also wrote the key work on how to read historical texts critically in his *Method for the Easy Understanding of History* (*Methodus ad facilem historiarum cognitionem*) in 1566.

Such ideas had circulated widely in the humanities for some time and were part of a broader method which linked any discipline dealing with documents; the work of Niebuhr and von Ranke in Germany or Langlois and Seignobos in France can be seen as the codification of these ideas for the newly emerging, academic discipline of history. However, there is a limit to the extent to which these models were at all applicable to the nascent discipline of archaeology; certainly insofar as archaeology was principally the study of materials already collected via other means, and then there was clearly scope for adopting some form of source criticism. Chiefly, this revolved around the problems of establishing the reliability of provenance and authenticity of artifacts – just as with source criticism. Such reliability was a critical issue for collectors, including archaeologists in the late nineteenth century; the problem of false antiquities and false provenances was ever present, especially with flints and other stone tools for the early prehistoric archaeologists (O'Connor 2007: 88–9). The classic text on this subject is by the Scottish archaeologist Robert Munro, whose *Archaeology and False Antiquities*, published in 1905, explored a number of contentious cases regarding the authenticity of antiquities, as well as famous forgers like Flint Jack (Munro 1905).

Though not explicitly stated as source criticism, Munro is clearly addressing the same issues as historians dealing with the authenticity of manuscripts. After addressing the importance of distinguishing natural from manufactured objects, Munro then devotes most of his attention to the problem of false antiquities. He stresses the importance of long-term experience and skill in assessing authenticity and laments the fact that there were so few institutions in Britain training archaeologists in general scientific skills, in comparison with France or North America (Munro 1905: 9–11). Most of Munro's advice on assessing authenticity of finds is based on the formal and material characteristics of artifacts themselves rather than depositional context; however, he also acknowledges a number of secondary clues, which include their stratigraphic position, association with other objects, and general patina (ibid.: 18). It is perhaps a little odd that Munro gives only passing mention to perhaps the two fundamental concepts of archaeological excavation – stratigraphy and find combination or association – but we have to remember that he was writing at a time when the concept of archaeological fieldwork was only just emerging; many archaeologists still did not excavate, so their principal methods inevitably focused on the objects themselves (Lucas 2010a). Yet Munro clearly recognizes the importance of field observation, as this reference to controversies from the 1860s makes explicit:

> For we must remember that archaeological science was then only in its infancy, and that those who furnished the most important part of the evidence were unskilled observers... Yet the crux of the whole matter originally lay in a simple matter of observation, merely to determine the precise circumstances in which the objects were found, and how they came to be placed there questions which could only be determined then and there by skilled observers.
>
> *(Munro 1905: 271)*

Munro's whole book was emphatically an explicit plea for systematic instruction in archaeology (ibid.: 280), and he recognized that the future of such instruction lay primarily in controlled excavation – as his concluding remarks make abundantly clear:

> For the future it is on spade-work we have chiefly to rely for any considerable increase to the antiquarian materials already preserved in our museums. But the spade can be used as an implement of destruction as well as for unearthing archaeological treasures. Success depends on the intelligence which guides the hand of the operator. Excavations conducted by incompetent and irresponsible persons may do irretrievable mischief by destroying evidence which in the hands of a skilled antiquary might prove to be a valuable discovery.
>
> *(Ibid.: 281)*

Munro specifically names Pitt Rivers as the role model for such controlled excavation (ibid.: 283), and it is perhaps inevitable that Munro's book was the first and last of its kind in Britain. By his own prediction, it was superseded by excavation field manuals, the first of which was actually published the year before Munro's book: Flinders Petrie's *Methods and Aims in Archaeology* (Petrie 1904). Subsequent books on false antiquities were largely historical (e.g. Cole 1955; Rieth 1967), whereas more methodological texts now tend to be primarily by and for art historians and museum curators.

Such concerns as authenticity were thus rendered almost irrelevant as soon as they were recognized; for it was precisely because archaeologists – unlike historians – could create their own source material by doing fieldwork themselves, rather than rely on its collection by others, that they could circumvent the whole need for source criticism in the first place. Thus, from the late nineteenth to early twentieth century, although there is a similar codification of archaeological methods as one sees in history, it is much more concerned with heuristics than source criticism – that is, with fieldwork and specifically excavation. As with history, though, such texts should be considered part of the desire for professionalization and academic autonomy. Unsurprisingly, the earliest such texts came from German archaeologists, such as Voss's *Merbuch Alterthümer aufzugraben und aufzubewahren* (*Introduction to the Excavation and Protection of Antiquities*, 1888; see Sklenář 1983: 114). Indeed, among the first large-scale excavations were those of German classical archaeologists such as Curtius at Olympia, which had a major influence on the development of German archaeology (Marchand 1996: 77–91). Yet similar publications from elsewhere soon followed, such as Petrie's *Methods and Aims in Archaeology* (Petrie 1904) and Droop's *Archaeological Excavation* (Droop 1915) from Britain. However, methodological or 'textbook' publications in archaeology tended to be dominated by either reviews of material culture by period or typological approaches (e.g. Déchelette 1908–1914; Müller 1888–1895), and it was not until after the middle of the twentieth century that excavation manuals become a common and widespread phenomena (see section on source criticism).

Nonetheless, one of the consequences of this different methodological emphasis in archaeology from history was that models from the natural sciences offered much better analogies for the archaeological record. Because archaeologists had to 'make' their own sources, they were more like naturalists collecting specimens or fossils; this is not to say that they saw the sources as constructed in the sense of fabricated: they constituted real evidence or facts. But whereas historians had to ascertain such facts filtered through human testimony and memory, the archaeologist had a much more direct access to the facts themselves in the form of concrete things. Their problem became how to establish reliability in the creation of testimony, not in the reading or reception of it. This was the critical issue in the natural sciences, as has been made very clear in Shapin and Schaffer's *Leviathan and the Air Pump*, which looks at the controversy between Hobbes and Boyle in the seventeenth century in terms of establishing the importance of observational and experimental procedure to the development of science (Shapin & Schaffer 1985). Central to this procedure was the importance of establishing reliability in reported testimonies of observations and experiments. This was exactly the problem archaeologists faced in relation to fieldwork – but it was not something historians faced.

It is for this reason that archaeologists often liked to describe their discipline as a science, especially those working in pre-Roman or pre-classical archaeology. It is also why much of what one reads in late-nineteenth-century archaeological literature makes either implicit or explicit reference to a Baconian epistemology founded on induction (e.g. Pettigrew 1850: 174–5). Collingwood made this point very explicitly when he argued that archaeology was a much clearer example of a Baconian science than history – even though his whole goal was to transform history into such a science (Collingwood 1944: 90). Such an epistemology received its most systematic articulation in the mid-nineteenth century by William Whewell, particularly in his book *Philosophy of the Inductive Sciences*; for Whewell, knowledge was 'obtained by a common process of collecting general truths from particular observed facts, which process is termed *Induction*' (Whewell [1847] 1984: 124). Although Whewell is mostly concerned with describing the acquisition of knowledge in the physical and natural sciences – or what he called the material sciences, he readily admits that the same principles of knowledge apply to the human sciences, although because they are not yet properly established or stabilized, they have not yet attained the same status with regard to generalized propositions or theories (Whewell [1847] 1984: 124–9). One sees this same sentiment repeated endlessly by archaeologists in the late nineteenth century, who were humbly admitting that they were still a new science. Indeed, during much of the nineteenth century there was a suspicion of theory; as the archbishop of York put it in an inaugural address to the Royal Archaeological Institute, the 'greatest peril to science is to theorise overmuch' (Thomson 1867: 86). Thomas Wright, in his preface to the highly popular *The Celt, the Roman, and the Saxon*, similarly warns archaeologists against the twin dangers of insufficient data and hasty generalization: 'The great obstacle with which the student has had to contend was, the want of examples brought together for comparison, which led him to continually make assumptions that had no foundation' (Wright 1861: vi). Such a sober attitude was widely shared and based on the perception that archaeology was a new science and needed to prove itself. To do so, it relied heavily on precisely the model of an inductive science as outlined by Whewell.

However, if Whewell's model of inductive science acted as an implicit guide for many archaeologists in the field, the issue of interpretation remained problematic; so long as one focused on collecting facts and pretending that the theory would come later, the issue of interpretation could be postponed. The general suspicion of theory meant that one sees little explicit discussion of how to interpret the archaeological record in the nineteenth century: the immediate goal was to go on collecting and hope that when one had enough pieces, the 'whole' would eventually materialize. This jigsaw view implied that the creation of archaeological sources, their collection, was in some sense teleological: it strove towards a certain point, namely the idea of the complete collection. Thus, for Charles Newton, as for most of his contemporaries, archaeology was filling in a gap in our knowledge of the past, a gap which he defined in terms of an era before printed literature (i.e. before the sixteenth century). The divide of history and prehistory familiar to us today did not exist for Newton, writing in the 1850s, rather the fracture (if it even can be called such) occurred much closer to the present. It is perhaps because of the short chronology that most archaeologists were working under at the time – typically about six thousand years of human history – that the issue of the fragmentary or incomplete nature of archaeological sources was principally an issue about the incompleteness of collections, not the survival of evidence. Archaeologists undoubtedly recognized the partial nature of their evidence, but the real gaps in the archaeological record related to our knowledge and were not intrinsic to the material: there was plenty of evidence out there; it just needed gathering.

Such an attitude is evident if one looks at one of the more obvious areas where the issue of preservation stands out: wetland archaeology. Excavations and recovery of archaeological remains from European wetland contexts, such as bog bodies and lake dwellings, are often perceived as an insight into the missing aspects of material culture (e.g. Coles & Coles 1996). Such findings are as old as archaeology and date back to the early nineteenth century, yet what is striking about the nineteenth-century accounts of such finds is the almost complete lack of excitement about the increased range of finds when compared to dryland sites (Coles & Coles 1989: 31). Reading through Ferdinand Keller's classic account of the lake dwellings, what strikes the modern reader is how the emphasis is almost reversed; rather than highlighting how lake-dwelling finds expand the repertoire of material culture known from dryland sites, Keller focuses all the discussion on recounting how such finds compare and match up to previous dryland collections (Keller 1866: 301–9). Thus, there is a predominance of extended discussions and illustrations of stone artifacts, metal objects, and pottery over texts and images associated with horn, wood, and textiles. This is perhaps the most telling indication of how the nineteenth-century conception of the archaeological record differed from our own.

Robert Munro's later synthesis of European lake dwellings would seem to take a little more cognizance of this than Keller (Munro 1890); for example, he recognizes the potential importance of such sites because of the nature of their abandonment, which was generally perceived as untimely or catastrophic rather than gradual:

> *It is, indeed, to such catastrophes that we owe much of our information, as the sudden interruption of busy life scenes in such a manner and especially when accompanied by circumstances that tended to preserve the ruins from decay, has been the means of supplying us, as it were, with a photographic picture of the habits, customs, and industries of the people; and it requires only a sufficient number of such instances to be able, from a comparative examination of the recovered relics, to construct a fair scale of the progressive civilisation and culture of the lake dwellers.*
>
> (Munro 1890: 496)

Yet at the same time, although Munro acknowledges the presence of objects which are not commonly preserved on dryland sites, this is not a point of major concern, and like Keller, he spends vastly more pages in considering the more conventional types of finds out of more durable materials. Like Keller before him, this chiefly relates to the need to provide a chronology for these sites and linking the finds into the three-age system and current artifact chronologies, which were largely built up from dryland sites. Indeed, herein lies the chief reason archaeologists like Keller and Munro did not spend time thinking about issues of preservation in terms of interpreting the archaeological record. It was precisely such durable finds that defined classification systems, and thus, in effect, the concept of completeness in terms of collections. The incompleteness of the archaeological record in the nineteenth century was primarily about incomplete collections, not incomplete survival. The issue really centred on how extensive such collections needed to be, as I discuss next.

The Total Record

The striving for completeness is clearly expressed in Eduard Gerhard's third thesis on archaeology:

> *The task of archaeology is to present not just a selection of art monuments, but the entirety of the monumental material, both for its own sake and in its consequences for literary, religious and individual relics; the entirety of all philological research and the total world view of ancient life.*
>
> (Gerhard [1850] 2004: 173)

This demand for total collections became a very prominent feature of nineteenth-century archaeology, especially in classical archaeology; it lies behind the notion of the corpus, a full and detailed collection of all known examples of specific artifact types. In this, it shared many similarities with philology and art criticism, not unsurprising given Gerhard's ascription of archaeology as a branch of philology (Andrén 1998: 15; Schnapp 1996: 304). Indeed, the first institutionally backed, large-scale excavations in the late 1870s, such as those at Olympia in Greece by Ernst Curtius or Pergamum in Turkey by Karl Humann, were explicitly intended to recover extensive collections of material as an antidote to the small-scale work that tended to predominate (Marchand 1996: 75–115). Alexander Conze, who had been excavating at Samothrace during the same period and had backed Humann's excavations at Pergamum, was particularly emphatic about the need to recover the full range of material culture. The task of 'big archaeology' was precisely to retrieve and comprehend 'whole cities and landscapes in their entirety . . . from images, inscriptions and all manner of minor art forms down to the most insignificant potsherd, to bring forth, with the united energies of [many] scholars, the finer characteristics of the grand picture' (Conze, quoted in Marchand 1996: 97). Such total archaeology was also inextricably linked to the need to separate archaeology as a science of history from aesthetics and art history.

In Britain, Thomas Pettigrew made a similar point in his address to the British Archaeological Association in 1850, lamenting the current state of collections of British antiquities, arguing that 'much has yet to be accomplished' (Pettigrew 1850: 167). Yet to some extent, the notion of a complete collection was at odds with the classificatory desire which was the cornerstone of archaeological method at this time. For the purposes of classification, one did not need to have every instance recorded, just representative examples of each type; multiple examples of the same served no purpose and added no new knowledge.

In his discussion of the utility of the corpus, Flinders Petrie actually makes this point quite explicitly; he argues that the corpus is essential to archaeology, but as a classification – once it has been constructed, it removes the need for total collections:

The practical utility of such a corpus *is found at once when excavating. Formerly it was needful to keep dozens of broken specimens, which were of no value except for the fact of being found along with other vases. Now the excavator merely needs to look over the* corpus *of plates, and writes down on the plan of the tomb say, B23, P35b, C15, F72, thus the whole record is made, and not a single piece be kept unless it is a good specimen.*

(Petrie 1904: 125)

Such an attitude was perhaps even more evident in the context of natural history, where it was regarded as a given and had the added advantage that it got around the problem of the incomplete survival of evidence (see the discussion of Lyell and the geological record in Bowker 2006: 67). Yet this was also precisely where archaeology or human history diverged from natural history: in the significance given to particularity. Not that archaeology was or is averse to generalization, just that the importance of the particular is not as easily dismissed as it is with natural sciences. Although archaeology adopted the same classificatory impulse as the natural sciences in the nineteenth century, because of its closer affiliation with history (at that time), it could never quite escape the relevance of the singular or unique. This was Mortimer Wheeler's point in commenting on Petrie's attitude to the role of the corpus:

> *The advantages of a scholarly* corpus *or yardstick need no further emphasis... and the extension of the* corpus-system *is certainly no less urgent now than in Petrie's day. But always with the proviso that it presents a very serious danger: it lends itself to a loose usage and to the overlooking of those subtle variations of form, the importance of which Pitt Rivers rightly emphasized. Generally speaking, only an evolved and largely mechanized industry offers suitable material for a corpus.*
>
> *(Wheeler 1954: 211–12)*

Exactly the same point was made by the British archaeologist William Greenwell half a century earlier; here, in 1865, he wrote about the importance of each find:

> *It may be thought that so many accounts have been given of the facts connected with primitive interments, that nothing can be added, and that any fresh record is only a repetition of well-known details, which can bring no additional data to the stock of knowledge that we already possess. Such is, however, a mistaken idea. No two interments present quite the same features, and each one that is examined is valuable, either as a confirmation of views not as yet based on a sufficiently exact or wide foundation, or as giving some new fact which may modify, or perhaps destroy, the theory which, in such matters, we are sometimes obliged to erect.*
>
> *(Greenwell 1865: 97)*

Contained here are two ideas about archaeological remains: one drawing on the popular Baconian or Whewellian view of induction as the foundation of knowledge (i.e. knowledge progresses only through the accumulation of facts); the other, about the limitations of generalization for a historical discipline insofar as each find is ultimately unique. There is a clear ambivalence in Greenwell's position – although he recognizes that some new finds may be repetitive, still some may not. Greenwell's ambivalence was not felt by one of his contemporaries,

Pitt Rivers, whom we saw referenced by Wheeler in the previous quote. Pitt Rivers is renowned for being the father of British fieldwork, as well as for his work on evolutionary typology, and he espoused a very firm position of the importance of total collection during excavation and its relevance for generalizing classification:

> *Excavators, as a rule, record only those things which appear to them important at the time, but fresh problems in Archaeology and Anthropology are constantly arising, and it can hardly fail to have escaped the notice of anthropologists, especially those who, like myself, have been concerned with the morphology of art, that, on turning back to old accounts in search of evidence, the points which would have been most valuable have been passed over from being thought uninteresting at the time. Every detail should, therefore, be recorded in the manner most conducive to facility of reference, and it ought at all times to be the chief object of an excavator to reduce his own personal equation to a minimum.*
>
> *(Pitt Rivers 1887: xvii)*

This tension was also brought out further in a short paper by Harlan Smith in 1911 titled 'Archaeological Evidence as Determined by Method and Selection' (Smith 1911). His concern was to highlight the interpretive problems of incomplete or biased collections, and he makes an explicit contrast between collections made by an amateur and those by a trained archaeologist:

> *The collection gathered by the connoisseur differs from the collection made by the scientist who endeavours to obtain, in an unprejudiced and disinterested manner, the evidence, the whole evidence, and nothing but the evidence. Archaeological material, being necessarily fragmentary, readily lends itself to misleading reconstruction.*
>
> *(Smith 1911: 445)*

Smith discusses the advantages of scientists going into the field to gather the collection for themselves, insofar as they strive to collect every scrap and fragment and thus gain a true cross-section of the whole material culture, not just special or unique finds. He likens the archaeological approach to a 'merchant's store of goods after he has taken his inventory and replenished his stock by filling up the gaps' (ibid.: 447).

Moreover, even once a full collection has been made, the archaeologist faces the dilemma of how much of this should be presented. Because one cannot, for lack of space or expense, show all objects in such a collection, one has to, perforce, show only representative examples of the more common types – but in doing so, one gives a false impression of the abundance of unique objects (ibid.). For Smith, the only way out of this dilemma was for the reader or visitor to pay close attention to accompanying text, which ought to rectify this impression.

In many ways, this tension between the general and particular still exists with archaeology and probably always will, indicating as it does, different views of the discipline as idiographic or nomothetic (Trigger 1978a; Lyman & O'Brien 2004). Yet there is a deep irony here. In promoting the particularistic nature of archaeology as a historical science, and thus the need for as complete collections as possible, one would imagine that the problem of the incomplete survival or preservation of evidence would have been of major concern. It was not; the problem of incompleteness rather always remained allied to the practice of collection or the production of *corpora*, not something intrinsic to archaeological remains – even if their fragmentary nature was cited as a justification for such complete collections. Incompleteness thus remained a matter of archaeological heuristics, not source criticism. This is clear in Pitt Rivers paper 'Principles of Classification' (1874), in which he decries the state of specimens in ethnological collections, which 'have not been obtained in sufficient number or variety to render classification possible' (Pitt Rivers 1906: 2–3). It is only from the mid-twentieth century that one starts to see a concern for this latter issue in relation to interpretation.

What changed at the turn of nineteenth and twentieth century was the attitude toward incompleteness; whereas Eduard Gerhard and Pitt Rivers had argued for the goal of the total collection or total record, a century later Hans Jürgen Eggers and Grahame Clark recognized that this was an impossibility. The change was already visible in the writings of Flinders Petrie in the first decade of the twentieth century:

> *In recording, the first difficulty is to know what to record. To state every fact about everything found would be useless, as no one could wade through the mass of statements... The old saying that a man finds what he looks for in a subject is too true; or, if he has not*

*enough insight to ensure finding what he looks for, it is at least sadly
true that he does not find anything he does not look for.*

(Petrie 1904: 49)

In short, Petrie is arguing for the idea of the selective record against
Pitt Rivers's call for a total record; as with Pitt Rivers, however, the
focus remains on archaeological heuristics (i.e. on the collection of
archaeological evidence), not on issues of preservation or survival –
this comes much later (see next section).

Martin Carver has discussed this difference between Pitt Rivers and
Petrie and has put it in the context of long-term traditions of British
fieldwork practices (Carver 1990). Carver argues that this difference
is linked to perceptions about the formation of knowledge, specifically
whether archaeological facts are found out there, in the ground to be
recovered, or whether they are produced by archaeologists in relation
to their questions (Carver 1990: 45; see also Carver 1989). However,
I think Carver was perhaps reading this dichotomy too much in terms
of the theoretical debates in archaeology of the 1980s about object-
ivism and relativism; nonetheless, it is true that Pitt Rivers and Petrie
appeared to have very different attitudes to the nature of evidence –
the one adhering to an inductivist position, the other adopting a more
problem-oriented, historical approach. But this was framed within different perceptions of archaeology as a science: Pitt Rivers with his
focus on prehistory and his alliance to the natural sciences, and Petrie with his focus on Egyptology and a more philological or historical
orientation.

This comes out very clearly in Petrie's discussion of the nature of
archaeological evidence, in which he draws explicitly on analogies with
legal evidence (Petrie 1904, chapter 10; 1906). Petrie discusses archaeological evidence under four headings: witnesses, material facts, exhaustion, and probability. For archaeology, witnesses are the historical texts
and inscriptions which may exist – and like witness testimony, they may
be completely unreliable. Material facts are artifacts or assemblages of
artifacts in context, but his discussion is interesting insofar as he uses
examples to illustrate how misunderstanding can occur but also can be
avoided. By 'exhaustion', Petrie means evidence by default – an archaeological example being the erasure of the name Amen on Egyptian
inscriptions; this act is not signed, but because no one but Akhenaten

is known to have done this, one can reasonably infer that any such act is by him, by default. Finally, there is probability, by which he means what today we would call circumstantial evidence – thus, knowing a general characteristic of a group such as the Saxons leads one to infer that the destruction of specific Roman towns was the result of Saxon attacks (Petrie 1906: 220–1).

Petrie's discussion is one of the first explicit and extended treatments on the nature of archaeological interpretation, and the alignment of archaeological with legal evidence can be considered part of a general humanistic attitude and the links between historical scholarship and jurisprudence, as related earlier (Franklin 1977). Similar parallels were later drawn by Collingwood in his book *The Idea of History* (Collingwood 1946: 266–8). Both considered the similarities to the legal process to be valid only up to a point, and Petrie stressed the open-endedness of archaeological enquiry, that '[h]appily archaeology is relieved from the terrible dilemma of being bound to come to a conclusion at once, as the law has to do' (Petrie 1906: 222). Collingwood made the same point years later (Collingwood 1946: 268). In Collingwood's discussion, however, the relevance of the analogy with legal evidence is spelt out more explicitly as part of a basic Baconian method of question and answer in which sources are treated as evidence to be subjected to inference. Collingwood was essentially arguing against a simplistic historical method, which he called scissor-and-paste history; by this, he meant a history which simply cut documents up into true and false or reliable and unreliable parts, and then pasted the reliable parts together into a narrative. Equally subject to his scorn, however, was a generalizing history, which he labelled as pigeonholing (ibid.: 263–6). In short, Collingwood was sceptical of the overemphasis on source criticism as historical method, because for Collingwood, the meaning of texts was as important as their reliability (ibid.: 260).

Significant though this is, it only partly explains why Petrie espoused a selective record as against the total record of Pitt Rivers. I would suggest that another element hinges on differences in practice, especially the material conditions of those practices. Pitt Rivers's excavations all occurred in Britain, and mostly but not exclusively focused on prehistoric settlements, such as the sites on his estate of Cranbourne Chase (Pitt Rivers 1887). The amount of material – specifically artifacts – he was dealing with was not on a vast scale. Petrie, in contrast, whose fieldwork was all based in Egypt, had to deal with material remains on a vastly larger scale. It may seem unsatisfactory to link Pitt Rivers's and Petrie's attitudes to archaeological collection on something as arbitrary and contingent as the location of their fieldwork, but it seems to me that the material nature of archaeological practice ought to be intimately connected to its conceptual nature. This is something I take up in much greater detail in Chapter 6, but to lend this notion some credence here, it is highly instructive to look at Mortimer Wheeler. Wheeler is the other key mythic figure in British field archaeology, and he is even largely responsible for Pitt Rivers's ascription as the father of fieldwork; Wheeler saw himself as the successor to Pitt Rivers and clearly praised him and his methods – quoting the same text about the total record as mentioned earlier (Wheeler 1954: 25–8). Moreover, in the same chapter from his *Archaeology from the Earth* in which he discusses the historical background to excavation methods, Wheeler also roundly condemns Petrie (ibid.:30). Apropos, it is strange in this connection that Carver (1990) places Wheeler in the same tradition as Petrie, not Pitt Rivers, simply because he saw archaeology more as a humanistic, particularizing discipline.

Yet there is a noticeable inconsistency in Wheeler's official guide to methods as presented in *Archaeology from the Earth* and his more personal reflections. In a paper presented to the Council for British Archaeology in 1950 titled 'What *Matters* in Archaeology?', Wheeler reflects on the differences between doing fieldwork in Asia and Europe; at Mohenjo-daro in Pakistan, Wheeler confesses to making compromises in method which he would not have done in Britain simply because of the sheer scale of the archaeology – compromises both in stratigraphic excavation and in total recovery of finds (Wheeler 1966: 107–8):

> [T]hese methods, undiluted, will not as a rule meet the Eastern problem. There the accumulation of soil is on average five times as great as in this country, and if a reasonable amount of horizontal excavation is to be accomplished – if we are to uncover enough of the plan to matter – the vertical digging must be speeded up. For example, at the end of my first month's work at Mohenjo-daro in Pakistan ... I sent back twelve bullock-wagon loads of selected pottery to base, but still had no idea what I was digging.
>
> (Wheeler 1966: 107)

Wheeler realizes that this contradicts his general adherence to Pitt Rivers's advice on the total record, but he argues that the idea of the total record is applicable only in some contexts and that a more select- ive approach is necessary in others. Wheeler also expresses the same ambivalence about the corpus, as referenced earlier – and probably for much the same reasons: explicitly, he talks about the limitations of generalization and classification, but implicitly (and this comes across much clearer from Petrie's own writing) it may also be a question of sheer excess of finds. Petrie was dealing with hundreds of thousands of pottery fragments, whereas Pitt Rivers was dealing with only hundreds. Faced with such vast differences, it is perhaps no surprise that Petrie promoted the corpus as a means of not having to keep all his pot- sherds, whereas for Pitt Rivers, the problem was the opposite – a deficit of material, hence his promotion of drawing and describing every single piece.

Wheeler thus stands hovering between the views of the total and selective records, but the point here is not that he is having the cake and eating it too, but his reasons for moving from one to the other view. It all comes down to the material differences in the archaeological record:

> We proudly proclaim the Pitt Rivers tradition but do not let us make a fetish of it. Were the General alive today and confronted with the relics of a great central civilization instead of the smudges of his peripheral slum he would, I have no doubt, echo fervently the words of Karl Marx and say[,] 'At any rate I am not a Pitt Riverist'.
>
> (Wheeler 1966: 109)

Of course, the question immediately arises, If this attitude is connec- ted to the material richness and scale of the archaeological record, why was it not an issue for scholars – like Eduard Gerhard – working in these areas in the nineteenth century? The answer is fairly simple: these archaeologists by and large did not go into the field; they worked with material deriving from collectors, antiquarians, and others. Con- sequently, they did not actually have to deal with problems at the coal face, so to speak; selections had already been made (see Gerhard's sixth thesis [1850] 2004: 174).

As archaeologists became more closely involved with fieldwork in the later nineteenth century, and in particular as the very manual aspect of fieldwork relied less and less on unskilled labourers over the twentieth century, one might expect to see archaeologists becoming more and more favourable to Petrie's views of the selective record – even if not his specific methods. But in fact discourses on archaeological method tended to remain more loyal to Pitt Rivers's view until recently. Philip Barker was a clear exponent of this idea, and associated with it, during the 1970s and 1980s, the idea of the archive objective (that the archive should be able to stand in for the site itself, or preservation by record) was widely promoted (Carver 1990; Roskams 2001: 35; these issues are also discussed further later in this chapter). One might suggest that the idea of the total record remains as ambiguous today as it did a century ago; what has changed, however, is the addition of another sense of incompleteness to the archaeological record. From around the middle of the twentieth century, the idea of incompleteness starts to be applied more explicitly to the question of preservation and survival of evidence, a shift from an archaeological heuristics to an archaeological diplomatics (i.e. source criticism). Increasingly, archaeologists became more concerned with the representivity of their sources than the selectivity of their recording and collection. In part, this happened because of the increasing influence of functionalist approaches to interpreting the past, as the archaeological record came to be viewed less as a set of cultural vestiges or relics and more as components of a social system.

Archaeological Source Criticism

THE SHIFT FROM AN ARCHAEOLOGICAL HEURISTICS to source criticism is very clear if one compares the works of Gordon Childe with those of Grahame Clark, two of the leading archaeologists in Britain during the first half of the twentieth century. Childe was certainly aware that he was dealing with partial evidence, but he was not perturbed. In his only book-length treatment of archaeological method, *Piecing Together the Past*, he dismisses the problem as something which can be resolved by recourse to ethnographic analogy or the rare cases where preservation is excellent: 'with proper precautions these gaps may partially be filled in by deductions from comparative ethnography as well as by the lucky finds' (Childe 1956a: 10–12). For Childe, one senses that the important issue remained one of archaeological heuristics, and in particular, the extensiveness of collections and the quality of fieldwork. This latter issue is made clear in his letter to Soviet colleagues, in which he urged them to improve their fieldwork techniques (see Klejn 1994: 95–9). Childe was thus somewhat conventional in his perspective on the archaeological sources, even if he did not write much about fieldwork methods himself. This attitude contrasts sharply with Clark's; whereas Childe devoted fewer than three pages to the question of preservation and survival of evidence in *Piecing Together the Past*, Clark gave a whole chapter of more than thirty pages to the same issue in *Archaeology and Society*, which was originally published in 1939, but went through two revisions. Clark promoted a concern with data quality totally different to Childe's, which generally revolved around the issue of survival, looking at the inherent qualities of material culture and their depositional conditions, which include both natural and cultural aspects (Clark 1957). Clark was quite explicit about the importance of this topic in relation to archaeological research:

> *The subject is one of supreme importance for three reasons: it largely determines the kind of site to be investigated when particular types of information are sought and the proper method to be followed in the actual work of excavation; and it affects profoundly that ultimate task of the archaeologist – the interpretation of his finds.*
>
> *(Clark 1957: 74)*

The differences may again be also partly related to the specific material conditions of their empirical work. Clark was no less keen than Childe to develop social and economic interpretations, but he may have been more acutely aware of the difficulties of such an ambition because his main research interests lay in earlier prehistoric periods (Palaeolithic and Mesolithic), whereas Childe's interests were emphatically in later prehistory (Neolithic and Bronze Age). The difference in the quantity and diversity of source material for these periods needs no special mention. However, this does not really explain the differences, because the same concerns felt by Clark were also being aired in Germany around the same time but over the same later prehistoric material that Childe worked with. The most explicit formulation of this concern was developed by Hans Jürgen Eggers in the 1950s, although the basic points had been made earlier by Karl Hermann Jacob-Friesen in the 1920s (Kristiansen 1978). Indeed, it is perhaps fair to say that, although in Britain issues of preservation were acknowledged, they generally did not become of great methodological concern. For example, although our contemporary perception of wetland research has clearly changed since the late nineteenth century and we perceive a much greater significance to the 'missing material culture' than, for example, Keller or Munro did (see e.g. Coles & Coles 1996), it is arguable how seriously archaeologists take this issue (see e.g. Evans 1989a). Moreover, material preservation is just one aspect to a much larger issue here, about representivity, which has been explored in most detail through the German tradition of archaeological source criticism.

The Central European Tradition: Archaeological Source Criticism

The German archaeologist Hans Jürgen Eggers was at the forefront of a major attack in the 1950s on interpretations resulting from Gustav Kossina's settlement archaeology, which had become the dominant paradigm since the 1920s. Specifically, it was argued that Kossina's culture-group distributions did not take account of the conditions of survival and recovery in the archaeological record (Härke 1991: 190). Even though Eggers continued the geographical tradition largely established by Kossina, the attention to the representivity of the archaeological record was an important development. In his *Einführung in die Vorgeschichte (Introduction to Prehistory)*, first published in 1959 and which became the standard German textbook for much of the later twentieth century, Eggers followed many concerns raised decades earlier by Jacob-Friesen but extended them:

> *Are archaeological finds applicable as historical documents, or are they not? We have already noted that history (in a narrower sense) and prehistory differ from each other based on the character of their sources. If we therefore want to understand the difference of the character of these two related sciences then we have to start with an analysis and criticism of their sources. That what is nowadays often understood as 'source criticism' in prehistoric archaeology, can be best read in the well-known work 'Grundfragen der*

Urgeschichtsforschung' [Fundamental Questions of Prehistoric Research] by Jacob-Friesen. He means there with 'finds criticism' the observation, if a find, i.e. an archaeological source, is authentic or counterfeit; if the finding place is assured, if the find proveniences are known, if it was lifted by a layman or salvaged by professionals during an archaeological excavation. Thus are these all questions which refer to the reliability of passing on a source – not to the reliability of the source itself. The historian also knows this kind of criticism. He names it 'textual criticism' – and often leaves this work to the philologist. But when the philologist has reconstructed the original text by the comparison of different types of written record or interpolation of a damaged inscription stone – then actually begins the critical analysis of the source by the historian.

(Eggers 1986: 255–6; trans. A. Daxböck)

This quote is important because it shows that Eggers was adopting a common distinction in history between external and internal source criticism and applying it to archaeology. The former, also called textual criticism, as he says, concerns the passing on of the source, which archaeologists now largely control because they themselves conduct fieldwork. Though still important, this was chiefly a concern of developing systematic field methods, as in the quote from Munro given earlier. The latter, however, was another issue, and for Eggers, of much greater concern, because it pertained to historical interpretation.

In short Eggers was saying that archaeological remains can lie – and not only because of issues of representivity (hence external criticism) but also because of the intentionality behind their original formation (hence internal criticism; Malina & Vašiček 1990: 106–7). He argued that archaeological evidence was not a face-value reflection of people's everyday behaviour in the past but was often mediated by their beliefs and ideology and could thus give a false impression if read as such. Thus, people were not buried in everyday clothing or objects, and the rate and manner in which people threw things away varied according to cultural systems of value (Eggers 1950). This has crucial implications for the nineteenth-century view of archaeological remains as an accidental record as discussed earlier and thus for Droysen's elevation of such sources as less biased than intended records. Eggers also introduced the concepts of living, dying, and dead culture (*lebendes*, *sterbendes, totes Gut*) as a way to articulate the manner in which the archaeological record is part of a continuous historical process linking past and present. In his paper 'The Problem of Ethnic Interpretation in Early History' ('Das Problem der ethnischen Deutung in der Frühgeschichte'), he argues that a living culture is one in which the meaning and use of artifacts are concurrent; in a dying culture, meanings may be preserved, but the objects are generally not in use; and in a dead culture, even the meanings have been lost (Eggers 1950). He recognized that cultures may die very slowly and in parts – for example, he cites ethnographic material from Pomerania, where clothing is replaced every five years and jewellery every century, but aristocratic and religious insignia goes back centuries. Eggers later modified this three-stage model (*Dreistufenmodell*) into living, dead, and rediscovered culture, the latter being what remained of the culture found by archaeologists (Eggers 1986; see also Härke 1997).

These ideas share some similarities with the development of formation theory in North America, which is discussed in Chapter 3 – but there are significant differences. Principally, Eggers views this from the perspective of source criticism and the present position of the archaeologist looking back; second – at least in the original scheme – he also stresses the continuity between living and dead cultures through the middle term of a dying culture; this middle term is totally missing from later North American thinking, which polarizes the archaeological record into living and dead, dynamic and static (but see Ascher 1968 and DeBoer 1983 for exceptions, discussed further in Chapter 3).

Eggers's ideas can, of course, be considered the continuation of an historical source-critical method in Central European archaeology. His ideas became very influential in Germany and Scandinavia, were developed by others (especially W. Torbrügge), and continue to form a basic part of archaeological method in Germany through the updated version of Manfried Eggert (e.g. Eggert 2001). But by the 1960s the influences of approaches from North America also started to have a wider impact. In 1978, Kristian Kristiansen attempted to advertise and update the European model of source criticism, and his intention was clearly influenced by the theoretical discourse of New Archaeology (Kristiansen 1978: 1). However, it is also clear that he came to see the development of an explicit source-critical method as a response or alternative to the

emerging North American (and anthropological) approaches to formation processes. Kristiansen's paper focused on three factors which he
regarded as central to a source-critical method. The first is the physical and environmental factors which affect the survival of remains; he
gives examples such as differential preservation in areas of Denmark
due to the extent of glaciations or sea-level change. The second concerns the affects of later cultural and economic factors on survival –
ploughing, quarrying, and even the absence of such activities which
might preserve relict landscapes. The third and final factor concerns
the nature of archaeological research and the selectivity of what is
recorded, such as through sampling strategies or attributes chosen for
description.

Kristiansen's approach can be summed up by the concept of representivity: 'source-critical analysis examines the effect of factors that have
influenced the representivity of the sources from the time they ceased
to be an active part of a culture' (Kristiansen 1978: 4). In the same
year (but published only in 1985), Kristiansen edited an impressive set
of papers examining the representivity of archaeological remains for
Danish prehistory, provocatively titled *Archaeological Formation Processes* (Kristiansen 1985). The contrast to the North American usage
of the term 'formation process' is very evident and no doubt intentional. The volume is largely about the factors cited by Kristiansen
affecting the preservation and nature of the archaeological record; a
good example is Baudou's paper, which links the extant distribution
of Bronze Age burial mounds in Denmark to intensity of cultivation
since at least the thirteenth century (Baudou 1985). These are generally either historical processes affecting the landscape or archaeological
procedures of investigation. Absent is any discussion of issues such as
discard or reuse, or of Schiffer's c- and n-transforms, which had started
to enter the literature in the early 1970s. What is interesting, however,
is that Kristiansen's definition of source criticism pertains to only one
aspect under Eggers's scheme – external criticism, not internal criticism. Thus, he focuses on the problem of the passing on of sources,
even if he extends it to include not just the context of recovery but
also intervening formation processes since original deposition. Eggers's
concept of internal criticism is largely absent, and indeed it is not until
the emergence of postprocessualism in the 1980s and an interest in
symbolism and ideology that one sees a similar concern for this issue

elsewhere. However, one could equally argue that formation processes do not belong to either internal or external criticism but sit uncomfortably somewhere in between; this issue is central to Chapter 3 and is not pursued further here.

A similar attempt to conjoin Eggers's Central European model of source criticism with formation theory from North America was made by the Czech archaeologist Evžen Neustupný (1993); his starting point is the familiar distinction between living and dead cultures that Eggers used – but noticeably, Neustupný drops the middle term of dying culture (Neustupný 1993: 45–6). Instead, he considers the relation between living and dead cultures in broad terms as a transformative process of reduction – both quantitative and qualitative – which he likens to entropy (ibid.: 47–8). For Neustupný, these processes can be classified into two types: exit transformations, which define the transition from a living to a dead culture, and subsequent transformations, which lead to further decay or disturbance of matter (ibid.: 49). This results in an extremely negative characterization of the archaeological record as a series of absences, which have to be restored through a process of reversing the transformations (conceptually) to get back to the living culture (ibid.: 67–72).

However, Manfried Eggert is probably the true heir of Eggers, perpetuating the idea of archaeological source criticism as central to method and theory in the German tradition. In chapter 4 of Eggert's *Prehistoric Archaeology: Theories and Methods* (*Prähistorische Archäologie: Konzepte und Methoden*; Eggert 2001), Eggert outlines the nature of the archaeological record in terms of historical sources, drawing heavily on the work of Paul Kirn, an early-twentieth-century German historian, in particular his adoption of Droysen and Bernheim's distinction between remains and tradition (or sources) as two different kinds of historical evidence – that is, accidental and intentional records, respectively (Eggert 2001: 45–7; see also Härke 1993, 1997). However, Eggert adds a second level of distinction between written and unwritten sources (i.e. things and texts); he argues that it is this second distinction that is more important to separating historical from archaeological sources – at least as Eggert defines archaeology, whose concern is chiefly pre- or protohistory (Table 3). Thus, Eggert sees historical sources as comprising all four possible types of source, whereas archaeology has access to only two and is thus impoverished

Table 3. *Types of Sources Available to History and Archaeology (Pre- and Protohistory)*

	Accidental (Remains)	Intentional (Tradition)
Written	History	History
Unwritten	History	History
	Pre- and protohistory	Pre- and protohistory

with respect to its evidence (Eggert 2001: 48–50). Because of this, he emphasizes a two-tier model of archaeological inference:

> *Prehistoric sources are materialised remains of the past. As a genuine part of this past, they can give certain information about the material habitus at this time. Everything else which goes beyond the materiality of these objects and contexts, is already an interpretation of these remains. And here it does not matter if these are statements about a bronze sword or postholes of a building. As soon as the material-level is left, it is about 'secondary' insights or 'conclusions'. Now it is up to the archaeologist to approach the area which is behind the material-level by using objects and contexts. It is only possible to investigate this significant 'non-material' aspect of sources and their past cultural context by using analogies and compare them with that which is already known.*
>
> (Ibid.: 100–1; trans. A. Daxböck)

This rather negative view of archaeological evidence and interpretation is somewhat surprising in such a contemporary context, yet Eggert is quite emphatic that because the meaning of objects lies in their sociocultural context, not in themselves – and because this sociocultural context no longer exists, such meanings often must remain inaccessible. This, for Eggert, is what largely defines the nature of archaeological sources and distinguishes them from historical or written sources (ibid.: 100). In contrast, Eggert draws on Droysen's nineteenth-century notion of the accidental source as one of the more advantageous aspects to archaeological sources, vis-à-vis many written and historical records. Yet Eggert is clearly wary of their bias, as previously expressed by Eggers in the 1950s, citing examples of burials and hoards as typical types of source material which cannot be read at face value (ibid.: 101–2).

Indeed, this is why, for Eggert, archaeological sources can fall into the category of intended records (tradition) as well as accidental records (remains), which is why, within archaeology, this distinction carries greater significance than that between written and unwritten sources (see also Härke 1997).

Otherwise, Eggert more or less follows the methods established by his predecessor Eggers, adopting the distinction between internal and external source criticism as those concepts apply to archaeological evidence and significantly bracketing the whole issue of formation theory in a footnote under a discussion of internal source criticism (ibid.: 109). He also draws on Eggers's notion of living and dead cultures and views source criticism as the attempt to get back to the living culture through what has been recovered of a dead culture, thus highlighting the problems of representivity. Furthermore, he adopts and modifies Eggers's applied approach to source criticism, in which emphasis is laid on the progression of previous research on any given topic. Thus, source criticism as practiced depends on a deep familiarity with the current state of research (*Forschungsstand*), analysis (*Bearbeitungsstand*), and publication (*Publikationsstand*) – the latter of which was specifically singled out by Eggert in contrast to Eggers, who subsumed it in the second (ibid.: 112–13).

Such approaches perhaps typify central European scholarship in the humanities and show how conceptions of the archaeological record are closely tied in to archive and literary production as much as – if not more so than formation processes. Indeed, the idea of archaeological source criticism never took on wide acceptance outside of Central Europe, just as formation theory and middle-range theory did not receive much attention outside North American and Britain (see e.g. Forslund 2004). They represent two very different approaches to the archaeological record, which – despite the attempts of Kristiansen or Neustupný to conjoin – could not be so easily translated into each other without serious loss to one or the other. Yet the same concerns one sees with Eggers were evidently shared in the Anglo-American tradition, only they took a very different trajectory. If one were to attempt a coarse translation of Eggers's view of source criticism into Anglo-American terms, then one could argue that they were expressed in the simultaneous but entirely bifurcated emergence of discourses about fieldwork and theory from the 1950s. Whereas for Eggers the two remained connected as aspects of source criticism (external and internal), in Anglo-American archaeology one sees a divergence as both fieldwork manuals and theoretical texts start to proliferate from the 1950s. In Britain alone, although the early twentieth century saw the publication of only a handful of field manuals, such as by Petrie (1904) and Droop (1915), from midcentury these increased dramatically (e.g. Atkinson 1946; Kenyon 1952; Wheeler 1954; Webster 1963). This increase in field manuals no doubt relates to the rise in students and university courses and the establishment and consolidation of archaeology as an independent subject, but it also testifies to a growing concern for controlling the production of sources or recovery of data – in short, external source criticism. Though initially connected to the simultaneous rise in theoretical discourse, the two gradually drifted apart so that by the 1990s, archaeologists were starting to question the atheoretical nature of fieldwork (see final section of this chapter).

This bifurcation between theory and practice (often simply not recognized by archaeologists outside the Anglophone world) might not have occurred had archaeologists in the Anglo-American tradition been more receptive to the German model of source criticism. However, one of the reasons source criticism may not have become a major part of British archaeological method may be tied to the similar lack of interest in it among British historians; as already remarked, for Collingwood source criticism was a limited method of interpretation in history insofar as the meaning of texts often weighed more than their reliability – although again, this view equated source criticism solely with external or textual criticism. Not that reliability was unimportant; it was just not all that mattered. In many ways, this is exactly the attitude that Childe was displaying in his book *Piecing Together the Past*, particularly when one considers that Childe's remarks on the survival of evidence occur in an introductory chapter, not in the chapter explicitly titled 'The Archaeological Record', which rather deals with the question of finds association and typology. It seems a peculiarly odd chapter title to a modern reader, but it reveals what Childe considered the principal methodological problem facing archaeologists: the interpretation of material culture per se rather than the archaeological conditions of its recovery. I take up this point further in Chapter 4. Yet despite Childe's lack of interest in fieldwork or the representivity of the evidence, as already made clear, quality of fieldwork did become a major concern for

British archaeologists in the mid-twentieth century. Yet it was particularly in North America that it was gradually connected to an explicit theoretical discourse around the interpretation of the archaeological record. The emergence of sampling theory, which developed in the late 1960s, became a core part of archaeological methodology in North America, Britain, and other parts of Europe and was effectively concerned with much the same sets of issues as external source criticism: representivity of the archaeological record.

The Anglophone Alternative: Sampling Theory

The Whewellian model of an inductive science remained fairly entrenched in Anglo-American archaeological thought for a long time, at least implicitly in regard to fieldwork as data collection, even if not always as an overt model for interpretation. Yet in the 1950s, it started to come under severe criticism, as is made clear in the work of Gordon Willey and Philip Phillips, who called this approach, rather aptly, a jigsaw view of interpretation:

> *For the most part the outlook was that, with sound field work, careful analysis, and classification, the archaeologist discharged his duties to science and society. The over-all problem, so far as it was envisaged at all, was seen as the bit-by-bit discovery of a pre-existing order in the culture-historical universe, the outlines of which would miraculously emerge when sufficient pieces were ready to be fitted together. Thank Heaven, archaeology was not a 'theoretical' science but something 'you could get your teeth into'.*
>
> (Phillips & Willey 1953: 615)

They – and others – argued for the need to rethink this inductive empiricism; however, it was not until the following decades that an explicitly new model, logical positivism, was adopted by some North American archaeologists to replace it. This is not the place to review the spate of papers and books that emerged in the 1970s arguing for a more deductive epistemology, often of the covering-law variety (for one of the most detailed reviews, see Gibbon 1989). Outside of North America, interest in this issue was more muted; in France, apart from Courbin's scathing review of the New Archaeology (Courbin [1981] 1988), a very different approach to explanation was taken, under the name 'logicism'

(Gardin 1979; Gallay 1989; see also Cleuziou et al. 1991). In Britain the response was divided between sheer revulsion against the jargon of science (e.g. Hawkes 1968; Hogarth 1972) and a more welcoming attitude (Clarke 1972, 1973, 1978), whereas similar interests in logical positivism had been emerging in Scandinavia (Malmer 1984; Johansen 1982; see also Myhre 1991). However, it is the connection of archaeological explanation to sampling theory that is of chief relevance here, a connection made very clear in Binford's review of the second edition of Heizer's *Guide to Archaeological Field Methods*, which came out in 1967 (Binford 1968b).

In Binford's opinion, Heizer's book was 'a guide for conducting nonscientific archaeological investigations', because it gave 'the impression that data collection can be learned by cookbook directives. If one wishes to give amateurs some appreciation for the complexities of archaeological research, then some attention to research design, data quality control, and sampling are necessary' (Binford 1968b: 807). In short, Binford was demanding three things of fieldwork: a need for greater reflexivity about why one was digging and thus which data were relevant; greater standardization of recording to avoid idiosyncrasies of the individual field worker and enhance data comparability; and finally greater attention to the representivity of the sample towards the actual population. All these elements – relevance, comparability, and representivity – filtered into archaeological practice over the following decade in the form of problem-oriented and research-directed excavation, pro forma recording techniques, and the adoption of sampling strategies in terms of systematic spatial coverage and object recovery (see Lucas 2001a: 52–61).

Yet such a process did not go uncontested; for example, Chenhall argued against this new formalization of fieldwork on two grounds; first, most archaeological fieldwork, because it was salvage, could not wait for the detailed project designs envisaged by Binford (1964) or Fritz and Plog (1970); second, it was a myth that material collected under such conditions was not useful for later research which had not originally formed part of the original collection process (Chenhall 1971). Chenhall's comments remain pertinent even today; indeed, although contemporary development-led archaeology has come a long way since the early 1970s, there is no doubt that project designs in much of archaeology are often formulaic and poor representatives of the original intention. A problem, of course, is that the selective excavation and recording of the archaeological record implied by the criterion of relevance clashes with the archaeological imperative for the total record, which is premised on the notion that excavation is destruction (Mayer-Oakes, quoted in Swartz 1967: 487–8; see also next section). Yet elsewhere, such as in Britain, archaeologists had been urging the idea of a question-led approach to archaeology for some time – it was made very explicit by Collingwood, who said that it was his experience in archaeology that impressed upon him the importance of a question-and-answer approach to history (Collingwood 1944: 25, 83–6; see also Atkinson 1956: 199).

If Binford and others promoted sampling theory as a means of securing quality control over data as part of the scientific method, it was others who revealed its more direct relationship to changing conceptions of the archaeological record. One of the first was George Cowgill, who in 1970 suggested seeing the archaeological record in terms of three populations: the ethnographic, the physical consequences, and the physical finds (Cowgill 1970). Cowgill argued that before any generalizations could be made, one needed to know whether the finite data population available to archaeologists was sufficient to make such generalizations. The problem as he saw it was that the archaeological record consisted of what he called a physical-finds population, that is, the physical consequences of human behaviour that have been preserved and are detectable; in other words, archaeologists do not have access to behaviour as ethnographers, not even to the physical consequences of that behaviour, but only to what remains of those physical consequences (Cowgill 1970: 162–3). Moreover, archaeologists often recover only a sample of this population. Cowgill saw that it was especially vital to distinguish the physical-finds population from the physical-consequences population – the former was usually a greatly reduced version of the latter, a point which was of course central to the development of formation theory (see Chapter 3). Cowgill then devotes the rest of his paper to exploring the problem of attenuation on statistical inference from such physical-finds populations – or rather samples thereof.

In 1975, Michael Collins extended Cowgill's ideas in a paper on sources of sampling bias, using the concept of a contingency sequence borrowed from palaeontology; the principal idea is that an original patterning of material culture (analogous to what might be observed in an ethnographic context) undergoes a series of reductions before it ends up as archaeological data: 'identification of the sequence of contingencies to which these patterns [of material culture] are subject provides a structure for evaluating our control of sources of bias' (Collins 1975: 27). Collins identified seven sources of bias:

1. Not all behaviour results in patterned material culture.
2. Of those that do, not all can enter the archaeological record.
3. Of those that do, not all will enter the archaeological record.
4. Of those that do, not all will be preserved.
5. Of those that do, not all survive indefinitely.
6. Of those that do, not all will exposed by the archaeologist.
7. Of those that do, not all will be identified and/or recognized by the archaeologist.

What is interesting about this list of biases is the continuity expressed between the processes of materialization in the past, preservation over time, and excavation in the present. Collins expressly described the problem as one of understanding the sequence of discontinuities between past behaviour and present remains of that behaviour (Collins 1975: 29). The importance of this list is that it connects the problem of the incompleteness of the archaeological record with the incompleteness of archaeological archiving and/or collecting, a connection which has largely been separated by formation theory or approaches to materiality (see Chapters 3 and 4). However, even contemporary sampling theory has largely lost this continuity, insofar as it deals primarily with the last two sources of bias on Collins's list. Such separation of the different aspects of the archaeological record is problematic – and of course forms a key impetus for this book – but it is a separation that has been increasingly codified in archaeological discourse (for further discussion of this issue, see Chapter 6).

Daniels proposed a similar scheme of seven stages of reduction in 1972, highlighting three causative factors: historical (relating to the living population), postdepositional, and research (Daniels 1972: 202–4). David Clarke also suggested a similar but more compacted scheme in 1973 (Clarke 1973: 16):

1. Full range of activity in the past
2. Sample and traces of (1) which have been deposited
3. Sample of (2), which survive to be recovered
4. Sample of (3) which is recovered

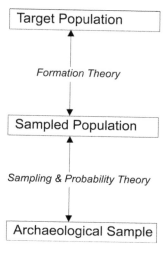

Figure 2. Schematic representation of the simplification of sampling theory and its separation from formation theory.

From this, Clarke proposed a series of theories to tackle the relationship between these domains – thus his predepositional and depositional theory dealt with the relation between (1) and (2), postdepositional theory with (2) and (3), and retrieval theory with (3) and (4). In addition, Clarke added two other levels of theory, analytical and interpretive, which linked all four domains (see also Chapter 5). Sullivan subsequently developed Clarke's ideas a little further, in particular focusing on the importance of trace production, thus linking up such approaches with incipient formation theory (Sullivan 1978).

In many ways, sampling theory today is a greatly reduced version of that proposed by Cowgill, Clarke, and Collins, insofar as it has been stripped of and disconnected from the theoretical issues of the archaeological record. This is effected by collapsing the various stages outlined here into two: target and sampled population, that is, the first and last domains in all the examples herein. This model also emerged at the same time in the 1970s (Chenhall 1971; Cherry et al. 1978) but has been much more influential in sampling theory over the long run; the reason is clear as Orton points out: this dual characterization immediately divides the whole issue into two separate domains, the relationship between the archaeological sample (i.e. what is recovered) and the sampled population (i.e. what exists in the archaeological record) on the one hand, and the relationship between the sampled population and the target population on the other hand (Figure 2). Sampling and probability theory in archaeology is thus mostly concerned with the former, whereas the latter is a theoretical question for formation theory. However, most critical is that from a sampling theory perspective, each of these domains – archaeological sample, sampled population, and target population – can be effectively black boxed in terms of their ontological status, for all that really matters is understanding what goes in and out (Orton 2000: 41, figure 3.1).

As a result of this black boxing, contemporary sampling theory largely addresses the archaeological record in terms of the representivity of archaeological samples to a target population in statistical terms. For example, consider the issue of pottery sherds, which represent broken fragments of once-whole pots. Although one approach, such as formation theory, might be interested in understanding the processes of breakage and dispersal, sampling theory would primarily be concerned with understanding how representative the sherds are of the whole pots. Thus, the first might pay attention to mapping and conjoining fragments and examining postdepositional wear through sherd size and abrasion, whereas the latter will explore the reliability of the various measures of quantification (e.g. count, weight, proportion) from which one can even infer degrees of brokenness. This is not to argue that the two approaches are incompatible or irrelevant to each other, only that they have diverged into two very different sets of theory. The theoretical issues which were held together in the unifying models of Cowgill, Clarke, or Collins swiftly became fragmented and carved up, to be addressed by separate theories such as formation theory and sampling theory.

Incompleteness and the Total Record

IF ONE WERE to summarize the changes to the concept of the archaeological record that have taken place since the 1950s, it would be around the idea of incompleteness; from Grahame Clark's general emphasis on survival and preservation to the more theoretical models of source criticism and sampling theory, the problem that increasingly preoccupied many archaeologists was how to deal with the fragmentary nature of the archaeological record. As discussed earlier, this was something that had always been recognized by archaeologists, but in the nineteenth and early twentieth centuries it did not seem to be of major concern – even

Childe was not too perturbed by this fact. For earlier archaeologists, the issue was more about incomplete collections, which was something that could be rectified by doing fieldwork themselves rather than relying on others, and concomitantly building up systematic and scrupulous methods of recovery. Yet because the issue was framed in terms of the collection, the key question was this: when was a collection complete? This had no easy answer, as it could turn endlessly on the tensions within classification, between duplicates and unique objects, and as we have seen, archaeologists often had very different opinions about the extent to which archaeological data was amenable to generalization in the form of classification. From the 1950s, this question became less urgent as the focus of incompleteness shifted from the collection to the material in the ground. Incompleteness of the archaeological record was no longer primarily about incomplete collections but about incomplete evidence or data. It is precisely for this reason that one sees the simultaneous emergence of a theoretical discourse centred largely on issues of epistemology. It is also why one sees a rise in methodological concerns, expressed through source criticism and sampling theory.

In emphasizing the issue of incompleteness and survival of evidence, it is perhaps no coincidence that archaeological source criticism and sampling theory emerged at the time they did. Since the late nineteenth century, there had been an awareness of the need to protect and manage the archaeological heritage in both Europe and North America, and one could no doubt trace this back even further (e.g. Cleere 1984). However, it is not until after World War II that land development and urban redevelopment on a massive scale led to the emergence in the early 1970s of the contemporary practices of cultural or archaeological resource management, which form the foundation of current legislation and organization (see e.g. Hunter & Ralston 2006; Johnson & Schene 1987; Willems 1998; Darvill 2004; Tainter 2004). The emergence of salvage or rescue archaeology brought the issue of preservation and destruction of archaeological remains to the forefront of archaeology and inevitably contributed to the shift in thinking about the incompleteness of the archaeological record discussed in this chapter. Archaeologists for the first time become acutely aware of the fragility of their source material and how easily it could disappear – and in large amounts; this is an awareness which has become crystallized in the contemporary notion of heritage as a nonrenewable resource. It is perhaps no surprise, therefore, that the issue of preservation in the present was extended into a more general reflection on the survival of the evidence and the incompleteness of the archaeological record. Moreover, there was a flip side to this recognition: archaeology itself contributed to this very destruction, a point which had been long acknowledged of excavation (see Lucas 2001b). This led to a seeming paradox: to understand the past, one needed to destroy its traces, yet if one wanted to preserve those traces, one was severely limited by the amount of information they could offer.

The Paradox of Excavation

The idea that excavation is destruction pervades almost all major texts about the process of excavation in the twentieth century (e.g. Petrie 1904: 48; Atkinson 1946: 16; Leroi-Gourhan 1950: 2; Wheeler 1954: 15, Kenyon 1964: 68, Coles 1972: 133; Barker 1982: 12). However, this paradox was heightened in the wake of rescue and salvage archaeology, simply because it sharpened the ethical responsibility of archaeologists towards their task in a way that, ironically, was probably not felt by those excavating unthreatened or 'safe' sites. It took the doubling of the threat of destruction – from both archaeologist and developer – to heighten awareness of this paradox. As a result, the burden placed on the archaeologist also seemed to double, which is precisely why one sees the emergence of two different responses to this paradox: partial or restricted excavation on the one hand, and total recording on the other hand. The first was premised on what is often known as the PARIS (preserving archaeological remains in situ) principle, whereas the latter was premised on the site archive acting as substitute form of preservation, that is, preservation by record (Corfield et al. 1998). For example, in Britain in the 1990s, heritage management promulgated very rigid versions of these two solutions in its policy statement PPG16:

> If physical preservation in situ is not feasible, an archaeological
> excavation for the purposes of 'preservation by record', may be an
> acceptable alternative ... From the archaeological point of view
> this should be regarded as a second best option. The science of
> archaeology is developing rapidly. Excavation means total
> destruction of evidence (apart from removable artefacts) from which
> future techniques could almost certainly extract more information

than is currently possible... The preservation in situ *of important
archaeological remains is therefore nearly always to be preferred.*

(Historic Buildings and Monuments Commission 1991: A13)

Although the language is different and perhaps a little softer, more or
less the same attitude is maintained in the new U.K. policy document
PPS5:

*There should be a presumption in favour of the conservation of
designated heritage assets and the more significant the designated
heritage asset, the greater the presumption in favour of its
conservation should be. Once lost, heritage assets cannot be replaced
and their loss has a cultural, environmental, economic and social
impact.*

(Department for Communities and Local Government [DCLG] 2010:
HE9.1)

*A documentary record of our past is not as valuable as retaining the
heritage asset.*

(DCLG 2010: HE12.1)

The first solution of partial excavation was proposed with the expectation that future archaeologists would do a better job. This notion was
not new (see e.g. Randall-MacIver 1933: 11; but see Droop 1915: 2,
for the opposite position). However, it became the subject of a heated
debate between Philip Barker and Olaf Olsen in 1980. Barker, like
others before him, explicitly acknowledged excavation as a form of
destruction, yet he was also an advocate of total excavation. Barker's
articulation of total excavation was largely viewed in terms of promoting large-scale horizontal or open-area exposure as opposed to limited
trenching, the idea being that one cannot understand a site unless he
or she excavates all or at least a sufficiently large part of it. Reynolds
and Barber made a similar point a few years later, linking criticisms of
the question-and-answer or problem-oriented approach to fieldwork
to the limitations of small-sample trenching (Reynolds & Barber 1984:
96). However, Barker was heavily criticized by the Danish archaeologist Olaf Olsen, who accused Barker – and others – of promoting a
free pass on the destruction of the archaeological record, a disease he

coined 'rabies archaeologorum' (Olsen 1980). Barker's response is very telling; for Barker, the issue is really about open area versus trenching and issues of sample size; he never advocated total excavation as a rule. But whereas Olsen seems resistant to total excavation in any situation (bar rescue work), Barker suggests that it is sometimes justified:

> *The argument must be put in perspective. Even I, rabid as I am,*
> *would not support the total excavation of Stonehenge or the removal*
> *of the Parthenon to recover the plan of the timber temple which may*
> *have preceded it. I would now be more than dubious about the*
> *excavation of Trelleborg and Fyrkat (were they still intact), since*
> *they are two among a very small group of such sites in the whole of*
> *Europe. But Hen Domen [a site excavated by Barker] is only one of*
> *many hundreds of motte and bailey castles in Britain, let alone*
> *Europe, which has thousands more, so that the total excavation of*
> *one example out of so many is not so heinous as it seems, and might*
> *provide, for the first time, a series of complete plans of a timber*
> *castle, which no amount of trenching would ever do.*
>
> (Barker 1980)

This is an interesting argument because it replays exactly the same issues as in the nineteenth century about complete collections but in reverse; how many examples of the same type of pottery do you need before you have enough? In classification terms, one is enough, but archaeologists always wanted as many as possible for their corpus, because no generalizing system could capture the particularity of history. Now the same argument is used but on its head: if you have hundreds examples of motte-and-bailey castles, surely one or two can be sacrificed to total excavation – one or two being enough, as examples of a general type. But Barker is not consistent on this matter, for in the introduction to his book *Techniques*, he reaffirms the idea that each site is unique (Barker 1982: 12). If so, how can one or two examples ever be enough? One sees how the ambivalence between archaeology as a generalizing and particularizing discipline remains and becomes ever more complicated as new conceptions of the archaeological record are developed. More generally, however, the ethos behind partial excavation – namely preservation in situ, could be argued to be paradoxical in itself; Martin Biddle, in a keynote address to the British Institute of Field Archaeologists in 1994, argued that if preservation is taken to its logical extreme, then there will be no more excavation and ultimately no more knowledge; as he says, 'We cannot conserve what we do not understand' (Biddle 1994: 17). Biddle asks, How will future archaeologists excavate a site better than us if they have no experience, no sites to practice on? Moreover, if future generations uphold this view, then excavation could potentially always be deferred to a never-arriving present, and a site will be preserved in perpetuity for no one, turning preservation into an oxymoron.

The second response to the paradox of excavation as destruction is by appeal to the record the archaeologist makes on site – the plans, sections, profiles, context sheets, notebooks, photographs, and so on. These justify the act of excavation and tacitly give it its scientific or academic status – or rather perhaps more significantly the possibility of evaluating this status. More important, these records came to stand in for the site, acting as a substitute, hence the idea of the archive objective or preservation by record (Roskams 2001).

The idea of an archive objective, however, was always equivocal; one of the earliest criticisms was made by Reynolds and Barber in their paper 'Analytical Excavation', where they attack the trend towards formulaic, pro forma recording methods, which they recognize was driven by the demands of rescue archaeology to produce results (Reynolds & Barber 1984: 97):

> *The emphasis on recording technique has been a response to this – an attempt to convert the whole site, lock, stock and barrel, into a physical record. In effect, this too often means that Observation (an essentially active process) gives place to passive mechanical recording; and in recent years the actual forms of recording on site have become geared increasingly towards 'direct archiving' and (limited) publication ... The potential of this is that the archaeologist is encouraged not to think about the uncomfortable facts about the site, but to try to put them (if 'facts' they be) into the archive for the future to elucidate.*
>
> *(Reynolds & Barber 1984: 97)*

Their criticisms of the mechanical nature of recording and, more important, the deferral of interpretation it engendered in many ways presented a new paradox which this was supposed to solve: to defer interpretation to some future point presupposes anticipating all possible information that any given future interpretation might make. This is patently impossible, as the history of archaeology shows only too well, and because it is, it throws into doubt the whole idea of the archive objective. Yet it is questionable how widespread or even deeply held this belief in the archive objective was; Roskams suggests that it may have been used more for rhetorical effect in helping to gain support for adequate finance than because of a real adherence to its philosophy (Steve Roskams, personal communication, 3 December 2010). Indeed, two issues need to be separated here: one is about the archive as an objective and complete record; the other is about the archive's ability to stand as the basis for subsequent interpretation or reinterpretation of a site. These two are not the same, and although many held to the latter, few may have really believed in the former.

Since the late 1980s, the notion of producing an objective record of archaeology in the field has been subject to intense critique (e.g. Carver 1989; Tilley 1989; Richards 1995; Bender, Hamilton, & Tilley 1997, 2007; Hodder 1997, 1999, 2000; Lucas 2001a; Andrews, Barrett, & Lewis 2000; Chadwick 2003). Yet ironically this critique has often been paired with a corresponding rise in the addition of more forms and methods of recording, such as a revived use of diaries alongside pro forma sheets, alternative graphic representations to plans and sections, adoption of video media, and even having an anthropologist on site (see e.g. Hodder 2000). One might be forgiven for thinking that this hyperrecording on an excavation actually reveals a persistent anxiety about the total record and thus indicates a subtle contradiction between theory and practice. In the sense that all archaeologists are taught that excavation is destruction and that a heavy ethical burden consequently rests on the record they produce, it is difficult not to feel this anxiety about the total record. Indeed, the issue ultimately brings us back to the importance of fieldwork in archaeology and the issue raised earlier in this chapter about the archive as testimony. Because archaeologists have to 'make' their own archives (unlike historians), their problem is primarily about how to establish reliability in the creation of testimony, not in the reading or reception of it. All the issues of source criticism and sampling theory are ultimately preceded by that of the quality of the record as it is made by archaeologists, which returns us to the original nineteenth-century problem of the incomplete collection. In summary, the two 'solutions' to the paradox of excavation as destruction turn out to lead to new paradoxes themselves, both of which, however, hinge on an unrealistic link between present practice and future expectation. At the heart of this paradox remains an anxiety about the incompleteness of the archaeological record.

··· 3 ···

Formation Theory

'FORMATION THEORY' is a term I use here to cover a variety of approaches which address the issue of formation processes and the archaeological record. It is important to distinguish formation theory from other approaches which overlap in subject matter, particularly source criticism and sampling theory (see Chapter 2). Although these latter approaches acknowledge formation processes, their general perspective and starting point is quite different, as outlined in the previous chapter. One way of characterizing this difference is in terms of temporal outlook – do we look at time backwards (from the present to the past) or forwards (the present as the future of the past)? Source criticism, sampling theory, and formation theory all view the archaeological record as a contemporary phenomenon, but they do so from quite different perspectives. One way of expressing this is through the dominant concepts deployed. Thus, source criticism and sampling theory start from the concept of incompleteness and try to fill in the gaps, whereas formation theory starts from the concept of a living or dynamic context and tries to understand its transformation into a static context. Formation theory, in a sense, thinks of the archaeological record as the end point, as the future of a past present, whereas source criticism and sampling theory largely view it as the starting point, the fragmented present of a past totality. This is what I meant by looking at time backwards or forwards. This difference is expressed in the nature of the methodological work associated with these respective approaches; for example, the study of artifact use-life and discard rates in the case of formation theory, and the importance of state of research or representivity in the case of source criticism and sampling theory. However, I admit the difference between the orientations is perhaps subtle and not always as clear as I have portrayed it; moreover, other factors weigh equally, such as different traditions (North America versus Europe) or even different perceptions of the scientific nature of archaeology (sciences versus humanities).

Formation theory itself is also not necessarily a uniform or coherent approach to the archaeological record. Although the most immediate reference might be to North American models of formation processes commonly linked to the work of Michael Schiffer from the 1970s (see Shott 1998), I draw on a much older and more international set of ideas in this chapter, particularly the principles of stratigraphy and geoarchaeological approaches. In that regard, it is useful at this point to make a key distinction within formation theory which structures this chapter: on the one hand, the formation of deposits, and on the other hand, the formation of assemblages. As we excavate a layer or deposit on an archaeological site, we typically separate the finds from the soil matrix; we record both, and we may sample the latter while retaining all of the former. We recognize that they comprise a connected unit and, as such, form the basis of all subsequent interpretation; yet in terms of archaeological analysis, this singular unit is more commonly split and then studied from one of two primary orientations: either as an envelope for the finds or as a physical entity in its own right. The first underlies the basis of assemblage formation approaches, whereas the latter, of deposit formation. With assemblage formation, the principal focus is on objects and how they end up in a certain spatial or depositional relationship; although the formation of the deposit may be of relevance, the chief interest always lies with the objects and linking them back to their predepositional context in a dynamic or living society. With deposit formation, in contrast, the primary focus is on the deposit itself as a whole; objects play an important role in interpreting such deposits, but they are just one aspect of many for which the primary focus is on the material matrix of the deposit and its temporal relation to other deposits.

I have partly taken this distinction between deposit and assemblage formation from Julie Stein's (2000) discussion of stratigraphy, but I use it in a slightly different way, which I discuss further herein. Some might argue that such a separation is forced, but it seems to me that the nature of empirical work in formation theory rather supports this division. As such, it raises the question of whether we should not devote more attention to thinking about bridging these two aspects, which, I argue, have pursued quite different trajectories. This is an issue I return to at the end of the chapter. First, I begin by exploring the two approaches as separate streams.

Stratigraphy and Deposit Formation

The Origins and Development of Stratigraphy

Stratigraphy is an extremely simple idea which was introduced into archaeology from geology. The concept is conventionally traced back to the late seventeenth century with the Danish scholar Nicolas Steno, whose dissertation 'Concerning a Solid Body Enclosed by Process of Nature within a Solid' ('De solido intra solidum naturalitur contento', 1669) encapsulates the basic principles still used today. It is interesting to retrace Steno's particular problem, though, and how this led to the ideas behind stratigraphy. The title of the dissertation actually sums up the problem: how can solid objects (e.g. fossils) occur within other solid objects (rock)? His solution to the problem was simple: the containing solid was once a fluid. The notion that fluids can transmute into solids and vice versa would have been evident in many contexts (e.g. ice or water, metallurgy), but to apply this idea to the surface of the earth itself was bold. Steno clearly drew on processes observable in the present to explain this (particularly the effects of water and fire), but more specifically, he suggested that different locales show these processes at different stages of their cycle, and he used examples from Tuscany to illustrate this (Steno [1669] 1962). The key idea, though, is thinking of solid bodies in fluid terms and thus through formation processes; from this came the secondary idea that once a fluid (i.e. sediment) solidifies, it provides a surface on which a new fluid can settle, and so on, thus creating a series of strata (ibid.: 7).

It was only in the eighteenth and nineteenth centuries that Steno's ideas were taken up and developed systematically through figures such as Werner, Hutton, Smith, and Lyell (Koutsoukos 2005; Stein 2000: 20–1). The concept of geological stratigraphy was subsequently codified as three principles: superposition, original horizontality, and original lateral continuity, all of which are evident in Steno's original thought (Doyle, Bennett, & Baxter 1994: 13–15). In short, these state that in any sequence of strata, the earliest lies at the bottom and the latest at the top (superposition); all strata are originally laid horizontally as a result of gravity (original horizontality); and all strata originally extended outward, thinning to nothing at their edges unless prevented from doing so by the edges of the surface on which they are deposited (original lateral continuity). Of these, superposition is by far the most significant. In practice, the recording of stratigraphy involves the identification and description of stratigraphic units, usually based on their mineral composition or lithography; the identification of these and the boundaries (or unconformities) between them provides the basis of a stratigraphic sequence. This sequence is then interpreted in terms of environmental history, which means examining the relationship between fossil organisms associated with particular rock and/or sediment types (Doyle et al. 1994). This combination of palaeontological and lithostratigraphic data is usually referred to as facies stratigraphy. There are many other specific types of stratigraphic analysis used by geologists today which focus on particular aspects such as event stratigraphy or sequence stratigraphy, which have enabled much more detailed and complex reconstructions of environmental history (see e.g. Doyle & Bennett 1998), but the basic principles first articulated by Steno remain intact.

There appears little doubt that the concept of stratigraphy entered archaeology from geology; from the earliest days, however, one can see a divergence between two ways in which the concept was adopted. The first retained close ties with geology, and especially the importance of seeing stratigraphy in terms of formation processes; the second largely ignored the aspect of formation and reduced stratigraphy to a relative dating tool by focusing solely on the sequential structure of strata. The first stream is primarily associated with Palaeolithic archaeology, inevitably perhaps, as this was also the closest to geology in subject matter, especially in connection to the establishment of the antiquity of humans (Grayson 1983). Indeed, one must remember that research in what was only later to be called Palaeolithic archaeology was in fact largely conducted by people we would call geologists or palaeontologists today. The key figures such as Joseph Prestwich, Hugh Falconer, William Pengelly, and even Jacques Boucher de Perthes, were all originally mostly interested in understanding the development of earth history in terms of environmental change, and the presence of human artifacts in strata also containing extinct fauna was a recurrent cause of debate in the earlier nineteenth century. The famous site of Brixham Cave which finally turned the tide in favour of deep time for the human species was excavated not to clarify this debate but to establish a better sequence for environmental history (Van Riper 1993: 80–1). It was the first cave site to be excavated in horizontal layers, with careful attention paid to the stratification of deposits and the vertical position of fossils in deposits; it was precisely because of these methods of stratigraphic excavation that, when artifacts turned up alongside extinct fauna, the scholars could be confident for the first time that humans had existed on the earth far longer than previously thought. It made scholars reassess earlier claims for human antiquity, such as John Frere's observations in the late eighteenth century and also those of contemporaries like Boucher de Perthes, both of whom had presented stratigraphic information on the context of artifacts. The difference lay in the controlled manner of recovery at Brixham Cave – stratigraphic excavation rather than stratigraphic observation (Van Riper 1993: 86–8).

Stratigraphy remained a key concept for Palaeolithic archaeology, and its geological origins and affinities continue into the present; it is probably not contentious to say that stratigraphy in Palaeolithic archaeology is almost identical to that in geology (e.g. Stern 1993). A similarly close link between the geological concept of stratigraphy and archaeology is found in the pioneering research in Denmark and southern Sweden on the later prehistoric shell middens, or kitchen middens (*kjokkenmoedding*), which was inaugurated in 1848 as part of an interdisciplinary project including the archaeologist J. J. A. Worsaae, the zoologist J. J. S. Steenstrup, and the geologist J. Forchammer (Klindt-Jensen 1975; Kristiansen 2002). This project established a precedent for three more subsequent researches on kitchen middens over the late nineteenth and twentieth centuries, which always included a close relationship between archaeology and natural sciences, the third of which (from 1939) was particularly productive and out of which developed a European ecological archaeology (Kristiansen 2002). However, the Danish case is somewhat unusual in a wider European context, where a very different approach to stratigraphy was developed in later prehistoric, classical, and Middle Eastern archaeology. Here, stratigraphy became largely reduced to sequence as a means of relative dating; as a result, the formation of deposits or strata was not a dominant concern, nor was their description – rather, strata were primarily considered 'envelopes' for artifacts, which enabled what one might even call stratigraphies of objects. In a recent review of the concept of stratigraphy, Julie Stein suggests that stratigraphy was not even considered relevant by archaeologists working in these periods until the 1970s, because they relied on other dating methods, such as seriation and historical documents (Stein 2000: 22–3). This is somewhat of an oversimplification and seems to conflate a number of different issues; European archaeologists most certainly used the principles of stratigraphy – they just used a stripped-down version which ignored the issue of formation processes and focused on the sequential structure.

This is very clear, for example, in Schliemann's work in the 1870s at Troy, where he adopted a broad concept of strata that related each strata to a different 'city'; he thus identified seven strata (and thus seven cities) within sixteen meters of archaeological deposits (Schliemann 1880; see also Schmidt 2002: 222); this has little connection to the complex, multilinear sequences of stratigraphy employed today and is more akin to the notion of phases or levels – but it still embodies the first principle of stratigraphy: superposition. However, it is clear that Schliemann did not ignore stratigraphy at smaller scales, as his examination of the walls of the third city-strata shows. However, such smaller-scale observations were not systematic, and there is certainly no attempt to construct an integrated stratigraphic sequence; there were simply the large-scale strata or levels which formed the key stratigraphic observations, and then small-scale, ad hoc observations. Schliemann's approach was not unique but rather adopted a model used by his contemporaries. Frank Calvert, for example, who was probably the original discoverer of the site of Troy and advised Schliemann on excavation methods, was also clearly familiar with the importance of stratigraphy (Allen 1995, 1999). Thus, although Schliemann's use of stratigraphy was extremely coarse by our contemporary standards, it followed and helped to set a model – building levels – which became widely spread in Near Eastern archaeology and was ultimately codified through the work of Robert Koldaway in the 1890s at Babylon (Micale & Nadali 2008).

Warburton has suggested that the stratigraphy of Schliemann and Koldaway was not really stratigraphy but typology, insofar as it was concerned primarily with architecture and establishing sequences of, and contemporaneity between, buildings (Warburton 2003: 3–10). Indeed, he claims the same about the work of William Albright and others, who constituted an alternative biblical school to the German school of Koldaway; the only difference is that Albright focused on artifacts rather than architecture. The key point, though, as Warburton argues, is that neither of these schools, which continue to dominate excavation methods in the Near East, use stratigraphy in its full geological sense, but rather stratigraphy reduced to chronology and sequence (Warburton 2003: 12). There is no doubt a lot of truth in this claim, and the same could indeed be applied more generally to later prehistoric and historical archaeologies elsewhere; certainly stratigraphy in classical archaeology largely follows this building-level and envelope approach to strata (Altekamp 2004). A similar characterization could be made of the development of stratigraphy in North American later prehistory, albeit through very different sets of concerns. The close relationship between seriation and stratigraphy resulted in the development of what has been called metrical stratigraphy (Phillips, Ford, & Griffin 1951: 240–1) or percentage stratigraphy (Lyman & O'Brien 2006), that is, using proportions of artifacts found at different levels as a means to establish chronological phases (Stein 2000: 28–31). The basis of this approach lay in excavating what appeared to be thick homogeneous deposits in arbitrary levels to wrestle out 'hidden' stratigraphies based on the vertical position of finds. In Britain in the late nineteenth century, Pitt Rivers was using much the same idea; by recording the depth of finds, he was assuming that the later artifacts lay above or higher in a deposit than earlier ones (Bowden 1991: 94, 155–6).

Originally, archaeologists were very clear on the distinction between this metrical stratigraphy (or what one might even call artifact stratigraphy, as opposed to deposit stratigraphy) and conventional geological notion of natural stratigraphy (Stein 2000: 29–30; Phillips et al. 1951:

241). They even distinguished the concept of level (an arbitrary unit) from that of layer or stratum to emphasize this difference; but as Stein points out, many contemporary North American archaeologists seem to have forgotten this and either conflate the two or simply think solely of artifact stratigraphy *as* stratigraphy (Stein 2000: 31). In Europe, the connection to the geological concept of stratigraphy remained much more solid with the focus on deposits. In Mortimer Wheeler's address to the Royal Society of Arts in 1927, the basic principles of stratigraphy (or stratification, as he calls it) are expounded through a series of examples, beginning with one from geology (Wheeler 1927: 816–17). Wheeler's examples illustrate not only the same basic principle of superposition of deposits but also the complexities of cultural stratigraphy and a keen awareness of the various formation processes involved.

Wheeler, of course, exerted a profound influence on excavation methods in Britain and elsewhere, especially the Near East through his student Kathleen Kenyon, and along with it, on the depositional concept of stratigraphy. Although Wheeler and Kenyon clearly saw stratigraphy primarily as a chronological method and in some ways were heirs to the building-level and envelope concept of strata, it is equally clear that they took the matter much more seriously. Berating a North American archaeologist working in the Near East who claimed that his site lacked any stratification, Wheeler retorts:

> *This, of course, is nonsense; by 'stratification', the writer quoted means merely 'continuous building-levels', oblivious of the no less important layers which on any site may be expected to supplement and interrelate phases of actual construction. The fact is that the observer had simply failed to observe.*
>
> (Wheeler 1954: 60)

With Wheeler, we see the importance given to every deposit and the full set of relationships between those deposits, an approach which was ultimately to be codified in Harris's matrix system. Moreover, these layers were not simply envelopes for finds either; the attention given to describing the physical composition of each deposit is also evident, even though it may been basic; Wheeler, for example, adopted a symbol key for denoting the nature of the soils in his stratigraphic sections during his work for the Archaeological Survey of India (Wheeler 1954:

77), a practice which became quite common in British archaeology. Nonetheless, most descriptions of deposits were fairly basic by today's standards, consisting of words such as 'gravel', 'sand', and 'loose earth'. More common, though, were terms which denoted something about the cultural nature of the deposit in terms of its formation: 'walls', 'floors', 'occupation deposits', 'destruction level'. It is only from the 1970s that one starts to see a separation of two types of description, or what is less appropriately but more commonly characterized as a separation of description from interpretation. Thus, on typical recording forms, there appears a physical description of the deposit in terms of lithology and then an interpretation, usually in terms of formation processes.

From this rather rapid review, it is fair to say that the archaeological concept of stratigraphy has been understood in many different ways in different times and places, and although the simplified accounts of Stein and Warburton between the deposit-oriented and artifact or typological-oriented concept of stratigraphy is unnecessarily polarizing, they have highlighted extremes on what is more of a continuum. That is, at one end, stratigraphy is reduced to mere sequence; at the other, it is enjoined with consideration of formation processes. The more important issue, though, is whether the formation processes implicated in archaeological stratigraphy are substantially different to those in geology – different enough to argue that the concepts in the two disciplines need to be thought in different ways.

Formation Processes of the Archaeo-Stratigraphic Record

R. G. Collingwood makes one of the first – and perhaps still most astute – observations on the distinction between geological and archaeological stratigraphy:

> Archaeologists had often called attention to the likeness between their own stratigraphical methods and those of geology, and a likeness there certainly was; but there was difference as well.
>
> If an archaeologist finds a stratum of earth and stones and mortar, mixed with potsherds and coins, on top of which is a layer of level flags, supporting more earth with potsherds and coins of a rather different type, it is easy to say that he uses these two sets of potsherds and coins exactly as a geologist uses fossils, to show that the strata belong to different periods and to date them by correlating

them with strata found elsewhere and containing relics of the same type.

Easy, but untrue. For the archaeologist, these things are not stone and clay and metal, they are building-stone and potsherds and coins; debris of a building, fragments of domestic utensils, and means of exchange, all belonging to a bygone age whose purposes they reveal to him.

(Collingwood 1944: 74)

What Collingwood is saying quite simply is that archaeological deposits and objects relate to human acts involving intentions and beliefs, and they cannot therefore be equated with natural deposits formed through entirely different processes. However, it was not Collingwood who inspired a reaction to drawing such a distinction between geological and archaeological stratigraphy – perhaps because most of his contemporaries agreed with him. Rather, it was Edward Harris. In his now-classic text *Principles of Archaeological Stratigraphy*, Harris, too, argues that archaeological deposits are different to geological ones, again because of the human involvement in their creation (Harris 1979: 36–7; see also Harris 1977: 88–9). However, Harris takes a very different line of argument from Collingwood for their distinction; for Harris, human formation processes 'transgress the natural laws of stratification' (Harris 1979: 37), which they do in two ways. First, by introducing a new agent in the transportation of materials, which creates very different stratigraphies, for example, the use of white quartz, mined from miles away and used to cover a burial mound. Second, by creating upright or vertical deposits, such as walls and buildings.

Despite these differences, however, Harris in many ways underlines the continuities between geological and archaeological stratigraphy; he affirms their common properties (Harris 1979: 38–41), and in the second edition of his book, he defines the laws of archaeological stratigraphy in terms of the three basic geological laws of superposition, original horizontality, and original laterality, merely adding a fourth – stratigraphical succession (Harris 1989). Indeed, there is something of a paradox in Harris's texts, which has perhaps created confusion in the ensuing debate. What is convincing in Harris's argument for separating archaeological and geological stratigraphy is that it is based on the assertion that the formation processes on archaeological sites are very different to those on 'natural' sites; what is ironic, though, is that in recognizing this, Harris then more or less separates the question of formation processes from his whole approach to stratigraphy so that his stripped-down version actually appears to be fundamentally the same as geological stratigraphy. The confusion derives from the over-emphasis in Harris's work on the stratigraphic sequence as an abstract set of relations, hence his elevation of the concept of interface (see also Brown & Harris 1993); he is concerned with the relation between units over and above the formation of units themselves. The very advantages of the Harris matrix as a means of presenting stratigraphy are also the cause of its limitations. The matrix strips down the notion of time to a bare sequence, and it strips down the notion of a stratigraphic unit to interfaces between units. Warburton makes the same criticism, arguing that Harris's approach is basically no different to that of Koldaway or Albright: stratigraphy as an abstractly sequential rather than a con-cretely depositional process (Warburton 2003: 12).

I think lumping Harris in with these late-nineteenth-century approaches is grossly simplistic, but Warburton has a point; indeed, as Stein argues, the geological or geoscientific concept of stratigraphy is just as concerned with interfaces and sequences, but it is also concerned with the depositional properties of stratigraphic units and the wider interpretation of a sequence. In a sense, the Harris matrix is a strati-graphy separated from formation processes, and Stein rightly questions this separation. Stein and Warburton bring stratigraphy back down to earth, so to speak, linking stratigraphy to the wider issue of deposition, which has been excised from Harris's approach.

What this means in practice is a reconsideration of what a strati-graphic unit is, in compositional and depositional terms, and particu-larly the processes behind its formation. A concern with soil and sedi-ment formation processes goes back to the nineteenth century, but such concerns were almost exclusively the preoccupation of those working on the antiquity of humans and Palaeolithic contexts (see Rapp 1987; Rapp & Hill 2006: 4–24), with the exception of Danish studies on shell middens (Kristiansen 2002). However, for later prehistory and histor-ical period archaeology, there was very little interest in such matters until the mid-twentieth century. One of the earliest papers to take up the question was 'Worms and Weathering', by Richard Atkinson (1957). This was followed a year later by the first systematic treatment of soils in archaeology by Ian Cornwall in his book *Soils for the Archaeologist* (1958) and then by Edward Pyddoke in *Stratification for the Archaeologist* (1961). In the latter book, Pyddoke emphasized the geologic and geographic context of archaeological sites and thus the importance of understanding natural formation processes to interpreting the archaeological record. The bulk of Pyddoke's book – nine chapters – focuses on natural agencies affecting stratification and deposition formation, from wind to fauna, with only one chapter devoted to human activity. In particular, Pyddoke drew attention to the dominance of an artifact-centred view of the archaeological record, and his book was an attempt to correct this imbalance by emphasizing a deposit-centred approach (Pyddoke 1961: 116). He furthermore rebuked archaeologists for their descriptions of deposits (e.g. 'grey rubbly layer', 'yellow sandy layer'), which he regarded as woefully simplistic and uninformative with regard to formation processes (ibid.: 121). This was the start of geoarchaeology.

The term 'geoarchaeology' seems to have been coined by Karl Butzer in 1973, and it formed a key part of his influential book *Archaeology as Human Ecology*, published a decade later (Butzer 1982; Gladfelter 1981: 344). The term and idea were quickly adopted in number of publications throughout the 1970s (e.g. Rapp, Bullard, & Albritton 1970; Davidson & Shackley 1976; Gladfelter 1977; Hassan 1979), and today there are several major textbooks outlining the methods and approaches of this subdiscipline, as well as the journal *Geoarchaeology* (Rapp & Hill 2006; Goldberg & Macphail 2006; French 2003). The basic principles and methods of geoarchaeology were essentially adopted from the earth and soil sciences, where the stress is on the process of deposit formation, or sedimentation, and where the distinction between depositional and postdepositional processes needs to be clearly defined (see e.g. Stein 2001). Although these processes are more commonly environmental in nature, they need not be, and indeed much work on smaller-scale deposit formation explicitly cites human agency, such as micromorphological analysis of floor layers (e.g. Matthews et al. 1997).

The geoscientific focus generated by such studies soon spilled over into discussions of stratigraphy. In the late 1970s and early 1980s, a workshop at the Belgian University of Ghent began to develop universal standards of classification and terminology for archaeological stratigraphy, which culminated in a preliminary guide. The guide quite explicitly considered archaeological stratigraphy as similar to geological stratigraphy, contra Harris:

> *Thus although the processes of archaeological and geological sedimentation are, generally, subject to different causes, and although man is much more involved in the first type of deposition than in the second, it seems that the two processes are subject to similar rules and axioms.*
>
> *(Gasche & Tunca 1983: 326)*

The authors of the guide, Hermann Gasche and Önhan Tunca, rightly pointed out, of course, that natural processes occur on all archaeological sites, but their relevance or identification is often downplayed; however, they do not justify their claim in the quote here – it is merely asserted, and they move on. The basis of their program was to establish types of stratigraphic units, of which three were initially proposed: lithologic, chronostratigraphic, and ethnostratigraphic units (ibid.: 327). The lithologic is clearly the primary unit, based on its petrologic composition, and from these, chronostratigraphic and ethnostratigraphic units are composed, either of single or multiple lithologic units; chronostratigraphic units are defined in terms of time intervals or phases, ethnostratigraphic units on the basis of common artifactual material. Obviously both chrono- and ethnostratigraphies can be created in different ways on the same basic sets of data, depending on variable definitions of a time interval or what constitutes a common group of finds. Also, they may or may not correspond with each other (i.e. respect the same boundaries). Gasche and Tunca's original guide was commented on and debated in a follow-up journal *Stratigraphica Archaeologica*, of which only two volumes were ever issued (for a review, see Linse & Stein 1997).

Yet this system is, in practice, almost identical to the methods of single-context excavation and recording associated with the adoption of the Harris matrix; there, the basic stratigraphic unit (a.k.a. context) is defined on the basis of its physical composition, which usually involves sediment description. Subsequently, the sequence of contexts, as they are arranged in a matrix, can be ordered into phases, but also spatially related groups, or any other kind of grouping based on artifacts or a combination of artifacts and architectural elements. If anything, the focus in the Ghent system on artifacts in their ethnostratigraphic units is somewhat limiting and clearly influenced by the idea of fossils in deposits associated with geological stratigraphy. Nonetheless, the broader point is that there is no substantial difference between archaeological and geological stratigraphy as defined by geoarchaeologists on the one hand, and proponents of the Harris matrix and single context recording on the other hand. The difference, such as it is, lies chiefly in that the latter is an abstract method of determining stratigraphic sequences, whereas the former puts more emphasis on deposit formation and how that is linked to stratigraphic sequence.

The question remains, however: if the formation processes on archaeological sites are different to those in natural environments, how does this affect our understanding of stratigraphy? Harris may have identified the crux of the matter, but his method does not actually address this issue. The challenge facing us is how to understand stratigraphy in terms of cultural formation processes (or a combination of cultural and natural processes – the distinction is admittedly highly problematic). One suspicion is that the stratigraphic terminology and concepts which have been emerging in Palaeolithic archaeology may not be as applicable to later prehistoric and historic sites, simply because the formation processes on Palaeolithic sites are more commonly natural processes (see e.g. Franken 1984). One can certainly define basic stratigraphic units in lithologic terms, but this surely makes sense only because lithologic description relates to natural depositional processes. The problem can be rephrased: it is not that geoscientific terminology and methods of description should be replaced by another, more cultural or social terminology but that our social and cultural terminology is woefully simplistic by comparison. The problem is brought into sharp relief when one considers the relationship between unit descriptions and interpretations in conventional single-context recording.

Consider the following hypothetical (but quite realistic) example of a stratigraphic unit or context:

Description: *Compact, mid greyish brown, sandy silt with occasional inclusions of fine charcoal (2%, <5mm) and subangular gravel (1%, <10 mm). Some iron panning around the edges of the deposit.*

Interpretation: *Pit fill*

We should ask, What is the connection between this detailed soil description and the fact that it is a pit fill? What does a pit fill mean? That it fills a pit undoubtedly, but how did it get in there? Where did it come from? How does it relate to the pit itself (apart from being stratigraphically later)? These are all legitimate questions, and they highlight the problem that the description itself does not help us very much. Why? Because the descriptive terminology was developed in relation to very different types of formation processes. But it also highlights the poverty of the interpretation – it actually tells us very little.

The Social Interpretation of Stratigraphy

There has been a lot of discussion about the fact that all excavation and recording is interpretive and that the distinction between description and interpretation is simply wrong (e.g. Hodder 1997). But it seems to me that at this level, the criticism misses the point. The description in the foregoing example is indeed interpretive, and so is the interpretation, but to call them both interpretations covers over an important issue. The distinction between these two interpretations is still valid because what it should do – but does not in this example – is reveal the links in reasoning between our perception of the deposit and our argument about how we think it was formed. This link is missing in the example because we have adopted a geoscientific approach to recording the deposit but a social or cultural approach to the interpretation of its formation. This lack of connection means that the one appears almost irrelevant in its detail, whereas the other is devoid of meaning because it is so generic and abstract.

I would not claim that this disconnection is true of all excavations or records, but it is common enough to suggest that there is a real problem. Warburton has suggested one approach, which distinguishes between what he calls analytical and interpretive stratigraphy; in the former, stratigraphic units and sequences are identified and described, following geoscientific conventions, whereas in the second, units are classified and explained according to their formation process (Warburton 2003). His interpretive stratigraphy is of more interest here because it deals with the issues of formation processes, and in particular, his separation of stratigraphic units in terms of intentional and unintentional acts is engaging, especially in the context of discussions in the previous chapter. Thus, an intentional deposit might include a wall, whereas an unintentional deposit includes all natural deposits but also some human ones, such as accidental accumulation of debris as a by-product of another activity. This is an interesting attempt to try and make explicit the ways in which we describe and interpret stratigraphy in terms of formation processes, and it also echoes an older distinction in source criticism between voluntary and involuntary sources (see Chapter 2). Yet it is also somewhat simplistic, especially in the notion of creating some kind of classificatory framework for archaeological deposits and interfaces in the same way one might do for natural deposits. The problem is that archaeological stratigraphy largely reflects the historical and social particularities of the people who created it, and these cannot easily be reduced to some general classificatory schemes. This is being made clear by innovative work carried out by Hodder at Çatalhöyük and by Berggren on the City Tunnel project in Malmö, Sweden, where attempts have been made to mediate between the need to broadly define features through general categorizations (e.g. pits, fire installations) and the need to not eclipse interpretation of such features through the simple act of naming (Berggren 2001; Hodder 1999: 94–5).

Consideration of the cultural nature of depositional practices is not new (for a recent historical review, see Joyce & Pollard 2010); in Britain in particular, the concept of structured deposition was developed in the 1980s as a way to think about stratigraphy in later pre-historic contexts in social terms (Richards & Thomas 1984; Hill 1995; Pollard 2008). One problem with the concept, however, is the ease with which it has been taken up, especially in British prehistory, without proper reflection of a wider understanding of depositional histories and formation processes (Brudenell & Cooper 2008). Another and related issue is that it has tended to be equated with a very specific type of practice – ritual (Pollard 2008: 43). The term, though well intended, resulted in creating a series of problematic dichotomies, whether explicitly as between ritual and regular deposits or implicitly in terms of structured versus unstructured deposits. The first distinction is highly problematic (e.g. Brück 1999), whereas the latter seems to invoke Childe's old distinction between meaningful association and random aggregation. A similar approach emerged a decade later in North America from within behavioural archaeology, such as William Walker's studies of ceremonial trash and the ritual structure of deposits, which attempted to see stratigraphic sequences and the life histories of archaeological features in ritual terms (Walker 1995, 2002, 2008). A recent volume linking up depositional practices with the concept of social memory offers a broad range of studies which draw on a lot of this early work, taking it in new directions (Mills & Walker 2008; see also Pauketat & Alt 2005). Various studies thus deal with deposition in terms of acts of concealment, whereas others look at how repetitive and routinized practices create long-term memories through citation of earlier deposits or break and remake memories through new enchainments between deposits.

Themes such as memory or even aesthetics (Pollard 2001) and disaster (Dawdy 2006) as a way of rethinking the social nature of stratigraphic sequences open up new possibilities for interpretation; however, the explicit connection to stratigraphy, and a theorization of stratigraphy in social terms, has only recently been made by Hodder and McAnamy and is the first real engagement with Collingwood's original recognition of the difference of archaeological stratigraphy. Insofar as archaeological stratigraphies are created by people, then stratigraphies ought to incorporate the intentionality of people in ways which are materially related to the nature of stratification. Drawing on the studies cited herein and many others, they offer simple examples to illustrate how certain formation processes can be interpreted in social terms; for example, raising the ground surface through platforms or mounds can be considered a form of political display or dominance, cleaning and scouring an act of purification or renewal, and hiding or concealing as forms of memory and/or forgetting (see Hodder & McAnany 2009). The authors are not offering a classification or arguing for any simple one-to-one correspondence between types of stratigraphic units or sequences and their social meaning – interpretation will always be contingent on the particularities of the record in question. Rather, they present a set of conceptual tools to think with; indeed, this is a long way from Hodder's earlier attempts to explore a social interpretation of sequence, which adopted a much coarser level of resolution (Hodder 1993, 1995).

Where does this leave us with the question posed at the beginning on the difference between the geological and archaeological concepts of stratigraphy? In some ways there is no absolute answer, for it all depends on how one defines the concept. At its most basic, all stratigraphy is about a set of spatial relationships between contiguous bodies of matter which are interpreted in processual terms – in short, Steno's original conception of bodies as fluids. The different forms of the objects and the interfaces between them are interpreted in terms of different formation events, and these events can be both successive and contemporary, as well as of variable duration. As soon as one starts to get more specific than this, then differences between geology and archaeology emerge – because the time scale and processes in geology are often very different from archaeology, one cannot always interpret either the relationship between bodies of matter or their formation in the same way. But neither are they completely different. Our question should not be about whether the two concepts are similar or different, but rather, as archaeologists, we should be concerned to understand the agencies and forces involved in the creation of these bodies of matter we encounter on our sites. These will inevitably be a complex mix of natural and social agencies (we might even call this a symmetrical stratigraphy), but the critical thing is to develop ways to link our observations of these bodies with our inferences about the agencies which created them.

Taphonomy and Assemblage Formation

Origins and Development of Assemblage Formation

As with the emergence of stratigraphy, a focus on formation processes in relation to objects rather than deposits can also be traced back to the late nineteenth and early twentieth centuries, but again there are two very distinct traditions to consider here. On the one side, there is taphonomy, a field which largely stems from Palaeolithic studies, and on the other side, the concept of find combination, which was developed in Scandinavia in association with the three-age system. Some of the earliest research in taphonomy revolved around the eolith debate, which concerned whether certain flint flakes and nodules were the product of human or natural agencies. Experiments on breakage and wear patterns were conducted to understand whether some of the characteristics observed on such objects could have been produced by natural forces (Grayson 1986; O'Connor 2007: 161–7). It was not until the 1960s, however, that such studies really took off, especially in relation to animal bones on early hominid sites (Brain 1967; Isaac 1967).

Indeed, in many ways zooarchaeology has been one of the few object-oriented specialisms in archaeology to incorporate formation theory (as taphonomy) into its standard methodology (e.g. Lyman 1994). This is no doubt because of the obvious links with palaeontology, where the concept of taphonomy was first developed (Gifford 1981; Holz & Simões 2005). The association of the term 'taphonomy' in relation to assemblage-based formation theory has been expanded by Holdaway and Wandsnider, who recently referred to this body of work as the 'taphonomic metaphysic' (Holdaway & Wandsnider 2008: 4; also see Dawdy 2008 for an even wider use of the term), although in general, the term 'taphonomy' is not usually equated with 'assemblage formation', which has much broader connotations.

The other tradition of find association or find combination was largely developed by the Danish antiquarians C. J. Thomsen and J. J. Worsaae in the mid-nineteenth century, when it was used as the basis of establishing intersite, regional chronologies and the three-age system itself (Gräslund 1976, 1987; Rowe 1962). This approach was much more focused on assemblages rather than individual objects, and its chief distinction was between closed and open (or accumulated) find combinations, the one referring to contexts in which objects can be considered necessarily contemporary (e.g. burials), and the other not (e.g. peat bogs). What 'contemporaneity' means, however, is not necessarily straightforward; Worsaae's original formulation implied contemporaneity of use (Worsaae 1849: 76), but he probably also assumed that they were made at similar times, too, contemporaneity thus being a broad chronological unit. Yet this definition is not the same as that which appears to be now understood in Scandinavian archaeology; Gräslund, for example, states that the distinction between closed and open find combinations is not based on the contemporaneity of the objects but on the event of deposition (Gräslund 1987: 7). Eggert makes the same point in his discussion of source criticism in relation to closed finds (*geschlossene funde*; Eggert 2001: 53), and this shift seems to go back to Montelius, who used the term 'secure find' rather than 'closed find' (Montelius 1903: 11; see also Klindt-Jensen 1975: 88). The complexity of such assemblage formation in terms of chronology is well recognized in current European traditions (for a full treatment, see e.g. Eggert 2001); indeed, the various distinctions amongst the dates of production, use, and deposition in relation to find combination was also articulated in a paper by Rowe half a century ago (Rowe 1962), distinctions used more recently by Olivier to show the multitemporal nature of an Iron Age burial (Olivier 1999).

Aspects of both the palaeontological tradition of taphonomy and the Scandinavian tradition of find combination relate to issues in assemblage formation theory, which is largely a North American development. However, both were largely connected to very different approaches to the archaeological record; the latter especially was more intimately a part of the Central European tradition of source criticism (see Chapter 2) and viewed assemblage formation largely in terms of chronological issues. North American assemblage formation theory, however, had a much broader concern and can be conventionally traced back to the work of Robert Ascher. In 1968, he published a paper called 'Time's Arrow and the Archaeology of a Contemporary Community', in which he characterized the problems facing archaeology as twofold: missing evidence and how to interpret what does survive (Ascher 1968). However, Ascher effectively separates the two issues and goes on to focus on the latter; in doing so, he invokes analogy as the basic tool to aid interpretation, a topic on which he also wrote a seminal paper in 1961 at the end of which he anticipated in abbreviated form the ideas expounded in the 1968 paper (Ascher 1961). As Ascher points out, every community is both destroying and renewing itself continuously, but at some point, renewal stops but destruction continues. At this point, Ascher suggests, a site moves from an 'inhabited phase' to a 'ghost phase' (Ascher 1968: 46). He also adds a third phase, the 'archaeological', to define when the site is exposed again by the archaeologist, although his main concern is with the transition to the ghost phase.

Drawing a parallel with astronomy and cosmology, Ascher employs the metaphor of entropy and time's arrow to characterize this process and the formation of the archaeological record: 'Since the connection between the archaeological present and the ethnographic past lies along the route of increasing disorder, the advancement of interpretation depends on knowing what happens along that route' (Ascher 1968: 52). Archaeological inference thus needs to reverse the path of disorganization; failure to understand this path means a failure to control or limit the range of inferences one can make. Ascher's paper used two case studies of contemporary contexts (a wrecker's yard and a

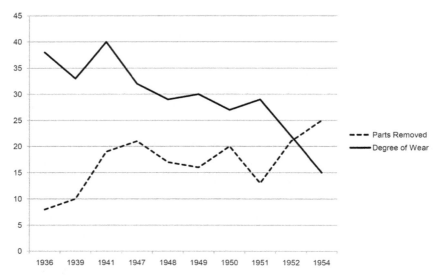

Figure 3. Transformation processes in operation at a wrecker's yard in New York in 1966; a sample of ten cars was recorded by Ascher's students, noting number of original parts removed and degree of wear, calculated on a scale of 1 to 6 (based on data from Ascher 1968: 45, table 1).

Seri Indian settlement) to explore this path of disorganization; in particular, his study of the Seri community highlighted three processes which increase disorder: smearing and blending, recycling and reusing, and broadcasting. There is, however, something of a contradiction in Ascher's first case study and his general theory of increasing disorder. In his example of the wrecker's yard, he shows two trends: one being the removal of car parts, the other being the process of rusting. Implicit here is a distinction which Schiffer would later characterize as c- and n-transforms, but what is significant is that although, from his tabulated data, the rusting does appear to increase over time, the removal of car parts shows a more variable pattern; on the whole, though, the older cars have more of their original parts than newer cars (Figure 3). This of course makes sense, as the newer cars might be more useful for recycling, but it contradicts the general theory of increasing disorder over time – if anything, it reveals how a process like recycling can introduce a pattern into an assemblage which goes against time's arrow.

This is where Schiffer's transformation theory, which he first articulated in a 1972 paper, improves on Ascher; Schiffer saw his theory as an important corrective to a more simplistic attritional or reductive view of formation processes, as exemplified in Ascher's entropy theory or sampling theory (Schiffer 1983: 676–8; 1987: 8–10). In such approaches, the problems were often perceived as largely quantitative (i.e. a reduction in data), whereas Schiffer was arguing for the importance of qualitative changes to the record, largely due to differential discard practices and postdepositional processes. Such processes are not solely reductive but also additive, and they can introduce new patterns into the record. Schiffer's first statement came out in 1972, a year before his doctoral thesis was awarded, in a paper called 'Archaeological Context and Systemic Context', where many of his key concepts are presented (Schiffer 1972). The initial prompt for the paper was his unease at the way archaeologists regarded spatial patterning in the archaeological record as a straightforward reflection of spatial patterning of past activities. In the opening lines, he disparagingly quotes Binford's use of the term 'fossil record' because of this connotation, which is ironic given the battle they were to later engage in over precisely that term (Binford 1981; Schiffer 1985). During the late 1960s and 1970s, spatial patterning had become an important aspect of archaeological interpretation, especially on Palaeolithic sites (for a recent review, see Wandsnider 1996). Schiffer's ideas were an attempt to mediate what he saw as two extreme views on the archaeological record:

> *Archaeologists have gone from the one extreme of viewing a site as spatially and behaviourally undifferentiated rubbish to the other extreme of viewing remains as mostly reflecting their locations of use in past activities. At this point, it appears that neither extreme is often the actual case.*
>
> (Schiffer 1972: 163)

Schiffer's middle road between the extremes was a flow model approach, which attempted to map the movement of objects through cultural systems. As did many at the time, Schiffer viewed culture as a system whose elements (i.e. artifacts, people, and other things) could be conceived in terms of flow models; for Schiffer, the aim was to understand this cycling process in terms of the life histories of individual elements (Figure 4). The key point in relation to the initial problem that Schiffer started with – spatial patterning – is for archaeologists to distinguish those elements of the archaeological record that have been discarded and those which have not:

> *Archaeological context includes all the materials found in a site,*
> *whether or not they are in specialized discard locations and whether*
> *or not they have been deliberately discarded by the past occupants of*
> *a site. It is well known, for example, that elements are found in*
> *every stage of manufacture and use. The way in which a site is*
> *abandoned – the variables operative at the time the occupants leave*
> *the site, or die without replacement – has demonstrable effects on*
> *the kinds and quantities of non-discarded elements found in*
> *archaeological context. Elements which reach archaeological context*
> *without the performance of discard activities will be termed* de facto
> refuse.
>
> *(Schiffer 1972: 160)*

In short, de facto refuse is material which has been abandoned midcycle to so speak and never reached the discard stage except by default; as such, it is this kind of material which is most reliable for inferring spatial patterning of past activities. However, even discarded material is valuable so long as one's spatial resolution is adjusted accordingly; here, Schiffer's distinction of primary and secondary refuse was presented to suggest that primary refuse (i.e. material discarded at its location of use) can still be used to infer spatial patterning of past activities (Schiffer 1972: 162). Schiffer brought a lot of his ideas together a few years later in the book *Behavioural Archaeology*, where the emphasis remained on artifact and assemblage formation. In many ways, assemblage formation theory remained focused on the issues first identified by Schiffer, particularly processes of abandonment and discard (e.g. Hayden & Cannon 1983; Staski & Sutro 1991; Cameron & Tomka 1993) or processes which delayed discard, such as curation and use-life (David 1972; DeBoer 1974; Binford 1979; Shott 1989, 1996a, 1996b). However, there seems little doubt that such studies reached their heyday in the 1970s and 1980s and have declined somewhat from the 1990s. Although they have by no means disappeared from the archaeological literature, nevertheless, with the exception of certain types of assemblages such as animal bones, few artifact studies systematically incorporate issues of formation theory in their methodology. The

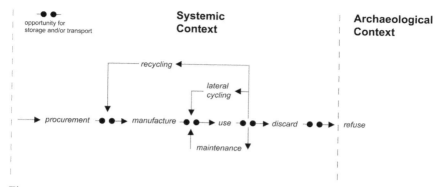

Figure 4. Michael Schiffer's flow model for durable objects through a cultural system (after Schiffer 1972: 158, figure 1).

reasons would appear to be related to the wider theoretical status of middle-range theory in archaeology which has always been more closely linked to assemblage-oriented approaches than deposit-oriented approaches.

In short, assemblage formation issues became seen as mere method, separate from general theory, and indeed often more relevant to simple, hunter-gatherer societies as well as perhaps an idiosyncrasy of a small group of North American archaeologists – a condition recently deplored by Shott (Shott 2005: 5). Indeed, there are some quite fundamental theoretical issues surrounding taphonomy and assemblage formation, which need to be addressed and have wider relevance for all archaeologists. One of the more provocative ideas is John Chapman's 'fragmentation thesis'; simply put, this argues that archaeologists have too easily assumed that the fragmented or partial nature of most archaeological finds is simply a product of accidental breakage or postdepositional factors and have thus never properly addressed fragmentation as a cultural or social practice. Although notions of ritual breakage or 'killing' have cropped up in the literature from time to time, Chapman's suggestion, based on his work in the Balkans, is that intentional fragmentation was far more common in prehistory than archaeologists have credited (Chapman 2000; Chapman and Gaydarska 2007). Chapman links such fragmentation practices to the reuse of fragments as a way of mediating fractal notions of personhood and associated social networks at various scales – a popular theme in the contemporary theoretical literature (e.g. Jones 2005; Fowler 2004). However, Brittain

and Harris have pointed out in a recent review that the notion of fragmentation does not necessarily have to connect to themes of personhood, or even the circulation of fragments which Chapman describes
under the term 'enchainment' (Brittain & Harris 2010). Nonetheless,
Chapman's critique that the issue of missing fragments has not been
adequately addressed but merely put down to general attritional effects
is important; on the contrary, Chapman argues that – on the basis of
examples of totally excavated settlement sites and closed graves – such
missing fragments may be missing because of deliberate removal and
circulation. If this is indeed the case, then it raises all kinds of questions
about traditional assemblage formation theory.

However, Chapman has been criticized for not fully considering the
means of distinguishing intentional from accidental fragmentation (e.g.
Bailey 2001), a critique responded to in his later, coauthored work
(Chapman and Gaydarska 2007; but see Last 2007). There is no doubt
that this is a difficult issue and not always easily resolved; however,
it seems indisputable that fragmentation is sometimes intentional and
that fragment reuse occurs, so whether or not one believes it was as
widespread as Chapman argues, it challenges our default assumptions
about the fragmented nature of the archaeological record. More generally, studies such as Chapman's have instilled an interest in assemblage
formation theory among many European archaeologists who had previously ignored it as a parochial and methodological issue. Whatever
the merits of the fragmentation thesis, it at least has the potential to act
as a bridge with the extensive and important literature on assemblage
formation which has been coming out of North America for the past
four decades, yet remains largely ignored by many European archaeologists. In the rest of this chapter, I revisit the basic theoretical issues
which first emerged with assemblage formation theory and explore the
more fundamental problems which revolve around the nature of time
and the archaeological record.

The Archaeological Parallax: Statics and Dynamics
As the title of his 1972 paper implies, Schiffer set up a basic opposition between the archaeological and systemic context. This collapsed
Ascher's three phases (inhabited, ghost, and archaeological) into two
(systemic and archaeological contexts), removing the middle, ghost
phase. Schiffer's initial definitions of systemic and archaeological

context were phrased in terms of his flow model of the cycling of objects through a cultural system. The archaeological context thus represents the state of elements once they had passed through this system while the systemic context indicated that such elements were still in the system (Schiffer 1972: 157). Put another way,

> *The archaeological record at a site is a static, three-dimensional structure of materials existing in the present. The remains in this site have undergone successive transformations from the time they once participated in a behavioural system to the time they are observed by the archaeologist.*
>
> (Schiffer 1975: 838; also see Schiffer 1976: 42–3)

The key point for Schiffer was that the systemic context was a behavioural system, whereas the archaeological context was nonbehavioural, and although this distinction could be mapped onto others such as past-present or unobservable-observable, this was only contingently true given that his broader model incorporated modern material culture studies (Schiffer 1976: 28). Schiffer's formation theory was, of course, just one component of a broader approach that he, along with colleagues Jefferson Reid and William Rathje, called behavioural archaeology (Schiffer 1975; Reid, Schiffer, & Rathje 1975), and which has maintained some kind of coherence as a particular theoretical school in North American archaeology (e.g. Skibo et al. 1995; LaMotta & Schiffer 2001).

In setting up this dual structure of systemic and archaeological context, Schiffer may have helped to create an ontological dichotomy, which Ascher had avoided by his middle term of the ghost phase. In fact the use of three phases was not unique to Ascher; Hans Eggers had adopted a similar tripartite scheme in his source criticism approach in referring to living, dying, and dead cultures (see Chapter 2). However, the influence of Schiffer's bipartite scheme was more powerful and has changed the way we think about the archaeological record and formation processes. A few years after Schiffer's 1972 paper, Binford started to express greater interest in formation processes, which he labelled 'middle-range theory'. Abandoning an early naive statement on the nature of archaeological remains as a 'fossil record' (Binford 1964: 425), Binford quite emphatically rejected the fossil metaphor in a paper from 1975, where he also uses the terms 'statics' and 'dynamics', which become his standard way of theorizing this record. For example, 'The archaeological record is a contemporary phenomenon. It is above all a static phenomenon. It is what remains in static form of dynamics which occurred in the past as well as dynamics occurring up until the present observations are made' (Binford 1975: 251).

This view was given more theoretical elaboration in his introduction to the volume For Theory Building in Archaeology (1977), in which he first uses the term 'middle-range theory' and links it quite explicitly to understanding formation processes (Binford [1977] 1983: 36). It is in the same paper that he also distinguishes it from general theory. The same themes are elaborated further in his book Bones: Ancient Men and Modern Myths (1981), in particular in the chapter on middle-range research. For Binford, in expressing the problem in terms of statics and dynamics, the key issue became how to infer dynamics from statics; this was, in essence, the basis of middle-range theory, namely to provide 'frames of reference', 'cognitive devices', or 'Rosetta stones' which permitted the archaeologist to convert observations on static phenomena into statements about past processes (Binford [1981] 1983: 416; see also Binford 1982a, 1982b).

The influence of this dualistic model promoted by Schiffer and Binford, has had a much more powerful appeal that the tripartite schemes of Eggers or Ascher; indeed, its influence was so strong that the Czech archaeologist Evžen Neustupný, under the influence of North American archaeology, rewrote Eggers's tripartite scheme of living, dying, and dead cultures into a dual opposition of living and dead cultures (Neustupný 1993: 45–6; see also Chapter 2). The only real attempt to suggest a less dualistic approach in North America was Warren DeBoer's notion of the archaeological record as preserved death assemblage (DeBoer 1983) which was heavily influenced by Cowgill's paper on sampling theory discussed in the previous chapter. DeBoer adopts a four-part schema of behavioural, discard, archaeological, and sample assemblage as an antidote to the simple dichotomy of systemic and archaeological context (DeBoer 1983: 21). DeBoer then talks about three types of processes (I–III) which intervene between these four assemblage states, but significantly, he only discusses the first and last – that is, processes between the behavioural and discard assemblages (type I), and those between the discard and sample

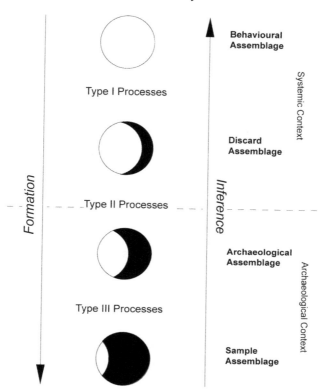

Type I Processes

Type II Processes

Type III Processes

Behavioural
Assemblage

Discard
Assemblage

Archaeological
Assemblage

Sample
Assemblage

Formation

Inference

Systemic Context

Archaeological Context

Figure 5. Warren DeBoer's taphonomic model of the archaeological record (after DeBoer 1983: 21), with Schiffer's division between systemic and archaeological context added.

assemblages (type III). Using the example of object size, he suggests how something as basic a physical quality as this has implications for both our understanding of processes of discard or deposition and processes of retrieval. Yet the complete omission of discussion of type II processes (between discard and archaeological assemblage) is very revealing, because it is these processes which cross the divide between Schiffer's systemic and archaeological contexts – and in a sense, also the divide between assemblage and deposit-oriented approaches to formation theory (Figure 5). It is this divide which seems to act almost as a blind spot in formation theory, a line in which it is difficult to join up the two sides. In a sense the line between the systemic and archaeological context demarcates two very different perspectives on the same object creating a parallax: on the one hand, the archaeological record as it appears to us in the present; on the other hand, the past processes which we suppose led to its creation. The problem is, the theoretical model used in formation theory not only does not link the two, but actually creates the parallax displacement in the first place.

Binford, Schiffer, and the Pompeii Premise

Although both Binford's and Schiffer's approaches are often lumped together, there are differences, which came to a head in the debate over the Pompeii premise (Binford 1981; Schiffer 1985). The term 'Pompeii premise' was coined by Ascher in 1961 in a footnote, where he first pointed out that the archaeological record is not a snapshot of a once-living community, stopped at a moment in time (like the famous site of Pompeii – or the lake dwellings as described by Munro, discussed in the previous chapter), but the remains of a community in the process of decomposition, interrupted by the act of excavation (Ascher 1961: 324). Binford redirects this notion of the Pompeii premise – and perhaps, Schiffer's original slight in 1972 towards Binford's use of the term 'fossil record', which Schiffer repeated in his *Behavioural Archaeology* (1976: 11) – towards Schiffer's characterization of transforms as distortions of an original cultural (i.e. systemic) context. Binford is stating, in no uncertain terms, that by using the term 'distortion', Schiffer is actually himself trying to recapture a Pompeii-like interpretation of the archaeological record, only one which is slightly more sophisticated than that contained in the Pompeii premise. Schiffer seems to be arguing that by taking account of these transforms and filtering them out, one can reconstruct the pristine, original cultural context as if it were some Pompeii situation – an ethnographic present, a slice of history. As Binford says: 'Schiffer wants to find Pompeii' (Binford 1981: 201). Binford has two specific problems with Schiffer's model which support his critique. First, it is unclear why Schiffer should separate his c-transforms from the systemic context (and by implication, his separation of correlates from transforms):

> For instance, Schiffer would view the event of a young boy cleaning out a hearth, taking the ash and other unwanted contents out of the house, and tossing it to one side as a C-transform distorting the juxtaposition of the hearth and ashes which obtained during the period of active fire in the hearth. From the perspective of the

occupants of the site, it was cleaning up. We may reasonably ask
how cleaning up should distort the relationship between the
archaeological record and the cultural system from which it derives.

(Binford 1981: 200)

In short, c-transforms are not distortions but simply part of the systemic context; and this leads on to Binford's second and related point: cultural systems are always in the process of entropy as well as renewal (a point Ascher had actually also made) – in short, they are always dynamic. Thus, there can be no original context, no Pompeii – this is always a product of the archaeologist's expectations, insofar as the archaeologist wants to recapture a specific moment; if so, then everything that comes after that moment is potentially distorting. Indeed, ironically, it has been shown that Pompeii itself does not conform to the Pompeii premise, as the process of abandonment was protracted, thus negating any notion that the site is a frozen moment in time, offering some kind of ideal, systemic inventory (Allison 1992; Bon 1997).

Schiffer's response to Binford's critique is remarkably brief (Schiffer 1985); indeed, rather than directly tackle Binford's points, which Schiffer simply dismisses as a misunderstanding of his views, Schiffer devotes the whole paper to re-presenting the problem of archaeologists who treat the archaeological record as if it were a direct reflection of the past systemic context. For Schiffer, this is the *real* Pompeii premise. Focusing on interpretations of floor assemblages in U.S. Southwestern archaeology, Schiffer shows how such floor assemblages cannot be straightforwardly read as if they were systemic inventories – that is, reflective of the full range and proportions of objects which are in circulation at any one time in the past systemic or living context. In this sense, the archaeological assemblage is a distortion of the systemic assemblage, or to put it another way, it is simply not directly representative of it. The difference between Binford and Schiffer really lies in how to respond to this problem; where Binford sees an irresolvable palimpsest suggesting that the systemic context actually needs to be studied at a larger temporal scale, Schiffer sees the challenge as dissecting the palimpsest to understand the small-scale events that produced it. Binford and Schiffer thus head in opposite directions, Binford towards general theory and explanations of large-scale processes, and Schiffer towards the microscale of activities in his behavioural archaeology.

Both, of course, are seeking generalizations, but at very different temporal scales. One could say that there is therefore no real contradiction between their views (see e.g. Tschauner 1996: 8–10; Shott 1998: 311–12). However, because of this divergence, they do differ on the how they see the relationship between middle-range or formation theory and general or social theory respectively. For Binford, although middle-range theory should be independent in evidential or methodological terms, substantively it should look to general theory for relevance (Binford 1983 [1977]: 36–7); for Schiffer, in contrast, his behavioural archaeology or reconstruction theory stands alone on both methodological and substantive terms (Schiffer 1988; see also Shott 1998: 312).

Given this difference, the key question is thus how one stands on the problem of the palimpsest; is it possible to dissect it or not? In some ways this becomes a caricature, a forced either-or, especially the way Binford paints it: either one aims to reconstruct ethnographic tableaux, or one seeks to explain longer-term processes. But it is debatable how far Schiffer and others ever tried to reconstruct Pompeii's or slices of history; Schiffer himself says the term 'reconstruction' as Binford uses it is inaccurate with respect to his goals (Schiffer 1988: 469). Rather, the question is what scale of aggregate behaviour one can realistically hope to obtain in archaeology. It is precisely such issues of scale in relation to the palimpsest nature of the archaeological record that was taken up by time perspectivism.

Time Perspectivism

Geoff Bailey coined the term 'time perspectivism' in his paper 'Concepts, Time-Scales and Explanations in Economic Prehistory' (Bailey 1981; see also Bailey 1987). Here, Bailey identified two conflicting assumptions about time used by archaeologists; one, which he called behavioural uniformitarianism, is that long-term patterns are simply the summation of short-term events as observed by us in our daily experience. This is clearly encapsulated in Schiffer's theory of behavioural archaeology. The other assumption, which he called time perspectivism, is that different processes are observable at different time scales and thus require different concepts and types of explanation (Bailey 1981: 103). Bailey suggested the two are not necessarily incompatible unless taken to extremes, but archaeologists need to be aware that they are assumptions, especially behavioural uniformitarianism. However, there is an obvious sense that time perspectivism is a broader and more ecumenical assumption than behavioural uniformitarianism, as it recognizes short-term events, whereas the converse is not true.

More than a quarter of a century after its inception, Bailey recently reviewed the concept in historical and personal perspective (Bailey 2008). He highlighted two principal aspects of time perspectivism: substantive and methodological. The substantive definition effectively recaps his 1981 statement, that different processes are observable and hence explicable at different time scales; the methodological aspect refers to the scale of resolution obtainable in archaeological data (i.e. the palimpsest nature of the archaeological record). This aspect is something he did not discuss in much depth in his original paper (Bailey 1981: 109–10) but that has received very detailed treatment in another paper, which I discuss later (Bailey 2007). One of the important consequences of the palimpsest nature of the archaeological record was how to respond to it; Bailey argues that under behavioural uniformitarianism, this becomes a real problem, because 'progressive loss of evidence and loss of resolution, especially as one goes further back in time, result in progressively worse data, by definition inadequate to answer the questions we really want to ask about the past' (Bailey 2008: 14). For Bailey, however, by adopting time perspectivism, this is much less of a problem, because the resolution of the data could be perfectly adequate to interpretations based on longer-term processes.

Bailey's retrospective on the concept of time perspectivism is interesting because it is quite clear that the theory has had limited impact on archaeological thought in the intervening decades; Bailey even identified three major causes for this. The first two are the importance given to the individual in contemporary archaeological (and social) theory on the one hand, and on the other hand, the need for linear narratives; time perspectivism which mostly works on time scales greater than individual lives and, indeed, on multiple time scales would clearly seem to confound both of these elements. How entrenched these elements are, however, is open to debate, and in fact if anything works against time perspectivism, it is probably the wider influence of social theory outside archaeology, which derives from studies of contemporary, and thus short-term behaviour, a point which Bailey noted in his original paper from 1981 (Bailey 1981: 103). Indeed, Murray's comments on the general reception of time perspectivism in archaeology are much more astute, in particular with regard to wider social theory, normalization, and the anthropological metaphysic (Murray 2008; see also Murray 1997; 1999). It is Bailey's last cause, however, which is perhaps the most damning – practical implementation. Although there have been quite important developments in methodological and theoretical discussions of time perspectivism (e.g. Stern 1993; Murray 1997, 1999), there simply have been very few empirical or substantive studies using time perspectivism which give us interpretations of long-term processes, beyond ones which highlight either a coevolution between human activities and geological or environmental change or the development of persistent places (see, for example, papers in Holdaway & Wandsnider 2008). And substantively speaking, there is nothing especially new in any of this.

The crux of the matter – methodologically speaking – boils down to the problem of the palimpsest and how one decides to interpret it, and this brings us ultimately back to Bailey's original contrast between behavioural uniformitarianism and time perspectivism. These two approaches are epitomized by the theory of accumulations research, on the one hand, and time averaging, on the other hand. The former derives from Schiffer's formation theory and, in particular, his discard equation, whereas the latter takes its cue from palaeontology and geology, which have of course been key influences on time perspectivism.

Time Averaging

Nicola Stern was the first to introduce the idea of archaeological assemblages as time averaged, taking the concept from palaeontology (Walker & Bambach 1971; Western 1980; Stern 1994, 2008). At its basis lies the disjunction between the accumulation rates of deposits and those of assemblages:

> *Sedimentary facies are time-transgressive phenomena whereas material debris accumulates as the result of instantaneous behavioural events; thus there is a discrepancy between the time scales of the geomorphic events and the behavioural events that interacted to create the archaeological record.*
>
> *(Stern 1993: 205)*

As a result, any assemblage of artifacts or bones or other material is an aggregate of multiple, separate events – a palimpsest. In palae-ontology, this has serious consequences, because in effect, it means that one can have fossils of different species which never cohabited, assembled together in the same sedimentary matrix. Translated into archaeological terms, the interpretive problem posed by this fact can be stated simply: how do we if know this aggregate is composed of similar events or different ones? If the same kind of activity is repeated, leading to similar deposition of objects, then the cumulative pattern is simply the same as the individual pattern, writ large. However, if differ-ent activities contribute to an assemblage, then the overall pattern will bear no necessary relation to individual patterns. This can be restated by saying that time-averaged assemblages are not necessarily average representations of the events from which they are formed.

Josara de Lange gives a clear illustration of this problem in discussing a hypothetical assemblage of animal bones amounting to 130 minimum number of individuals (MNI) which have accumulated over five hun-dred years (de Lange 2008: 154–6). She points to three possible scen-arios which could lead to the same assemblage, each scenario broken down into ten blocks of fifty years. In Scenario 1 each fifty-year period repeats the same pattern, whereas scenarios 2 and 3 exhibit quite differ-ent patterns in each period, which in scenario 3, also include a hiatus of activity for three periods (see Figure 6). Moreover, although de Lange's case is purely illustrative, taking the arguments of time averaging fur-ther, one obvious observation is that even her fifty-year periods are time averaged; she would no doubt agree, and in fact it is quite clear that almost all archaeological assemblages are time averaged or pal-impsests in a quite fundamental sense. This spells out the problem very clearly, but it also raises a potential spoiler for archaeology of massive proportions; simply put, if one accepts that any of de Lange's scen-arios (or more) is equally probable, then surely the data patterns which archaeologists find are quite simply arbitrary. Bailey would say this is true – but only from the perspective of behavioural uniformitarianism, which always seeks to explain patterns on the microlevel. One might compare this temporal aggregate to a spatial aggregate, such as a poll on consumption habits nationwide; no doubt such a poll would mask regional variation, and even other variables such as income, gender, ethnicity, but that does not necessarily mean that a comparison of, say, British and French consumer habits is still not informative. But does the same argument apply to temporal aggregates – if one compares two sites which both cover a span of five hundred years, can one say that differences or similarities in their faunal assemblages are meaningful in any way?

The crucial question here, which de Lange does not address, is, At what point does an assemblage become time averaged? Is it as soon as there is more than one event of object deposition? But this begs the question of what counts as a singular event of object deposition, and here we are back to the problem of whether or not one is dealing with repetitive and/or routinized events. When are two events distinct enough for us to call them two separate events or components of a single event? A collection of coins in the bottom of a wishing well may be the accumulation of fifty years of throwing events, but are these different events or simply components of one singular, protracted event – especially as each event is effectively a repetition of the previous one and takes its meaning only *through* this repetition? One of the reasons this question has not been raised in discussions of time averaging is surely because of its origins in palaeontology. The presumption of time averaging in palaeontology is that the relationship between the deposit and the assemblage is temporally arbitrary, that there is no synchronicity between the formation of deposits and the longevity and life cycles of creatures whose remains are encased in such deposits. However, can the same be said of many, if not most, archaeological deposits? Surely one of the features of deposition on most archaeological sites is that they are the product of intentional activity by human beings, not natural processes (i.e. structures, floor layers, middens) – as discussed earlier in this chapter. It is therefore quite justifiable to assume that the link between assemblage and deposit formation is not necessarily as arbitrary, even if there is a disjuncture between the time scales of the formation of, say, a floor layer and the individual acts of object deposition on that floor.

This raises what is a common element of time perspectivism and time-averaging studies in archaeology; they have largely been conceived and applied within Palaeolithic archaeology when the conditions of the archaeological record are most comparable to palaeontology – Stern's work on hominid fossils in East Africa is a case in point (Stern 1993,

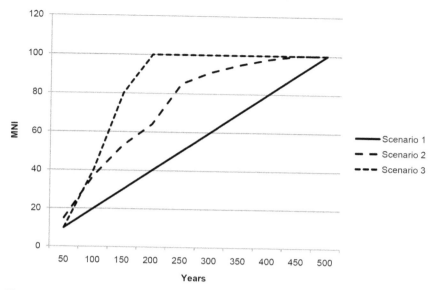

Figure 6. The problem of time averaging: cumulative graph showing changing composition of three hypothetical faunal assemblages at fifty-year intervals (data from de Lange 2008; adult numbers only). Combined over a five-hundred-year period, all three assemblages would appear identical.

1994; see also contributions in Holdaway & Wandsnider 2008). In such cases, the temporal relation of deposit to assemblage formation is undoubtedly a real problem when the time scales of the two processes are also different, and it is also obvious that one can find similar instances for any period of the archaeological record. However, in most cases in later prehistory and historical archaeology, the archaeological record, depositionally speaking, is quite different to that in palaeobiology, and in fact the relation between deposit and assemblage deposition is by no means necessarily arbitrary. As such, the presumption that time-averaged assemblages are not average representations is less likely to be true. There is, however, no question that this needs to be made explicit and even argued for by invoking supporting evidence. What it suggests is the need to understand the relationship between assemblage and deposit formation in individual cases, and to recognize that what counts as a mixed assemblage is relative to our understanding of the processes of deposition in a cultural or social context. This is where accumulations research has provided a useful counterapproach to time perspectivism.

Accumulations Research

Accumulations research is one of the more prominent, contemporary spin-offs of Schiffer's work on formation processes; its primary focus is on how materials accumulate in the archaeological record and the implications that has for occupational duration and population size (Varien & Mills 1997; Varien & Ortman 2005). The methodological basis of the research lies in Schiffer's basic discard equation, which attempts to quantify the rate at which any given artifact type is discarded (Schiffer 1975: 840; 1976: 60; 1987: 53); his equation is simple:

$$T_D = St/L,$$

where T_D is the total number of artifacts discarded; St the number of artifacts in use at any one time (i.e. systemic number), multiplied by the total period of use; and L is the use-life of the artifact. The key point of this equation is to highlight the important effect use-life can have on the ratio of artifacts in an archaeological assemblage. For example, if object x lasts twice as long as object y, one would expect it to be represented in the archaeological record only half as much. This does not mean, however, that there were only half as many x's as y's in the living or systemic context – x and y may have been present in equal proportions; only because y had a shorter use-life, it was discarded and replaced twice as frequently as x. This simple reasoning straightaway suggests potential problems when archaeologists are using proportions of objects in assemblages as proxies of proportions of objects in use at any one time, and thus inferring the relative importance of different activities on the basis of this assumption (e.g. Ammerman & Feldman 1974). As a consequence of this realization, a lot of ethnoarchaeological research since the 1970s has focused on estimating use-life of artifacts (primarily ceramics; for a review, see Varien & Mills 1997; see also Shott 1989, 1996a).

One of the problems with such cross-cultural research, however, is that it revealed quite a lot of variability, as a result of a number of factors, from accuracy of data collection to variables affecting use-life, such as function, frequency of use, and number of similar objects in use at any one time. In the case of ceramics, use-life estimates ranged from less than one year to nearly twenty years, although more than 70 percent had a use-life of fewer than five years (Varien & Mills 1997: 151).

To counter this problem, research by Mark Varien and colleagues work-ing in the Southwestern United States has focused on archaeological rather than ethnographic material to get around some of these prob-lems. Using what they call a strong archaeological case – the Pueblo Duckfoot site in Colorado, which was almost totally excavated and closely dated to a twenty-five-year time period using dendrochronol-ogy – the archaeologists had tight control on the number of households, the duration of occupation, and total discard assemblage (see Varien & Potter 1997; see also Lightfoot 1993). On the basis of the analysis of cooking pots – which offer one of the best types of ceramic because of their short use-life and high turnover – they could easily calculate the discard rate using Schiffer's formula and site data, without recourse to any ethnographically derived values. Moreover, they adjusted the cal-culations using two other variables – whether all the vessels were new at the start of occupation and whether each vessel was used consecutively or in rotation. Their study resulted in historically and culturally specific values of discard rates for cooking pots which could then be applied to other Pueblo sites and used to make inferences on occupation duration, which also had wider ramifications about understanding longer-term patterns (Varien & Ortman 2005).

The research by Varien and colleagues – though not free of assump-tions – has shown how archaeologists can generate middle-range the-ory from archaeological rather than ethnographic data, and data which are culturally specific rather than universally applicable. However, one of the key sets of variables here is the relationship between use-life and occupation duration, which bears directly on the issue raised by time averaging. Accumulations research suggests that understanding the systemic context works only if the time duration is long enough – in the case of cooking pots, five years (Varien & Potter 1997: 207); for example, if occupation duration is shorter than the use-life of an object, then that object may not appear in the archaeological record of that site at all. For the archaeological record to be at all repre-sentative of the actual and full range of objects in use, occupation has to exceed the use-life of all objects (Mills 1989). In short, to get a representative picture of material culture in use requires the very process of accumulation which time averaging suggests obscures this picture. This is a paradox. On the one hand, time perspectivism tells us that the aggregate nature of assemblage formation implies that we cannot get ethnographic tableaux but only longer-term patterns (see e.g. Shott 2008); but on the other hand, accumulations research tells us that to get at the systemic context, we need these aggregations or palimpsests.

This may or may not be an actual paradox; time perspectivism always seems to overplay this notion that archaeologists informed by behavioural uniformitarianism are seeking snapshots of the past. This is patently false – they are as much reliant on aggregates as time perspectivists, only of shorter duration. What both time perspectivism and accumulations research share is the importance ascribed to palimpsests for actually seeing patterns; they diverge, however, when it comes to the question of whether such patterns are explicable in terms of shorter-term processes (as demonstrated by accumulations research) or longer-term ones (as argued by time perspectivists). It seems to me that much of this difference hinges on whether the assemblage and deposit formation are related in some way and, perhaps also more generally, how much attention is given these two components. There is no doubt that accumulations research is emphatically embedded in the assemblage-oriented approach to formation theory, but time perspectivism seems to straddle the divide; although with a primary interest in assemblage formation and the problems of interpretation it poses, the palaeontological and geological background of time perspectivism makes it more aware of the importance of a deposit-oriented approach than accumulations research. But then it may be precisely for this reason that it remains a peripheral theory in archaeology; one could suggest that although time perspectivism has made us more aware of the problems of assemblage formation in respect to time, it ignored the potential cultural connections between deposit and assemblage formation because of its palaeontological influences. How do we bridge these two elements of the archaeological record?

Palimpsests: The Intersection between Deposit and Assemblage Formation

Linking Deposit and Assemblage Formation

The two aspects or streams of formation theory which I have discussed in this chapter – deposit oriented and assemblage oriented – are not necessarily seen as distinct by all archaeologists; Schiffer has clearly modified his ideas which began with a narrow focus on objects and assemblages towards including deposits (cf. Schiffer 1972 and 1976 with Schiffer 1983 and 1987), whereas many geoarchaeologists explicitly cite the broader theoretical justifications for formation theory which were developed by Schiffer and Binford in relation to assemblages (see e.g. Rapp & Hill 2006: 19). However, Shott in a recent paper discussing the relation between formation theory and middle-range theory implied that the term 'assemblage-formation theory' was synonymous with 'formation theory' (Shott 1998: 311). This may have been an inadvertent slip, and in the end, he uses simply 'formation theory' as a principal label – but it is telling, nonetheless, of the historical distinction between the two streams. Indeed, these two different streams might even be seen as reproduced within different approaches to archaeological stratigraphy, one artifact oriented, the other deposit oriented (Stein 2000), although I think this is not quite accurate (see the earlier discussion in this chapter). Thus, despite the apparent unity of the concept of formation theory and formation processes, there remain different emphases and perspectives.

These emphases, which manifest themselves in terms of the deposit-oriented and assemblage-oriented perspectives, seem at first to largely revolve around stages in the modelled formation of the archaeological record. In particular, one can suggest that the emphasis in assemblage-oriented approaches lies predominantly (but not exclusively) in the relationship between predepositional activities and deposition itself, whereas deposit-oriented approaches are more concerned with the relation between depositional and postdepositional processes. For example, if one compares Schiffer's flow model, in which the stress is on the break between systemic and archaeological context (see Figure 4), with Stein's model of the formation of the archaeological record, with its stress on sediments and weathering (Stein 2001, figure 1.3), this emphasis is quite clear. This difference also explains why there has been relatively little ethnoarchaeological work on the relation between depositional and postdepositional processes as compared to that on the relation between predepositional activities and deposition. Studies such as McIntosh's on mud-wall decay (McIntosh 1974) or Gorecki's call for a postmortem ethnoarchaeology (Gorecki 1985) are extremely rare in the body of ethnoarchaeological research, and indeed one recent textbook explicitly suggests that such studies fall more properly in the realm of geoarchaeology (David & Kramer 2001: 95).

There has, however, been equally little experimental work on such processes, even from a geoarchaeological perspective (cf. Coles 1973, 1979; Ingersoll, Yellen, & MacDonald 1977; Harding 1999; Stone & Planel 1999; Mathieu 2002; Outram 2008); part of the reason may no doubt be the longevity of research implied in such studies, compared to studying the relation between predepositional activities and depositional processes – although even the latter can benefit from so-called longitudinal studies (David & Kramer 2001: 136). For example, the experimental earthwork project on Overton Down in England was conceived in the late 1950s and initiated in 1960 with the expectation of running for more than a century. The overall objective of the project was and is to study short- and medium-term changes effected on an earthwork and buried artifacts to help bridge the gap between contemporary observations of environmental processes and the much longer time scales with which archaeologists are concerned. This involves examining the site at progressively longer time intervals over a 128-year period; so far, results from six examinations have been published (Jewell 1963; Jewell & Dimbleby 1966; Bell, Fowler, & Hillson 1996), with the next intervention intended for the year 2024 and the final one in 2088. Such a project requires a stable institutional framework to ensure continuity, as the initiators of the project could not possibly live to see its completion. It will also provide a real test case against conclusions such as Gorecki's that most postdepositional effects occur in the first five years, whereas a site fifteen years old differs little from one that is five hundred years old (Gorecki 1985: 188).

These distinctions between deposit- and assemblage-oriented formation theories suggest that there may be a deeper ontological rupture in our conceptions of the archaeological record than we are willing to admit. For on the one hand, we have the concept of deposit, which is fairly congruent with what we encounter in the course of fieldwork; we excavate deposits and describe them – they are, in a sense, the principal object that we observe. But the concept of assemblage is another matter; we do of course excavate assemblages, but these are largely defined by their depositional envelope or context; the concept of assemblage we use as archaeologists at the empirical level does not necessarily bear any relation to the concept of assemblage implied in living contexts through ethnoarchaeological research (for a fuller discussion of the concept of assemblage, see Chapter 5). Indeed, one might say that this is precisely the problem which assemblage-oriented formation theory was built to deal with. But can it? Indeed, it is primarily in the concept of assemblage that we come up against the problem of what I called the archaeological parallax – an ontological disjunction between systemic and archaeological contexts. This is a problem which is intimately related to the concept of the palimpsest, as already intimated. Indeed, it is precisely through the concept of the palimpsest that deposit and assemblage formation theory link up.

Origins and Development of the Palimpsest Concept in Archaeology

The idea of a palimpsest refers to the ancient practice of writing, erasing, and rewriting on the same surface – originally wax tablets but later medieval manuscripts. This term emphasizes the material aspect of texts, of writing, yet one which also highlights the memory of such material acts of inscription; this connection to memory is something that will become of central importance to my later discussion. A palimpsest is thus a document which, to varying extents, preserves the marks or traces of earlier acts of writing beneath the visible, uppermost marks of the last act of inscription. In short, the palimpsest encapsulates the dual process of inscription and erasure. Archaeologists have used the metaphor of the palimpsest to describe the archaeological record since the early twentieth century; originally employed to characterize the nature of the historic landscape (Crawford 1953; Randall 1934), it was later taken up to apply to the archaeological record tout court (Binford 1981; Bailey 1981; Foley 1981) and became a fundamental idea behind the theory of time perspectivism (Bailey 2007; Holdaway & Wandsnider 2008).

The earliest uses of the concept of palimpsest in archaeology were applied more generally to the landscape rather than the archaeological record per se; Maitland is often credited with being the first to employ the term at the end of the nineteenth century, but his is a passing reference in parentheses and moreover one directed at maps rather than landscapes, as Bowden has pointed out (Maitland 1897: 14; Bowden 2001: 43). Yet in a review of geographical and landscape approaches to archaeology published in 1934, Randall quotes Maitland, but clearly blurs the metaphor so that the distinction between maps and the land-scape becomes unimportant:

> *The face of the country is the most important historical document*
> *that we possess. Upon the map of England – 'that marvellous*
> *palimpsest' – is written much of English history: written in letters of*
> *earth and stone, of bank and ditch, of foliage and crop.*
>
> *(Randall 1934: 5)*

Randall's review was heavily and explicitly indebted to the two pioneers of landscape archaeology in Britain, Cyril Fox and O. G. S. Crawford; indeed, it was Crawford who was really the first to use the concept of palimpsest about the landscape in a systematic way (Bowden 2001; Johnson 2007: 58–9). In a chapter of his book *Archaeology in the Field* (1953), titled 'Deciphering the Palimpsest: Roman Roads', he opens with the classic statement:

> *The surface of England is a palimpsest, a document that has been*
> *written on and erased over and over again; and it is the business of*
> *the field archaeologist to decipher it. The features concerned are of*
> *course the roads and field boundaries, the woods, the farms and*
> *other habitations, and all the other products of human labour; these*
> *are the letters and words inscribed on the land. But it is not easy to*
> *read them because, whereas the vellum document was seldom wiped*
> *clean more than once or twice, the land has been subjected to*
> *continual change throughout the ages.*
>
> *(Crawford 1953: 51)*

For Crawford, deciphering this palimpsest involved both fieldwork and map study, and the key to success was to focus on a single element at a time – like a Roman road (Crawford 1953: 59). As with Randall, in many ways the distinction between the map and the landscape in Crawford is not always rigid, a point which takes on added relevance in Chapter 6. For now, however, it is more important to point out that this use of the palimpsest concept is one which clearly articulates the dual processes of inscription and erasure, but also one in which the history of these processes is dissectible and the landscape reconstructable into phases or periods (e.g. Iron Age, Roman, and Saxon; Crawford

1953: 51). In short, the palimpsest offers another type of sequence to stratigraphy, a 'flattened' stratigraphy, if you like. This view of the palimpsest is somewhat different to that which emerged in discussions about the archaeological record in the 1980s.

In 1981, three different papers were published which all used the concept of palimpsest in describing the character of the archaeological record in relation to interpretation – papers by Bailey, Binford, and Foley (Bailey 1981; Binford 1981; Foley 1981; see also Bailey 2008: 13–14). Geoff Bailey invoked it as a fundamental justification for time perspectivism:

> *A sample of archaeological sites, animal bones, molluscs, or any other type of subsistence data, large enough for reliable interpretation, often represents a palimpsest of activities ranging over a period of at least a hundred years to several thousand or more. It refers not to the activities of individuals, or even individual societies, but to larger aggregates of behaviour, reflecting average tendencies which persisted over long periods of time.*
>
> *(Bailey 1981: 109–10)*

In the same year, Lewis Binford wrote his scathing attack on Schiffer's view of formation processes, which he viewed as a misguided attempt to reconstruct the sequence of past events, akin to a palaeoethnography. Here the palimpsest nature of the archaeological record was used to support his argument:

> *I have never viewed the reconstruction of prehistoric lifeways in the form of prehistoric ethnographies to be an appropriate goal for archaeology in general. It has been clear to me that the time frame of ethnography is largely inappropriate for archaeological research. Rates of deposition are much slower than the rapid sequencing of events which characterizes the daily lives of living peoples; even under the best of circumstances, the archaeological record represents a massive palimpsest of derivatives from many separate episodes. Any structure and repetitive pattern of association and covariation must derive from the operation of 'systemic events', or dynamics, with a much longer term, more rigidly determined organization than*

is true of those observed in the lives of persons and groups who
embody the ethnographer's perception of time and human systems.

(Binford 1981: 197)

Foley's use of the term was also invoked in much the same way as in Bailey and Binford, as a means of pointing to the longer-term processes which the archaeological record gives us evidence for, rather than the short-term, ethnographic scale of events (Foley 1981).

It is clear that with these three archaeologists, the concept of palimpsest has a very different meaning from what it did for Crawford and British landscape archaeology. For Crawford, palimpsests contained the possibility of dissection and thus reconstructed sequence, whereas for Bailey, Binford, and Foley it was the very impossibility of dissection that justified an archaeology of the longer term (but see Carr 1987). It should be emphasized that this is not necessarily a negative view; as Bailey points out, it is a limitation only if one considers the goal of archaeology to reconstruct short-term sequences (Bailey 2007: 203). It becomes a virtue if longer-term processes become the central subject of investigation. Subsequent landscape archaeologies have tended to draw more on this latter implication than the one articulated by Crawford (e.g. Rossignol & Wandsnider 1992; Wilson 2004). The concept has remained an important one in relation to time perspectivism but has rarely been treated theoretically outside of this school of thought; indeed, the first and so far only detailed and systematic review of the concept was published only in 2007 by Geoff Bailey, who argued that the term actually entails multiple categories (Bailey 2007).

Bailey suggests that five different types of palimpsest can be distinguished. The first are true palimpsests, by which he means a situation in which all or most traces of previous activity have been removed before the latest; in such cases, they differ little from a single-episode occupation. The second type are cumulative palimpsests, wherein earlier episodes of activity are preserved but so mixed or inseparable that it is impossible to dissect the sequence of activity; this, according to Bailey, is probably the meaning most archaeologists have when they think about palimpsests and links to the issues of time averaging discussed earlier. The third category is spatial palimpsests, which are a variation of the second; whereas in cumulative palimpsests the activities all occur in the same general locale, in spatial palimpsests the activities are in separate yet adjacent and/or overlapping areas which may permit some dissection – although Bailey is still sceptical that such dissection is possible in most cases. The fourth type are temporal palimpsests, by which Bailey means assemblages of material which themselves derive from different times, even though their deposition might be a single episode; Olivier's analysis of an Iron Age grave is given as a prime example of this kind of palimpsest, where the grave goods and other objects date from different times (i.e. are differentially aged). Finally the fifth category is palimpsests of meaning, in which because of its life cycle or biography, an object collects meanings as it moves between social contexts; it may even undergo modification, such that it was used as one thing when originally manufactured, but may have had a completely different function (and appearance) by the time it is finally deposited.

Bailey's discussion of the varieties of palimpsest is extremely important, not least because it is the first time an archaeologist has actually attempted to problematize and explore the complex meanings implied in its use. Indeed, as Bailey convincingly argues, the concept is central to any understanding of the material world, simply because material objects endure, and in enduring, they incorporate the dual processes of accumulation and erasure, central to the concept of palimpsest:

> *In short, palimpsests are neither exceptions, nor inconveniences, nor oddities that need to be transformed into something else before they can be interpreted and understood. On the contrary, palimpsests are universal, an inherent feature of the material world we inhabit. They are not some distorted or degraded version of a message that needs to be restored to its original state before it can be interpreted. To a large extent, they* are *the message.*
>
> (Bailey 2007: 209)

The centrality of the palimpsest to understanding the archaeological record and the historicity of the material world in general have been explored even further and more philosophically by Laurent Olivier (Olivier 2001, 2008). For Olivier, the paradox of the present is that it incorporates both transformation and preservation – that it looks forward to the future and back to the past, simultaneously. Olivier takes the concept of palimpsest and aligns it with that of the memory-object (*objet-mémoire*), insofar as the essential property of any memory-object is not so much what it inscribes but the preservation of inscription: 'The current state of the present – as it is *physically* – basically consists of a palimpsest of all the durations of the past that have been recorded in matter' (Olivier 2001: 66). The basic paradox of the memory-object (and of the palimpsest) is that memory can only be preserved in it, to the extent that something else is lost or forgotten (Olivier 2008: 200); that is, any new event associated with an object always threatens to eradicate previous associations. Olivier's adoption of the concept of memory to describe the archaeological record is extremely useful and one which I draw on in a later chapter. However, beforehand I wish to pull together these recent thoughts on palimpsests by Bailey and Olivier and rework them a little into a more coherent scheme.

Rethinking Palimpsests and Formation Theory
The most important observation to make is that the concept of palimpsest can be applied not just to deposits (as in Bailey's first three types), but also to assemblages (type IV) and objects (type V). Indeed, Olivier's alignment of the palimpsest concept to the memory-object is extremely significant in this regard. The second observation is less praiseworthy; one of the most striking aspects about these discussions of palimpsests is the almost complete lack of cross-reference to the concept of stratigraphy. The paper by Hodder and McAnany discussed earlier in this chapter incorporated the concept of palimpsest into their broader discussion of social stratigraphy but in a very misleading way (Hodder & McAnany 2009). There, the concept of palimpsest is used to refer to a set of stratigraphic processes which have no intentional link to earlier ones; this would seem to include all natural stratigraphies but also cases of unintentional disturbance or the unintentional location of features on top of earlier cultural remains (ibid.: 9). Although the idea being discussed is important, labelling such processes 'palimpsests' is unfortunate and obfuscating in the light of conventional understandings. Nonetheless, in arguing that palimpsests are simply a type of stratigraphic process, the authors do highlight, albeit unintentionally, the broad similarities between the two terms. For if we think about palimpsests in relation to stratigraphy, both concepts essentially revolve around the same two processes: deposition and/or inscription, and erasure and/or cutting.

Indeed, stratigraphy cannot be thought of without simultaneously thinking of the palimpsest. This comes out very clearly when stratigraphy is reduced to bare sequence, as it has been suggested that the most common understanding of archaeological stratigraphy is as codified in the Harris matrix (Stein 2000; Warburton 2003). Insofar as the strength of stratigraphic analysis lies in understanding the temporal relations between units, it ignores the temporality of the units themselves (Lucas 2001a: 161–2). In foregrounding sequence, we encounter the problem of contemporaneity. How do we deal with the variable time spans over which different units were formed? We generally assume that any given unit is isochronous (i.e. formed at the same time), but this is purely relative; one unit may have taken fifty years to form (e.g. floor layer), another, fifty minutes (e.g. grave). How does one deal with this allochronicity between units, and what are its implications? Archaeologists have of course developed various means of grappling with this problem, from scientific dating techniques to traditional typological cross-dating, but the significant point is that although stratigraphy gives us a sequence of events, this sequence or these events may not necessarily be meaningful at the level at which they are identified. In short, at the heart of stratigraphy lies the problem of contemporaneity, which is directly related to the concept of palimpsest.

To develop our understanding of the historicity of materiality, we need to draw on all of the concepts being discussed here: palimpsests, memory-objects, and stratigraphy. All three share the same basic temporal structure. But we also need to know how they differ. This is where Bailey's classification of categories of palimpsests starts to be less helpful, because it attempts to present a range of cases or exemplars rather than focus on the basic processes involved. I would suggest that we need to foreground the processes of inscription and/or erasure, rather than the product (e.g. palimpsests, stratigraphy, memory-objects). Thus, at one extreme, if a true palimpsest is the total erasure of all previous activity prior to the latest, at the other extreme, a true stratigraphy might be the total preservation of all previous activity in a dissectible sequence of strata. In the first case, history, in a sense, starts anew as all traces of the past are erased; although locally this can happen, in general, it would amount to the impossibility of history as all connection between present and past is severed. In the second case, all of the past is preserved in the present, and again, although locally this is conceivable, in general, it would also lead to the impossibility of history as all distinction between the present and past would be severed. In short, the dual processes of inscription and erasure are always localized and always lie between these two extreme points – one might even say that it is a condition of history (if not of time itself).

But there is a further dimension to these processes of inscription and erasure – namely the order or sequence in which such events take place. It is one thing to have traces of the past preserved in the present; it is another to be able to dissect an order or sequence in such traces. This brings us to the classic definition of the palimpsest in archaeology (Bailey's cumulative palimpsest – and the spatial type): preservation of objects from the past but no preservation of their order or sequence of deposition. In contrast, stratigraphic sequences do preserve such an order – as did Crawford's concept of palimpsest when applied to the landscape. This issue of the preservation of sequence or order (rather than simply preservation of elements, traces) is what really matters in many ways, and one way to characterize it is in terms of entropy; that the issue of historicity in the material world is not just about the tension between the two processes of inscription and erasure but also about the two processes of order and disorder (Figure 7). Rather than attempt

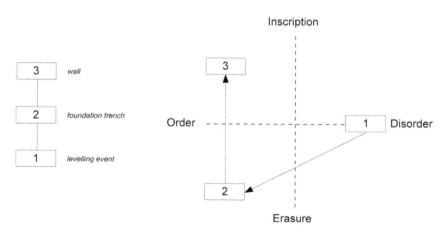

Figure 7. Stratigraphic matrix of a simple sequence of three units, transposed onto an entropy grid; each unit is defined in terms of the degree of order or disorder implicated in its formation and whether it adds (inscription and/or positive) or subtracts (erasure and/or negative) material from a specific locale.

some kind of classification of palimpsests or even broad separation of stratigraphy from palimpsest, it is more useful to recognize the archaeological record as the intertwining of these two separate processes. In fact, I would argue that there are no true palimpsests or stratigraphies out there – these are simply ideal concepts, limit points on a continuum, and in fact most elements we encounter lie somewhere between these limits.

In ending this chapter in discussing palimpsests, I have tried to show how the concept provides the bridge between deposit and assemblage formation; it lies at the intersection of these two aspects of formation theory, and it is this concept which we really need to work on in relation to the archaeological record. This is picked up again in Chapter 5, but for now I complete my survey of received views of the archaeological record by turning to the last approach, that of material culture.

4

Materialized Culture

THE CONCEPT of material culture is a nineteenth-century invention, one bound up with the broad development of anthropology and archaeology but also implicated in the emergence of mass production and mass consumption in nineteenth-century society (Buchli 2002). In 1851, London staged one of the most spectacular shows ever seen: the Great Exhibition. It was one of the first of several such events staged in the Western world intended to celebrate the marvels of modern technology and design, and although its full title was the Great Exhibition of the Works of Industry of All Nations, it was clearly an act of self-promotion on the part of Britain and its position in the global political economy. It can, however, equally be considered a manifestation of the degree of material entanglement affecting an industrialized nation like Great Britain in the mid-nineteenth century. Seven years later, a rather different event hit London. During an unusually hot summer in 1858, the River Thames, which was overflowing with sewage, started to smell – and smell really badly. So badly, in fact, that it became known as the Great Stink. It was the last straw in a cumulating set of problems for the city and resulted in the construction of new sewage and waste disposal systems for the capital. I think it is an irony that in the same decade that London celebrated its global power through an exhibition attesting to its wealth of material goods, it also suffered from the very excesses created by such wealth. The scale of waste – of rubbish – is inseparable from that of material entanglement.

Perhaps, then, it is no coincidence that the 1850s is often seen as the decade marking the birth of archaeology in England, that a nation so obsessed by its own materiality takes a systematic interest in the materiality of its past. But the symmetry goes further, for what made the new discipline of archaeology distinct was that it was precisely interested in all aspects of past materialities, and it especially made a point about collecting everyday and mundane artifacts as well as what might be considered pieces of more art-historical interest (see Chapter 2). Fundamentally, it was as interested in rubbish as it was in special deposits like burials. One might, then, suggest that what characterized – partially at least – the birth of scientific archaeology was (middle-class) imagination and fascination with superfluous matter, whether manifested by repulsion in the context of urban waste or attraction in the context of urban museums. The archaeological object and city rubbish share this in common – they are both matter which exists outside of contemporary society in the sense of being unintegrated and unconstituted. The difference is that they are moving in different directions; rubbish is matter that was once constituted and has become deconstituted, whereas the archaeological object is matter that was deconstituted but has become constituted. The constituting act is – predictably – modelled on that which modern industrial society performs in the production of its goods. It is no coincidence that when B. E. Hildebrand was organizing an exhibition in the Museum of National Antiquities of Stockholm in 1866, he employed an aesthetics directly copied from an exhibition of modern mass-produced items of the same year (Almgren 1995: 27).

What I want to explore in this chapter is how material culture has been conceived within archaeology over the past 150 years and, in particular, its ontological status. Thus, I am not so much interested in material culture as I am in materiality from a cultural or social perspective. One of the problems with the term 'material culture' is that it begs the question, Is culture therefore normally immaterial? The problematic status of this qualifier 'material' in front of culture has been raised before (e.g. Lucas 2001a: 177; Thomas 2007: 15), and exploring this issue forms a large part of this chapter. However, one could turn the question around and ask, What does the term 'culture' do in front of a concept like materiality? Indeed, as we shall see, this is precisely the position we are in today, and this whole chapter could be summarized as the shift from the former to the latter question. In between lies a history of ambiguity around the concept of material culture and its ontological status.

The Material Arts in the Nineteenth Century and the Externalization Thesis

PERHAPS *the* overarching concept which defined much of nineteenth-century research in both archaeology and anthropology was that of civilization or culture – the former term was more common in Britain and France at the time, whereas the latter prevailed in Germany (Stocking 1987: 20). The adjectives 'civilized' and 'cultured' could be applied to individuals as well as whole societies, if not the whole human species; as gradational concepts (rather than simply binary, such as civilized and uncivilized), they could also be used to map variation among contemporary peoples – both between societies and within them (i.e. class differences); and finally they provided a general model for human history when linked to the idea of progress (i.e. cultural evolution). In a sense, the applicability of the concepts of culture and civilization was almost universal when it came to the study of human society and history, for they provided a way to integrate the human sciences into a single field. But what was culture? Definitions varied, and of course the history and the development of the concept go back even further, to the eighteenth century (e.g. Kroeber & Kluckhohn 1952). In archaeology, useful summaries also track its various meanings over time (e.g. Trigger 1978b; Watson 1995).

Clearly, the culture concept today is very much dormant (but by no means defunct), a decline that started some time ago (see e.g. Yengoyan 1986), and some of the reasons for that are connected to the story in this chapter. But I am not really concerned here with reviewing its history so much as understanding its link to the concept of material culture and, in particular, the process of materialization as it was understood in the nineteenth century. Perhaps the fundamental notion of culture or civilization is that it was an expression of the human mind, which could manifest itself in diverse ways. But this manifestation was not equivalent to materialization, and the opposition of the mental and material needs to be viewed in a much more nuanced light. It seems to be quite evident that the notion of material culture was used as a qualifier to the more general concept of culture, which by implication ought to have been immaterial. This may be true and, in fact, may have been so obvious it never needed stating – but it seems to me that the important distinctions made in the nineteenth century were not between the material and immaterial, but the internal and the external, and to understand materialization, we need to understand this relation. All culture was in a sense an external expression of an inner mental state, but some expressions were more immediate than others, that is, more direct expressions of the mind. To some extent, this discourse has its parallel in physical anthropology and nineteenth-century studies of craniometry, in which physical characteristics of the brain and skull were linked to mental development (e.g. Gould 1981); philosophically, it might even be traced back to Hegel's interest in phrenology, in which he explicitly links it to his philosophy of objectification (Hegel 1977: 185–210).

One of the problems, however, is that in nineteenth-century anthropological texts on culture, the term had become almost so embedded in discourse that discussions about its ontological status are hard to find. In Edward Tylor's *Primitive Culture*, in which the classic definition of culture is given in the first lines, it is a vague and loose collection of phenomena; the bulk of the book is devoted to the process of dissecting the details and classifying the various elements (Tylor [1871] 1913). A far more revealing insight into the ontology of culture – and thus material culture – is to be found in his earlier work, *Researches into the Early History of Mankind* (Tylor 1865). Like the later work, this book is an attempt to historicize the concept of civilization; he even opens with a definition of civilization which anticipates and resembles his more famous one from *Primitive Culture*. However, it is the development of the argument in *Researches* that is significant, for it follows a certain logic of externalization in which the various elements of civilization are treated in order, according to the degree of immediacy with respect to the mind; the reason being that the less immediate (i.e. more externalized) an aspect is, the more it is prone to the effects of history, and thus the more difficult it is to identify general laws of human civilization (Tylor 1865: 3). For Tylor, the most immediate expression of the human mind lies in gestures and gesture language; it is worth quoting at length here:

> *The power which man possesses of uttering his thoughts is one of the most essential elements of his civilization. Whether he can think at all without some means of outward expression is a metaphysical question which need not be discussed here . . . To* utter *a thought is literally to put it outside us, as to* express *it is to squeeze it out. Grossly material as these metaphors are, they are the best terms we have for that wonderful process by which a man, by some bodily action, can not only make other men's minds reproduce more or less exactly the workings of his own, but can even receive back from the outward sign an impression similar to theirs, as though not he himself, but someone else had made it.*
>
> (Tylor 1865: 14–15, emphasis in original)

Two things are very clear from this quote; the first is the centrality of this notion of externalization. This is not unique to Tylor; indeed, the notion of externalization plays a key role in Marx's concept of objectification as elaborated in his *Economic and Philosophical Manuscripts* (1844 [1975]). The basic idea of objectification also underlay Marx's distinction of human from animal labour as articulated in *Capital*:

> *We propose labour in a form in which it is an exclusively human characteristic. A spider conducts operations which resemble those of a weaver, and a bee would put many a human architect to shame by the construction of its honeycomb cells. But what distinguishes the worst architect from the best of bees is that the architect builds the cell in his mind before he constructs it in wax. At the end of every labour process, a result emerges which has already been conceived by the worker at the beginning, hence already existed ideally. Man not only effects a change of form in the materials of nature; he also realizes his own purpose in those materials.*
>
> (Marx 1976: 283–4)

Objectification, however, involved not just externalization but also reinternalization (Marx [1844] 1975: 328–9; for a more general discussion of this concept in anthropology, see Miller 1987, part 1); Marx thus saw externalization as just one phase of a dialectical process, a difference which is crucial, as is seen towards the end of this chapter. The second thing to draw from Tylor's quote relates to his reference to the metaphorical nature of the materiality of this process; such externalization was not literally to be considered a material process, and thus gestures, language, speech, and so on, were not primarily considered material phenomena. This supports the need for the qualifier 'material' in the term 'material culture' when referring to objects or things. Tylor devotes just two chapters to such material culture in this book, although he never uses that particular term itself; moreover, the chapters deal with the development of stone tools and cooking utensils and are treated simply as indirect sources of the development of the human mind. To find a more concerned perspective on material culture, one can turn to Pitt Rivers.

Pitt Rivers, like Tylor, regarded culture as the 'emanation of the human mind' (Pitt Rivers [1875] 1906: 21); for him, the idea of studying culture, or rather aspects of culture, such as language or artifacts, independent from the human mind was absurd, a point he makes explicit in his key paper 'The Evolution of Culture'. There, he argues that in tracing the history of objects or words, one must remember that they do not descend from other objects or words but express historical connections between ideas:

> *These words and these implements are but the outward signs or symbols of particular ideas in the mind; and the sequence, if any, which we observe to connect them together, is but the outward sign of the succession of ideas in the brain. It is the mind that we study by means of these symbols.*
>
> (Pitt Rivers [1875] 1906: 23)

However, although Pitt Rivers clearly shared Tylor's view of culture as the expression of the mind, he also gave more importance to what he called the material arts (like Tylor, Pitt Rivers did not use the phrase 'material culture') and ranked them on an equal footing to language: 'Words are ideas expressed by sounds, whilst tools are ideas expressed by hands; and unless it can be shown that there are distinct processes in the mind for language and for the arts they must be classed together' (Pitt Rivers [1875] 1906: 25). This symmetry is extended further when

Pitt Rivers argues for the importance of studying the 'grammar' of the material arts, establishing clear parallels to language (ibid.: 29). Nonetheless, he recognized that there were differences between the two prominent expressions of the mind (i.e. language and the material arts), chief among which was that language was much more mutable than the material arts. Pitt Rivers pointed out that a word can change each time it is uttered, whereas a tool or weapon more or less remains stable once made and can endure for generations (ibid.: 27). As an example, he contrasts the uniformity of Australian weaponry against the diversity of names for the same object, due to the different languages and dialects spoken. This labile property of language is true, however, only until the invention of writing, when words are stabilized through incisions in stone, impressions on fired clay, or ink on parchment. It is the implications of this that were crucial, for they suggested that before writing (i.e. in prehistory), the material arts were more stable than language (ibid.: 29) and therefore are the best source for studying the distant past. Ironically, though, Pitt Rivers's scheme would not hold up today, either for texts or for objects; just think about contemporary digital forms of inscription, like Wikipedia, which result in highly fluid texts. Moreover, Buchli has raised the same issues with regard to objects through new rapid manufacturing technologies (Buchli 2010).

A key issue in Pitt Rivers's discussion is this broad division between language and the material arts; this is nothing new, and we have already seen how earlier Charles Newton had divided archaeology up into three branches – the oral, written, and monumental (see Chapter 2) – which encapsulate the same basic opposition. Indeed, Newton is very explicit about the primacy of language as one component of human civilization, from which other things such as customs and manners derive: 'Symbolic acts and gestures, tokens, forms, ceremonies, customs are all either supplementary to or the substitute for articulate speech' (Newton 1851: 4). Moreover, like Pitt Rivers, he suggested that oral language and its supplements were the least useful for archaeologists because they were so transient. For both Pitt Rivers and Newton, writing obviously occupies an ambiguous middle position between spoken language and the material arts – it was language, but it was language which had been stabilized, and thus it came closer to the material arts while still sharing a basic affinity to spoken language insofar as it was a more immediate expression of mind than mere artifacts. Like Pitt Rivers,

Newton thus emphasized the significance of distinguishing stable from transient expressions of the mind:

I said that man was the only animal that imitated in a material external to himself; who, in other words, practised painting and sculpture. To draw and to carve are natural to man; speech, gesture, and music are his transient – sculpture, painting, and writing, his permanent means of utterance.

(Newton 1851: 17)

Newton's interests in material culture lay more towards the aesthetic than Pitt Rivers's favouring of the utilitarian, but all were grouped together under the monumental or material arts, even if Newton was more explicit in the division between artwork and handicraft, which in turn were subdivided into constructive and imitative art, and useful and decorative handicraft, respectively (Newton 1851).

Materiality then comes to be defined by the stability of the externalization process – that is, the extent to which the process of externalization produces a body (i.e. object) independent of that from which it sprung. An ambiguity, however, still surrounded the concept of material culture, because writing was clearly considered a form of stable externalization, yet it was generally not classed with the material arts but considered a part of regular culture, like spoken language. This ambiguity is revealing, because it suggests the assumption of a subtler, yet fundamental difference between language and material culture, which was not about the stabilization of externalization but about immediacy – that is, the directness of expression (Table 4). Even if Pitt Rivers made the hand the equal of the ear as bodily tools for expressing ideas in the mind, there remained an implicit belief that language was a more direct or clearer expression of ideas than objects, which is more obvious in the

Table 4. *Grid of Externalization Implicit in Nineteenth-Century Views of Culture, Defined by Two Characteristics: Immediacy and Stability*

	Stable and/or Durable	*Labile and/or Ephemeral*
Direct and/or Immediate	Writing	Speech and gesture
Indirect and/or Distant	Material arts	Material arts

writings of someone like Tylor. Yet as Pitt Rivers's allusion to the hand and ear makes clear, this question of immediacy (and thus materiality) needs to be linked into sensory modes of experience. Moreover, Pitt Rivers is equivocal on this issue; sometimes he links the hand (touch) to materiality, and at other times, the eye (sight): 'the word is the tool of the ear, the implement the tool of the eye' (Pitt Rivers [1875] 1906: 27). This ambiguity about the sensory qualities of material culture, being linked to both vision and touch, may be partly explained by the ambivalent position of writing, as already mentioned, but it may also tie in to a deeper valuation of the senses.

The opposition of the ear and the eye was by no means an idiosyncrasy but drew on a tradition of vision supplanting sound (and indeed other sensory experience) as the most direct link to the mind. The emergence of this ocularcentrism, as Martin Jay has called it, can be traced to the Enlightenment and Cartesian rationalism (Jay 1993), and one could suggest that Tylor's elevation of the primacy of gesture language over spoken language was even a version of this, just as Pitt Rivers's importance of the stable over the mutable (and written language over spoken language) was linked to the eye and the ear, respectively. Conversely, however, materiality cannot be equated with visibility – quite the contrary, if anything. The connection among immediacy, materiality, and the valuation of the senses needs to be seen in relation to where the boundary between observer and world is drawn. This is made very clear in Jonathan Crary's analysis of the emergence of a new kind of observer and philosophy of vision, which developed in the nineteenth century (Crary 1992). Whereas in the Enlightenment model of ocularcentrism, the eye served as an almost neutral mediator or window between the world and the mind (represented metaphorically by the camera obscura), by the mid-nineteenth century the eye (and indeed all the senses) was no longer considered a neutral transmitter but an active participant in creating mental images. As a result, the locus of the boundary between subject and object or inner and outer shifted from mind and world to mind-body and world. Translating this in terms of the concept of culture as the expression of mind, the key distinction was therefore between corporeal and extracorporeal culture, and it was the latter which was classed as material culture. On the one side of this divide were expressions like language, customs, manners, beliefs, and on the other side, weapons, tools, and buildings. What is

ultimately at stake here in the issue of immediacy and sensory perception is the boundary of the human subject in relation to the external
world; the material arts clearly lay on one side of this boundary, language on the other. In the end, immediacy of expression always trumped
stability of expression, which is why ethnology and history always sat
in a better position than archaeology at the table of the human sciences. The influence of this presumption of immediacy continues to
have a powerful effect on the status of these disciplines, even today.

Functionalism and the Materialist Reinterpretation of Materiality

THIS NINETEENTH-CENTURY view of material culture and materialization as the expression or externalization of mind remained a core
assumption well into the following century, but it was also to undergo
a radical change under the influence of functionalist interpretations of
culture. Although most archaeologists in the nineteenth century saw
material culture as an expression of human history – either in the particular or in the general (i.e. as evolution), little attention was given
to its relations to the wider environment. It was first and foremost,
an 'emanation of the mind', as Pitt Rivers called it (Pitt Rivers [1875]
1906: 21). Thus, even when Pitt Rivers talked about the evolution of
culture, it was of a Spencerian or Hegelian kind rather than Darwinian,
a development of the internal faculty of the human spirit. The same can
be said of his Scandinavian contemporaries even if they cited Darwin as
their paradigm; archaeologists like Hans Hildebrand and Oscar Montelius made quite explicit references to the affinities between typology
and biological evolution during the 1870s and 1880s, equating types
with species (Gräslund 1987: 101–7). But as Gräslund has pointed out,
these affinities either were meant as loose analogies or implied a gross
misunderstanding of Darwin's theory on the part of these scholars;
either way, there was certainly little concept of material culture being
adaptive – this came only in the latest manifestations of a Darwinian
approach to typology, such as is found in Åberg (1929) and Gorodzov
(1933).

A functional interpretation of material culture seems to have emerged
quite early in the twentieth century, and although it may have been

partly inspired by biological analogies, another influence no doubt came via the Durkheimian approach to ethnography. However, it manifested itself in two quite different ways in the Anglophone and Francophone traditions, which I discuss next. I spend most time discussing the former, even if in many ways the latter has more contemporary relevance, as we see towards the end of this chapter. This is partly because in the French tradition, after the pioneering work of André Leroi-Gourhan, developments shifted away from the concerns that are most relevant to this chapter – at least until very recently, when new work has started to bridge the gap with the Anglophone tradition. This is picked up at the end of the chapter.

The Anglophone Tradition: Materialism and Material Culture

One of the earliest functionalist texts in the Anglophone tradition is that of the English archaeologist O. G. S. Crawford. Writing in 1921, he describes in explicit terms material culture as 'extra-corporeal limbs', developed as a means of enhancing human interaction with the environment (Crawford 1921, chapter 1). However, Crawford was also still working under the inherited nineteenth-century view of culture as the externalization of mind, as the following quote illustrates: 'Primitive tools were the highest existing functions of brain made manifest. Like language, they are the incarnation of intelligence. That, for an archaeologist, is the gist of the matter, and that is why he spends his time studying them' (Crawford 1921: 17–18). The archaeological record was thus comprised 'of a most intimate kind, these *disjecta membra* which man has left lying about, these cast-off limbs of his extra-corporeal evolution' (ibid.: 19). Crawford's external limbs, however, were not only externalizations of the mind but also tools to facilitate human adaptation to the environment, which is why the environment is such a prominent feature of his work. This dual aspect to material culture – the externalization view inherited from the nineteenth century and the new functionalism – was to remain throughout much of the twentieth century, but with the latter gradually eclipsing the former. Crawford's geographical background undoubtedly played a part in his adoption of functionalism, but his views on the importance of the environment were not unique (see e.g. Trigger 2006: 317) and were, of course, to become increasingly integrated into mainstream archaeology between the 1930s and 1960s.

However, it is with Gordon Childe that we see functionalism taken up to reconfigure the whole field of prehistoric archaeology in Europe. Like Crawford, Childe adopted an environmental and adaptionist view of material culture, as is made abundantly clear in his classic paper 'The Changing Methods and Aims in Prehistory', published in 1935 (Childe 1935: 10–11). Indeed, Childe explicitly acknowledged Crawford's book in this respect, but he also, unlike Crawford, made extensive use of the term 'material culture' and may even have been responsible for its popular adoption in archaeology. Childe's concept of material culture, however, shows a clear shift from the nineteenth-century concepts of the material arts or monuments. For by 'material culture', Childe means specifically those objects which are adaptive: 'Material Culture, as defined here, is just the assemblage of devices that a community has invented or learnt to enable it to survive or expand' (Childe 1935: 11) or elsewhere, 'we see material culture as an adaptation to an environment' (ibid.: 10). In contrast, all other objects Childe refers to as 'spiritual culture'; material culture thus includes tools, vessels, cultivation plots, and dwellings, whereas spiritual culture includes amulets, tombs, sculptures, and decorative styles (ibid.: 14). This sounds extremely odd at first, but in essence, Childe is simply reserving the term 'material' for a materialist definition of material culture. This is a distinction he retains until his death and that is repeated in his book *Piecing Together the Past*, published two decades later (Childe 1956a: 44).

The distinction is, however, somewhat in tension with his argument about the process of materialization, for he seems to want to equate a materialist view of history with the process of materialization itself:

> *To make a D scraper, collect a flint nodule (1) at full moon, (2), after fasting all day, (3) address him politely with 'words of power', (4) ... strike him thus with a hammerstone, (5) smeared with the blood of a sacrificed mouse ... Technical and scientific progress has of course just been discovering that (1), (2), (3) and (5) are quite irrelevant to the success of the operation prescribed in (4). These acts were futile accessories, expressive of ideological delusions. It is just these errors that have been erased from the archaeological record.*

> (Childe 1956a: 171)

This text reveals two things: first, as Trigger pointed out, it shows quite explicitly Childe's acceptance of a distinction between a true and false consciousness (i.e. rationality versus ideology; Trigger 1994: 22). The second is that material durability, if not materialization itself, is entangled with this distinction. The last sentence of the previous quote is very telling in this respect. However, despite what he says, Childe was obviously aware that the archaeological record was full of such 'delusions' and 'errors'; his solution was to interpret those that did survive as somehow contributing to the primary function of survival, via an indirect or secondary mode – a superstructure (Childe 1935: 14; 1956a: 44). This is a familiar argument in cultural materialism, where what appear to be totally unmaterialistic practices, such as beliefs in witches or food taboos, are argued to actually perform an adaptive role in society (for a classic of this genre, see e.g. Harris 1974).

This materialist definition of material culture had quite significant implications for archaeological epistemology and led in the 1950s to a heightened concern for the limits of archaeological inference on both sides of the Atlantic. As in Britain, functionalist and ecological interpretations of material culture were being increasingly pressed elsewhere, both in Europe (e.g. Tallgren 1937) and in North America (Steward & Setzler 1938; see also Bennett 1943). In Central Europe, Kossina's settlement archaeology (*Siedlungsarchäologie*) – which saw material culture distributions as manifestations of different ethnic and/or racial groups and was importantly influential on Childe – was being revised along more functionalist lines by scholars such as Ernst Wahle, Hans Eggers, and especially Herbert Jankuhn (see e.g. Kuna & Dreslerová 2007). However, it was in the United States, with Walter Taylor's critique of contemporary U.S. archaeology, that the message of a functionalist approach to material culture was most loudly proclaimed (Taylor [1948] 1983). One of Taylor's key points was to critique a naive or narrow empiricism in archaeology – that is, that interpretation of archaeological evidence was not limited solely by lack of data but also by a lack of the right theoretical attitude:

> *While it is perfectly true that all the evidence for a complete cultural context cannot be obtained by archaeologists from archaeological sites, it is equally true that all evidence cannot be obtained by*

historians and ethnographers from their sources either. Since . . . only the events and not their inferred relationships are empirically demonstrable in any study dealing with man's past, the difference between the archaeological, documentary, and ethnographic records is merely one of degree, not of kind, and the archaeologists should not consider that the limitations of their finds impose interpretive structures upon them any more than upon other students dealing with past actuality.

(Taylor 1983 [1948]: 96)

Taylor's argument was, of course, set within a wider theoretical framework which linked archaeology to history and ethnography as part of a broad, integrated vision of the human sciences (Deetz 1988). This was nothing new, even if his particular version was. However, Taylor's argument did raise important questions about the limits of archaeological inference, which were taken up much more explicitly by the British archaeologist Christopher Hawkes.

The limits of archaeological inference were becoming an increasing topic of concern during the second quarter of the twentieth century; Randall-MacIver, writing for *Antiquity* in 1933, argued that 'the only possible subject of archaeology is the *material* output of man, the visible products of his hands', arguing that human thoughts, beliefs, and feelings were beyond its ken (Randall-MacIver 1933: 6, emphasis in original). Only by analogy with historical and ethnographic sources, he suggested, could one make inferences about such materials – yet at the same time, analogy was becoming increasingly suspect (Wylie 1985). In 1954, Hawkes published a paper in which he considered the relevance of Taylor's book for European archaeology and the limitations of the conjunctive approach (Hawkes 1954). For Hawkes, without access to texts, the archaeologist's comprehension of the ways of thinking or cognition of past societies remains extremely difficult, an obstacle that the conjunctive approach can by no means overcome (Hawkes 1954: 161). Hawkes summarized his argument in the famous four-step ladder of inference: at the bottom were production techniques which were easy to infer from archaeological remains; then came subsistence economies; then social and/or political institutions; and finally at the top of the ladder, religious institutions and spiritual life (ibid.: 161–2). For Hawkes however, this ladder of inference also presented archaeologists with a dilemma: the most secure inferences were those that most pertained to human behaviour in its most animal state, whereas those least secure, its most human state. That is to say, archaeological inference is fairly sound when dealing with generic aspects of humans in their relation to the environment but very shaky when it comes to their more specifically human qualities. As he summed it up, 'what it seems to offer us is positively an anticlimax: the more human, the less intelligible' (ibid.: 162). This is Childe's materialism but this time applied to epistemology, not ontology – that is, materialism is not so much indicative of a successful externalization as it is of a successful archaeological interpretation – or at least one in the absence of texts or other sources pertaining to a society's mode of cognition (Figure 8). This is allied to the notion that the very material nature of archaeological data lends itself more to a materialist interpretation, a somewhat more arguable, if not downright fallacious, idea, even for cultural materialists (see e.g. Price 1982: 727).

One of Hawkes's students, Margaret Smith, elaborated on these problems, characterizing the issue in terms of cultural relativism; if one does not know a past society's mode of thought or reasoning, how can one infer what the reasons are for a certain pattern in the archaeological record? She used the example of yam gardens on the Trobriand Islands, studied by Bronislaw Malinowski – the size of these gardens and their productivity were far larger than necessary for subsistence because they incorporated a certain aesthetics which included intervisibility (Smith 1955: 5). She argued that archaeologists digging up the remains of such gardens would make wrong inferences about population size as well as about the specific functions of certain features. Such spoiler arguments from ethnography (a.k.a. cautionary tales) were to become common in the archaeological literature in the 1960s, but Smith's point is more specific. She wants archaeologists to stick to inferences in which the interpretation can be translated back to the set of observations which generated it; in short, she wanted inferences to be nonampliative and, in effect, a mere redescription of those observations (ibid.: 5–6). Thus, for her, reasonable inferences include statements about the movement of goods such as gold lunulae during the Bronze Age in Western Europe, while unwarranted inferences include statements about chieftainships in the past:

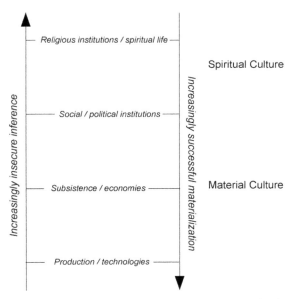

Figure 8. Hawkes's ladder of inference juxtaposed with Childe's division of material and spiritual culture, revealing the symmetry between materialization and materialism; even though scaling the ladder became progressively harder (in the absence of texts), the uppermost rung was also less relevant to the broad sweep of history, as it was full of delusions and errors.

You can infer, i.e. proceed by argument, from archaeological remains to some aspects of prehistoric economics, and reasoning will take you to a limited range of social practices . . . But to expect an archaeologist to infer from a hut to chieftanship . . . is nothing less than a demand for logical alchemy.

(Smith 1955: 6)

For Smith, archaeologists needed to adjust their inferences to the nature of their data and not attempt to mimic history or ethnography; archaeology should produce very different accounts:

A recognition that archaeological evidence, when it is confined to material remains, demonstrably supports only a limited range of conclusions about human activity, is incompatible with too ambitious a programme for archaeology. It is incompatible, as I see it, with an attempt to 're-create the past' in any real sense, or with a

*claim to recognize prehistoric societies from their surviving relics, so
that the subject could be compared either to history or to social
anthropology.*

(Ibid.: 7)

The following year, Eoin MacWhite added to the discussion with
his seven stages of interpretation, drawing on both Hawkes's ladder of inference as well as North American models of the stages of
archaeological interpretation after Gordon Willey and Walter Taylor
(MacWhite 1956: 4). His table is a corresponding mix with classification and chronology at the bottom (levels I–II), moving up through
ecology (III), economy (IV), history and sociology (IV–VI), and psychology at the top (VII); as one ascends the levels, one moves from firm
deductive logic to intuition (ibid.: 6). Most of his paper is concerned
with exploring his levels IV to VI and the concept of culture which is
seen as central to sociological and historical interpretation, which may
have contributed to its subsequent obscurity. Moreover, Chang was
later to criticize this model, especially for the way it placed classification at the bottom, as if typologies were unrelated to sociological or
historical questions (Chang 1967: 13).

Such pessimism (or realism, depending on your point of view)
reached its peak with Raymond Thompson's paper, also published
in 1956, titled 'The Subjective Element in Archaeological Inference'
(Thompson 1956). Thompson argued that archaeological inference
depended on two steps: the first was to assess the quality of the data
for its potential (indicative quality), the second to bring in probative
evidence to test any proposed inference (probative analogy). In short,
Thompson was making a common distinction between the processes of
discovery and justification in interpretation, where justification always
relied on analogy at some level, because one is always inferring a particular range of sociocultural behaviour from material remains. However,
Thompson's famous conclusions on these steps is that in both cases, a
subjective element in the form of the background, skills, and intelligence
of the archaeologist plays the key role in developing a plausible inference. They are required to come up with a good idea to begin with, but
they are also necessary when testing an inference, because it relies on
finding suitable analogies and demonstrating their relevance. Although

perhaps not contentious with regard to the first, they were downright depressing when applied to the second. Yet what is often forgotten is that at the end of his paper, Thompson does not see that yielding to professional competence as the final arbiter of inference is necessarily cause for despair; indeed, the very fact that to be an archaeologist, one needs training and education suggests that such an individual quality is enframed in a social context. One could thus read Thompson's paper as an early commentary on the social construction of archaeological knowledge, although I think this would be taking it too far. Nonetheless, in some ways it is far less restricting and prescriptive than the papers by Hawkes, Smith, or MacWhite. Yet to the new archaeologists who entered the debate a few years later, it was read as a complete withdrawal from any attempt to constrain interpretation; if Hawkes and the others were too limiting, at least they recognized the need for objective measures of evaluation.

For all that, it was precisely such narrow perspectives on archaeological evidence that had originally prompted Taylor and would later inspire Binford to promote an archaeology almost without limits (Binford 1968a). Yet to achieve this, they agreed with Smith and MacWhite on one point: the inference had to uphold the most rigorous of empirical testing. But what Hawkes's ladder of inference implied, fundamentally, was a materialist conception of material culture and the archaeological record in epistemological terms, to match Childe's ontological version. Such materialism was, of course, of a very vulgar nature, partly founded on an orthodox Soviet model of Marxism as well as Darwinian adaptation (see e.g. Friedman 1974), and it was one which was to become increasingly debated in the subsequent decades. One of its consequences, however, was the emergence of an opposition between the mental and the material, which was to inform much of the initial backlash against postprocessualism – a point to which I return. To understand this opposition, however, it is critical to see how the original nineteenth-century view of externalization had been modified by its intersection with functionalism.

Although the functional view of materiality may have shifted the focus of interest, the nineteenth-century idea that material culture and materialization were still ultimately expressions of mind remained strong, even in archaeologists like Childe and Taylor who were at the theoretical vanguard at this time (see e.g. Binford 1982a: 162). Taylor was particularly emphatic that 'culture is a mental construct consisting of ideas' (Taylor 1983: 101). For Taylor, material culture was still about a process of externalization of ideas, which he spelled out quite explicitly:

> *These ideas are not themselves observable. They are objectified and made observable through the action-systems of the body, being activated in the form of behaviour that is observable both visually and audibly. In turn this behaviour results in material objects such as axes and automobiles, and non-material manifestations such as dance patterns, musical tones and rhythms, styles of graphic and fictile representation, etc. . . . Thus we are dealing with three orders of phenomena, two of which pertain to culture and are thus cultural, but only one of which is culture.*
>
> (Taylor 1983: 101–2, emphasis in original)

Thus, culture is exclusively mental; behaviour and material culture are only expressions of culture, of the mind. Moreover, Taylor takes this to its logical extreme by describing the term 'material culture' as fallacious, as culture by definition is unobservable and nonmaterial; indeed, he points out that even behaviour is nonmaterial, reproducing the nineteenth-century distinction between corporeality and materiality (ibid.: 102). Furthermore, the implications of this for the limitations of archaeological inference were quite clear: not all behaviour materializes, or fossilizes as he called it, which meant that some behaviour – and thus some ideas – was forever out of reach to archaeologists (Taylor 1983: 113). Where Taylor's view differs from the nineteenth-century concept, however, is in the mediating role of behaviour; between the mental and the material. If one compares this to Pitt Rivers, for example, the material arts were direct expressions of the mind, just of a different kind to others like language and so on. In many ways, this marks a shift from a more complex understanding of externalization in which it was defined by two axes (immediacy and stability; see Table 4) to a simpler, linear notion of externalization, one in which behaviour starts to take on a more central and mediating role (Figure 9).

Figure 9. New, simplified model of externalization that emerged in the mid-twentieth century, showing the increasingly central importance of behaviour as the mediating concept between mind and material culture.

Very much the same view can be found in Childe, especially in two of his last books which deal more explicitly with archaeological method – *Piecing Together the Past* and *A Short Introduction to Archaeology*, both published in 1956:

> *All archaeological data are expressions of human thoughts and purposes and are valued only as revelations thereof.*
>
> (Childe 1956b: 11)

> *The archaeological record is constituted of the fossilized results of human behaviour, and it is the archaeologist's business to reconstitute that behaviour as far as he can and so to recapture the thoughts that behaviour expressed.*
>
> (Childe 1956a: 1)

> *Archaeological data are all changes in the material world resulting from human action or, more succinctly, the fossilized results of human behaviour.*
>
> (Childe 1956b: 1)

The latter two quotes are more interesting because they reveal the mediating role of behaviour and indeed could have almost been written by Binford in his early days, before he developed his middle-range theory (e.g. Binford 1962, 1964). Moreover, Childe repeats Taylor's statement that not all human behaviour fossilizes, citing the ephemerality of speech or the movement of troops on the battlefield (Childe 1956b: 1). The point is, though not free of the Victorian notion of externalization, the inclusion of the mediating role of behaviour was critical in the reconfiguration of the concept of materialization and material culture in the mid-twentieth century, and essential for the subsequent abandonment of the externalization thesis altogether. The anticipation of this behavioural turn is nowhere more evident than in the following quote from Childe, where what mattered was no longer the mental source but the material effect:

> *For all culture finds expression in action – action in the material world. It is indeed through action alone that culture is maintained and transmitted; a belief that exists only in somebody's head forms no part of culture and has no existence for history or anthropology. Some of the actions dictated by, and expressive of, culture effect durable changes in the material world. All such fall within the purview of archaeology. It is indeed just these human actions that have provided the material out of which archaeological cultures are constructed.*
>
> *(Childe 1951: 33; also see Childe 1956b: 10–11)*

Crucially, behaviour or action now mediated between mind and material culture, and although material culture could still be described as the expression of mind, it was always through the mediation of practice. Childe may have been an idealist, but he was even more of a materialist, if one can put it in such contradictory terms.

The Francophone Tradition: Techniques and Tools

A radically different and new version of the externalization thesis is given in the Francophone tradition, under the influence of Darwinian evolution and Durkheimian functionalism, particularly by the father of this tradition, André Leroi-Gourhan. Although first sketched by Marcel Mauss in the 1930s in his paper 'Techniques of the Body', it was Leroi-Gourhan who developed Mauss's ideas in the context of material culture. Mauss's essay raised the importance of how different societies or cultures use their bodies differently, in all kinds of situations; one of the examples he gives is how during the First World War, British and French soldiers could not effectively use one another's spades when digging trenches, because each had grown accustomed to very different techniques of digging (Mauss 1973: 71). However, Mauss put most emphasis on the bodily performance, whereas the spade and objects involved in other such techniques receded into the background. What Leroi-Gourhan did was elevate the importance of the object to equal status in his analysis of techniques, and it is thus largely his work which became the impetus and inspiration for subsequent scholars in the French tradition. His first key works were the two volumes *L'Homme et la matière* (1943) and *Milieu et technique* (1945), which not only provided an encyclopaedic review of tools and techniques but, more important, a novel approach to analysing them. Specifically, he focused on the particular properties of materials (e.g. hardness, plasticity), types of actions (e.g. cutting, heating, bending), and types of materials and forces involved (Audouze 2002: 283; Naji & Douny 2009: 412). Out of this work came his concept and theory of the operational sequence (*la chaîne opératoire*), which is almost synonymous with the Francophone school of techniques and has been adopted by many scholars outside this tradition.

The operational sequence became central to Leroi-Gourhan's next and better-known work, *Le geste et parole* (1964), translated as *Gesture and Speech* (1993). It is this work that articulates a new version of the externalization thesis, and the operational sequence lies at the heart of it. The importance of the operational sequence is that it focuses on the interaction between the human body and the material world and, in effect, is a way of analysing techniques; from Mauss he inherited the importance of gestures and their effects, but he underlined the importance of tools:

> *Techniques involve both gestures and tools, sequentially organized by means of a 'syntax' that imparts both fixity and flexibility to the series of operations involved. This operating syntax is suggested by the memory and comes into being as a product of the brain and the physical environment.*
>
> *(Leroi-Gourhan 1993: 114)*

Leroi-Gourhan envisaged this interaction in long, evolutionary terms, seeing the evolution of techniques as an extension of biological evolution. Thus, a large part of the book is taken up with the evolution of the human body, particularly the importance of the hand and face as the two organs associated with two of human's most prominent traits: tools and language. Indeed, he treats tools and language as almost symmetrical in the sense that both can be analysed through the same operational logic and that their evolution has occurred in tandem. His basic idea is that techniques (and language) evolve in terms of an increasing exteriorization of their operation:

> *In animals tool and gesture merge into a single organ with the motor part and the active part forming an undivided whole. The crab's claws and jaws are all of a piece with the operating program through which the animal's food acquisition behaviour is expressed. The fact that human tools are movable and that their characteristics are not species related but ethnic is basically unimportant.*
>
> *(Leroi-Gourhan 1993: 237)*

Tools are thus an external organ, performing a function previously done by a part of the body – the first stone chopper externalized the cutting function of the incisors. But this is not simply Crawford's extracorporeal limbs (as discussed earlier in this chapter); it is crucial to realize that it is not just the tool that is being externalized but the whole operation or function. The critical chapter in the book which addresses this general theme is that titled 'Gesture and Program', in which Leroi-Gourhan argues that humans have progressively exteriorized more and more of their organs and functionality – first tools (since the Palaeolithic); then muscular and motor power (since the Neolithic); and finally the brain, with its programming and memory function (since the twentieth century). The move from the chopper to the computer represents an evolution of exteriorization of techniques. This concept of exteriorization thus differs quite radically from that given by Pitt Rivers at the end of the nineteenth century; Pitt Rivers's model was an externalization of mind, whereas Leroi-Gourhan's is an externalization of function or organs (Figure 10).

Leroi-Gourhan's legacy certainly lies more with his development of the operational sequence as a means of analysing technology or material culture in French archaeology and anthropology than with his grander evolutionary vision. Indeed, the school that emerged in the 1970s around his work, with scholars such as Robert Cresswell (who founded the journal *Techniques et Culture*, an important venue for publication in this field) and Pierre Lemonnier, has largely retained a much more specific focus on the operational sequence and questions of technological choice (Lemonnier 1993b). While clearly situating

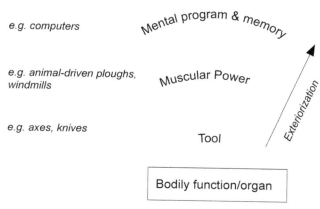

Figure 10. Leroi-Gourhan's view of the exteriorization of techniques in evolutionary perspective. Unlike the nineteenth-century view of an externalization of mind, this is an externalization of functions or organs.

technology in a social context and understanding operational sequences as informed by social logics, such scholars have tended to keep the notion of technical systems as a distinct component of society and separate from other, nontechnical systems (e.g. magic, religion). In a sense, this same distinction underwrites that of function and style (see Lemonnier 1993a: 10). More recent developments by some French anthropologists have attempted to extend the concept of techniques and operational sequences to a much wider range of phenomena and, in fact, take it back to Mauss's original discussion of techniques of the body. This is an issue I return to at the end of this chapter when I consider current rapprochements between the Anglophone and Francophone traditions. Before that, however, I bring the story up to date in the Anglophone tradition and show how it subtly transformed the externalization thesis by dropping all interest in mind and shifting its attention to behaviour.

Although in some ways this behavioural turn shares some similarities with the performative approach implicit in the operational sequence, there remained a fundamental difference. Whereas the Francophone tradition looked at performance or practice as the space in which gesture and matter interacted, in the Anglophone tradition, practice (as behaviour) largely just replaced mind as the origin of material culture. Material culture thus became expressive of behaviour instead of mind; but that expressive relation remained a very poor and simple way to articulate the relation between people and things compared to the concept of techniques and operational sequences devised by the Francophone tradition. The most theorized attempt to explore the relation between behaviour and material culture in the Anglophone tradition is that developed by Michael Schiffer and colleagues, called behavioural archaeology, and in places, there is some resemblance to the Francophone approach. For example, Schiffer talks about behavioural chains, which are similar to operational sequences in the way they break down production processes into key stages or steps. However, until recently, Schiffer maintained a rather simplistic theoretical approach to the relationship between behaviour and material culture, subsuming it under the notion of correlates, that is, regular associations between patterns of behaviour and patterns in material culture (e.g. Schiffer 1975; 1976). I return to Schiffer's more recent work later; first, let us step back to the emergence of the behavioural turn in archaeology.

From Function to Meaning and the Impasse of Poststructuralism

IRVING ROUSE may have been one of the first archaeologists to dispense with the notion of mind altogether in his discussion of culture and material culture. In his work *Prehistory in Haiti: A Study in Method*, he affirms that material culture is not, strictly speaking, culture but only an expression of culture (Rouse 1939: 15). Moreover, he interjects behaviour between material culture and culture, as Childe and Taylor did; but thereafter he departs quite radically, for instead of placing the mental at the source of – and thus equivalent to – culture, he talks about standards of behaviour (i.e. social norms of practice), which he describes as forces (ibid.: 17). Culture is thus not mental but a set of social forces which partially (along with other elements) determine behaviour, which in turn produces material culture. This shift may reflect the more general influence of Parsonian social theory in the states with its Weberian emphasis on social action. One could of course interpret these forces in mental terms, but it is telling that Rouse avoided all use of the word. Rouse's conception of material culture was thus in many ways ahead of its time, but because he ultimately invoked a normative conception of culture – mental or not – it was nonetheless lumped with other idealist approaches (see e.g. Binford 1965: 203–4). It is only with Binford that the mentalist conception of culture was finally and publically deconstructed.

In a seminal paper from 1962, 'Archaeology as Anthropology', Binford famously described culture as the extrasomatic means of adaptation for the human organism, after Leslie White (Binford 1962: 218). We have already seen how this idea is not new, but found at least as far back as O. G. S. Crawford in the 1920s, where it interlinked with the nineteenth-century view of externalization. Ironically, however, for Leslie White it was the mental faculty of what he called symbolling which lay behind this extrasomatic means of adaptation: the first few lines of White's book which Binford used actually read as follows: 'By culture we mean an extrasomatic, temporal continuum of things and events dependent upon symbolling' (White 1959: 3). This was moreover a recurrent and prominent theme of his work; it provided the foundation of his approach:

> [Culture] is the name of a distinct order, or class, of phenomena, namely those things and events that are dependent upon the exercise of a mental ability, peculiar to the human species, that we have termed 'symbolling'. . . It is an elaborate mechanism, an organization of extra-somatic ways and means employed by a particular animal species, man, in the struggle for existence and survival.
>
> (White 1949: 363)

With Binford, however, the primacy of the mental element of culture is dropped and in fact becomes just a subsystem of a larger entity incorporating the technological, social, and ideological. These divisions are again taken from White, who actually suggested four categories or components of a cultural system: ideological, sociological, sentimental, and technological (White 1959: 6–7). It is interesting that Binford dropped the sentimental component, by which White meant the human faculty for emotions. Yet for White, the mental was not a subcomponent but part of all four elements; thus, Binford also dropped White's insistence that all four components were mediated by symbols, even the technological – for it was only symbolic mediation which enables tools to evolve and thus separated human tool use from animal tool use (ibid.: 7). Thus, in Binford's reworking of White, the mental is reduced and equated with the ideological. Nonetheless, all three of Binford's subsystems, like White's, ultimately operate for the survival of humans and thus have some adaptive function, and material culture can therefore be classed according to one of the three functions – the technomic, sociotechnic, and ideotechnic. Binford's definition of material culture is thus materialist in much the same way as Childe's, and instead of Childe's distinction between material and spiritual culture, Binford invokes the opposition between function and style in material culture; moreover, just as spiritual culture could be functional, so style could be argued to perform an adaptive function in terms of maintaining group cohesion (Binford 1962: 220).

It is with Binford's systemic conception of culture that the externalization theory of mind is finally jettisoned; certainly, the functionalism of Childe and Taylor was an essential prelude for this, but where they still upheld the mind as the ultimate source, Binford completely displaces it. Binford did what Pitt Rivers abhorred – detached the study of material culture from mind. This shift is even more explicitly presented in his paper 'Archaeological Systematics and the Study of Culture Process' from 1965, in which he criticizes the normative view of culture for its idealism:

> *In summary, a normative theorist is one who sees as his field of study the ideational basis for varying ways of human life – culture. Information is obtained by studying cultural products or the objectifications of normative ideas about the proper ways of life executed by now extinct peoples. The archaeologist's task then lies in abstracting from cultural products the normative concepts extant in the minds of men now dead.*
>
> *(Binford 1965: 203)*

In contrast, Binford's view of culture, as an extrasomatic means of adaptation, is decentred and dispersed within a system of elements:

> *In cultural systems, people, things and places are components in a field that consists of environmental and sociocultural subsystems, and the locus of cultural process is in the dynamic articulations of these subsystems. This complex set of interrelationships is not*

explicable by reduction to a single component – ideas – any
more than the functioning of a motor is explainable in terms of a
single component, such as gasoline, a battery, or lubricating oil.

(Binford 1965: 205)

In quite important ways, this rearticulation of material culture avoided some of the problems raised by the crisis of inference which emerged in the 1950s. This was explicitly spelt out in the opening chapter in *New Perspectives in Archeology*, in which Binford takes on the limits-of-inference arguments which make, he claims, naive assumptions about the nature of archaeological evidence, in which imperfect preservation is translated into limited knowledge (Binford 1968a: 20–23).

This reasoning is functionally linked to a methodology that limits the
archaeologist to generalizing about the 'facts' he uncovers. Since
preservation is always imperfect, inferences from the facts of
material culture to statements about the non-material culture move
us away from the primary data and thus diminish the reliability of
our statements.

(Ibid.: 21)

For Binford, '[i]t is virtually impossible to imagine that any given cultural item functioned in a sociocultural system independently of the operation of "non-material variables" (ibid.), and thus one could not possibly argue that inferences of material culture were more sound at the technological level. Indeed, Binford found the 'dichotomy between the material and non-material aspects of culture itself and the relevance of this dichotomy for a proposed hierarchy of reliability' as suspect (ibid.). Yet Binford's views on this were to subtly change; certainly his initial optimism for including ideotechnical explanations waned, as did any interest in past people's beliefs, which he came to regard as irrelevant in a lot of cases when explaining material culture. But more important, his position on the dichotomy of material and nonmaterial reversed, largely in response to the emergence of postprocessualism, as was made very clear in Binford's critique of Hodder in the 1980s:

We study material things, matter in various forms and arrangements.
To equate these forms, distributions and patterns of association with

an ideational 'system' seems to be strange at best. Systems of adaptation are material systems composed of matter and energy sources. Information may be important in organizing and integrating a system, but it is not the system. Culturally organized systems of adaptation are no less concrete and materialistic. They are composed of things, places, persons, resources, communication channels, energy pipelines, etc. We do not find 'fossilized' ideas, we find the arrangements of material which derive from the occupation of a system of adaptation culturally integrated at some level. I don't have to know how the participants thought about the system to investigate it as a system of adaptation in a knowable natural world.

(Binford 1982a: 162)

Binford's emphasis on the materiality of the archaeological record here seems to use exactly the same argument that he criticized Hawkes and others for, more than a decade earlier; this is partly true, yet one also needs to bear in mind that Binford is making an unspoken distinction between two senses of nonmaterial culture – one which refers to internal, unobservable beliefs and ideas, and another which refers to external, observable processes and events. One could suggest that Binford is being consistent with his earlier position, insofar as he regards the concept of materiality to include the nonmaterial processes. Yet Binford's distinction between the two senses of nonmaterial culture (which depended on somewhat simplistic notions of the mental in relation to observability and the externalization thesis) means that he does ultimately reverse his position and retain – albeit in modified form – the dichotomy between the material and nonmaterial which he so rightly criticized in his earlier paper.

For even if Binford had managed to decentre the position of mind and reject the externalization thesis of material culture which had held sway so long in archaeology, his systemic model was nevertheless not a complete break. On the one hand, the key concept of functionalism – behaviour – introduced by Childe and others retained a central place. Indeed, already in Childe's writings, one senses that behaviour (what people did) was more important than mind (what they thought), and with Binford this is made even more explicit. Moreover, behaviour in some ways simply replaced mind as the source of material culture: material culture remained dependent and secondary to something else, and all Binford did was substitute behaviour for mind. On the other hand, the particular form of the relationship between behaviour and material culture was very different to that between mind and material culture. If the latter was understood in terms of emanation or external- ization, the former was largely a causal relation, the effect of particular interactions between human behaviour and its environment. It was the self-creation of a dynamic system rather than the externalization of an inner, mental realm. This difference is significant because Hodder's position is essentially much closer to Binford in this respect, yet with some obvious and important qualifications.

Hodder inherited from processualism the centrality of the relation- ship between behaviour and material culture (e.g. Hodder 1986: 11); he emphatically does not return to a nineteenth-century emanationist view of material culture but rather wanted to understand material culture in relational terms to what people do. The general preference for the term 'action' or 'agency' over 'behaviour' by Hodder and others, while indicating a theoretical difference on one level, also reveals continu- ity on another (see e.g. Skibo & Schiffer 2008: 24). However, unlike Binford, Hodder argued that such behaviour could not be understood without reference to people's beliefs or ideas about their world:

> *All actions take place within cultural frameworks and their*
> *functional value is assessed in terms of concepts and orientations*
> *which surround them. That an item or institution is 'good for'*
> *achieving some end is partly a cultural choice, as is the end itself.*
>
> (Hodder 1982b: 4)

In an ironic sense, Hodder was simply reinserting Leslie White's emphasis on the mediating role of the symbolic faculty which Binford had silently elided – although for very different reasons. Hodder's cri- tique of functionalism, which was launched in his paper 'Theoret- ical Archaeology: A Reactionary View' (1982b), was one of several texts by him in the early 1980s in which he argued that the rela- tionship between behaviour and material culture needed to be under- stood through the lens of social structures of meaning – hence his repeated statements that material culture was meaningfully constituted (see especially Hodder 1982a, 1984, 1986). Moreover, for Hodder this was not optional – it was ineluctable, and for anyone to claim that archaeologists can effectively ignore that was simply delusional (see e.g. Hodder 1992: 16–18). For Binford, in contrast, accepting this meant being trapped in an impossible dilemma of either imposing our own cultural understandings on the archaeological record or presupposing the very thing we are trying to find out, that is, other cultural perceptions (Binford 1989: 31). The important point, however, is that when Binford removed mind from behind behaviour, Hodder did not reinstate it; rather, he interposed something else between behaviour and material culture. This something else was meaning; for even though Hodder often uses the word 'mind' and related mental phenomena like beliefs, ideas, and meanings, his invocation of the phenomena avoids all discussion of externalization but rather focuses on their social nature (Figure 11). Moreover, he is explicitly antinormative about this social nature and highlights the relation between individuals and their cultural-historical context in the production of beliefs and ideas. Thus, it would be fairer to say that Hodder's main interest is not in mind but meaning – which is an external and observable phenomenon.

This marks a significant departure from nineteenth-century views, and of course, Hodder was clearly drawing on the general linguistic turn in the humanities and social sciences at the time. In a paper which most explicitly drew on this influence, Hodder argued against the opposition between internal thought and external behaviour, the one pertaining to meaning, the other to function, which he saw condemned archaeology to materialism and the lower rungs of Hawkes's ladder (Hodder 1989a: 254–5). Drawing on poststructuralism and the notion of texts, Hodder showed how meanings are embedded in the material world and thus equally external:

> The movement from language to text within post-structuralism is an important one for archaeology. Rather than placing an emphasis on the abstract thoughts that lie behind material culture, the archaeologist can accept the material world as itself contributing to the structuring and constituting of thought. The text (or material culture) derives its meaning from its specific role within the context of practical action.
>
> (Hodder 1989a: 257)

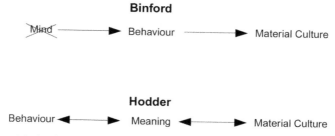

Figure 11. Binford's (*top*) and Hodder's (*bottom*) views of the relation between behaviour and material culture; Binford makes the important move of excising mind from the equation and thus jettisoning the externalization thesis, whereas Hodder inserts the role of meaning between behaviour and material culture.

Hodder was of course keenly aware of the differences between texts (as language) and material culture and, in particular, that unlike words, the relationship between material culture and meaning was often not arbitrary. Indeed, he pointed out that the material nature of artifacts acted as an anchor to constrain the otherwise-arbitrary nature of signification, in terms of their inherent natural properties which made them, in Pierceian terminology, closer to icons or indices rather than purely arbitrary symbols (ibid.: 258–60; see also Preucel & Bauer 2001; Preucel 2006; Keane 2005). It was this material anchoring that for Hodder was used as a way to reconcile a dichotomy between function and meaning; the material nature of objects could be analysed functionally, providing a functional or primary, denotative meaning, but this is often related to a secondary, connotative meaning in a nonarbitrary way. Thus, the connection between an arrowhead used for killing (primary meaning) and its perception as dangerous (secondary meaning) is by no means arbitrary.

Hodder's arguments about the material grounding of material meanings was in part an attempt to respond more explicitly to what he saw as the excessive positions taken by some archaeologists under the influence of poststructuralism (e.g. Bapty & Yates 1990; Tilley 1990), where there can be no such anchors (see Hodder 1992: 161–2; see also Buchli 1995: 189–91; 2004: 181). Yates, for example, used Jacques Derrida's famous phrase 'there is nothing outside the text' to upbraid Hodder for using the concept of materiality as a way to break out of the chain of signification, as the absent signifier at the heart of his notion of context: 'Material culture as a sign is turned against itself, such that the *materiality* of artifacts acts to break the flows of difference' (Yates 1990: 157, emphasis in original). But it was also a response to earlier critics of his work who regarded the whole textual metaphor as particularly problematic, insofar as it seemed to ignore the material conditions of social existence (Barrett 1988). For Hodder, the materiality of material culture was thus a given, a brute fact of existence which prevented a free flow of signifiers and thus grounded meaning; for Yates, this was a cop-out.

In a way there was a real dilemma here faced by postprocessualists in the early 1990s: on the one hand, accept that the meanings in material culture were completely in the eye of the beholder (or reader), and thus that archaeological interpretation was essentially free floating and a complete construct of the present. On the other hand, accept that the materiality of material culture acted as some kind of anchor or point of reference, outside the arbitrariness of the sign, which allowed archaeologists the possibility, at least, to understand past meanings. It would be fair to say that postprocessualism on the whole took the second option, but this was by no means straightforward, because taking this route seemed to imply that, unless one redefined materiality in a different way, one inevitably fell back on the dichotomy between function and meaning – or in Patrik's terms, the physical and textual models of the archaeological record (Patrik 1985). Shanks and Tilley's discussion of the problem in 1987, for example, stressed the polysemy of material meanings but also the concreteness of the object, but without really exploring what that concreteness was (Shanks & Tilley 1987: 114–16). Even Hodder's attempt to reconcile the two appears problematic, to say the least, for one could argue that he does not actually explain how the primary, denotative meaning of a thing relates to its secondary, connotative one but relies on our own cultural perceptions to make this leap. Thus, in his example cited earlier, the link between the killing function of an arrow and its symbolic value as dangerous is evident only because of our own cultural preconceptions. Thus, even if one agreed that materiality was nonarbitrary, the link between this and its social perception surely remains so. One should also note that this was never a problem for functional or materialist views of material culture, as materiality and function – defined in material terms – were part of a continuous ontology. In short, the gap between function and meaning remained unbridged.

The Return to Things: Materiality in Contemporary Archaeological Discourse

IF ONE WOULD define the 1980s and early 1990s as the heyday of semiotic approaches to material culture, from the mid-1990s to the present, the keyword has been materiality (e.g. Meskell 2005; Miller 2005). This has been expressed in different ways; for example, many processualist-oriented archaeologists started to address aspects of ideology and cognition in terms of materialization, a notable paper being that by Elizabeth DeMarrais, Luis Jaime Castillo, and Timothy Earle titled 'Ideology, Materialization and Power Strategies' (DeMarrais et al. 1996). However, their concept of materiality explicitly draws on the nineteenth-century notion of externalization, and they define 'materialization as the transformation of ideas, values, stories, myths, and the like, into a physical reality – a ceremonial event, a symbolic object, a monument, or a writing system' (DeMarrais et al. 1996: 16). Even though they go on to stress that ideas are not primary in materialization but rather a recursive process, this is still about externalization and, in many ways, is simply a renewal of the initial optimism of New Archaeology to address ideology, which was prematurely stalled in the 1970s (but see DeMarrais et al. 2004 for a more developed approach). An alternative and more critical discussion on materiality has come from postprocessual writings, perhaps precisely because of their prior position of being influenced by semiotics, and it is therefore this stream that I focus on here.

As with the influence of semiotics, this interest in materiality is wider than archaeology, and its discussion has often been at a cross-disciplinary level. A general interest in material culture outside archaeology developed over the 1980s, in particular in the way social life was increasingly viewed as constituted through the material world, rather than material culture simply being a reflection of society (Bourdieu 1977; Appadurai 1986; Miller 1987). The culmination of this was to establish the simple fact that things matter (Miller 1998), and indeed interest in material culture by the 1990s had spread across most of the social sciences and humanities, as well as, of course, created an interdisciplinary field of material culture studies (e.g. Miller & Tilley 1996; Buchli 2002). However, as Daniel Miller suggests, much of this work relied on a vulgar and untheorized concept of what things are: it lacked a theory of materiality (Miller 2005: 7). It is thus critical to try to understand how the current discourse on materiality relates to the problem highlighted at the end of the previous section, especially in light of recent calls in archaeology for a return to things (e.g. Olsen 2003; Domanska 2006a, 2006b).

This problem was restated in Buchli's commentary on material culture in the edited volume *Interpreting Archaeology*, based on a conference at Cambridge in 1991, during which materiality was equated with physicality: 'In discussing the appropriateness or inappropriateness of 'text' towards the understanding of material culture, a common distinctive feature of material culture has been continuously invoked... namely the fact that material culture is a thing, hard, durable and physical' (Buchli 1995: 189). In some ways, Buchli's characterization is close to the vulgar concept of materiality, which Miller was to later criticize; yet Buchli qualifies this physical notion in various ways, the most significant being through the aspect of durability. This is something I come back to, and certainly something which Buchli elaborated on in later work (e.g. Buchli 2004), but the most influential development in the concept of materiality in archaeology, initially, related more to its sensory qualities than to its temporality (Buchli 2004: 184). For example, in the same section of *Interpreting Archaeology*, Filippe Criado highlighted the visible property of materiality in the archaeological record, and adopting the Marxist notion of material culture as objectification, he makes a strong argument that objectification is in, quite important ways, about the will to visibility (Criado 1995). The return of the externalization thesis in these discussions of materiality would become very common, as we shall see, but what is immediately interesting in Criado's argument is the link between materiality and textuality through the concept of visibility. For it is precisely the sensual qualities of materiality that became increasingly crucial in grounding the concept of materiality in concrete ways (Buchli 2004: 184). It is precisely those sensual qualities that are highlighted in phenomenological approaches to materiality, thus tacitly evoking the underlying ontology of material culture expressed in the nineteenth century, as we saw in the case of Pitt Rivers.

The introduction of phenomenology into postprocessualism can largely be linked to two British archaeologists, Julian Thomas and Christopher Tilley. Theoretically, the origins of both of them lay in poststructuralism and the semiotic approach (e.g. Tilley 1990, 1991, 1993; Thomas 1991), but by the mid-1990s, they had started to work with ideas inspired by phenomenology, in particular the works of Martin Heidegger (Thomas 1996) and Maurice Merleau-Ponty (Tilley 1994). Tilley was more explicit in his adoption of the term 'phenomenology', and indeed, Heidegger can be called a phenomenologist in only the broadest sense of the word. Nonetheless, what united both was a focus on the importance of embodied experience, or being-in-the-world. It is the implications this had for materiality that I explore here, and in this respect, Thomas is a more useful guide (Thomas 1996: 70–8; see also Thomas 2006). Drawing on Heidegger's writing on 'things' (e.g. Heidegger 1970), Thomas argues that the notion of the thing as a brute physical object is itself a product of a particular relation (or way of being) between humans and the world, one which distances subject from object and contrasts with a more embedded notion of objects as relational. Importantly, this suggests that the concept of materiality cannot be defined independent of human engagement with things, and thus its meaning will change according to the nature of this engagement. Indeed, ultimately, materiality itself ought to have a history (ibid.: 77). Defining materiality as physicality is thus simply defining it according to one particular relation of human being-in-the-world – and one which is peculiarly modern at that. In later texts, Thomas emphasizes the importance of seeing materiality as a process, as materialization 'in which the physical world is gradually disclosed to us' (Thomas 2000: 154; see also Thomas 2004, chapter 9; Thomas 2005b, 2006). This notion of disclosure emphasizes the importance of a relational rather than a substance ontology of materiality; that is, the nature of things does not reside in some essence but emerges through its relations with other things – more specifically, human beings (Thomas 2004: 214–22).

Certainly, the importance of defining materiality in sensory or perceptual terms has been one of the most important contributions of a phenomenological archaeology and has also helped broaden the concept of the materiality by attempting to decentre the dominance of the visual (Hurcombe 2007; Edwards, Gosden, & Phillips 2006; see also important work in the anthropology of the senses: e.g. Howes

2004; Classen 1993). One of the problems with this sensory conception of materiality, however, is that it could be seen as repeating the
error of poststructuralism but on the phenomenological rather than
the semiotic plane – it removes any fixed point of reference. Indeed,
it is quite telling that Thomas has to refer to a physical world which
is disclosed – but what is this physical world if it is not the detached
world of natural science? One way out of this dilemma is to posit basic
structures of human experience, as Tilley does – not so much a universal grammar of cognition as Hodder had originally suggested, but a
common framework of perception grounded in the human body (Tilley
2004: 4–10). Thus, Tilley talks about basic concepts such as front and
back or left and right as grounded in the very structure of corporeal
existence. But even this leaves a lot of room for ambiguity, and it is
perhaps for this reason that Tilley, in response to a paper by Ingold
on materiality, interestingly reaffirms a distinction between the brute,
physical world and the social world of things; for Tilley, materiality
as a concept is quite emphatically about the social nature of things, in
contrast to physicality:

> To put it another way, there is on the one hand a processual world
> of stones which takes place oblivious to the actions, thoughts, and
> social and political relations of humans. Here we are dealing with
> 'brute' materials and their properties. On the other hand there is
> the processual significance stones have in relation to persons and
> sociopolitical relations. The concept of materiality is required
> because it tries to consider and embrace subject-object relations
> going beyond the brute materiality of stones and considering why
> certain kinds of stone and their properties become important to
> people.
>
> (Tilley 2007: 17)

It is not often that one sees an explicit statement like this in current
discussions of materiality, and in fact it seems to me that it is precisely
the ambiguity between physicality and materiality which underlies some
of the more recent calls for a return to things in archaeology.

One of the first to make such a call was the Norwegian archaeologist Bjørnar Olsen in a paper titled 'Material Culture after Text: Re-
Membering Things' (Olsen 2003; see also Olsen 2006), an argument he

has recently expanded into the book *In Defence of Things* (Olsen 2010). Following Miller, Olsen opens with the observation that the materiality of social life has been largely ignored in social theory. But then he goes further and suggests that even the resurgent field of material culture studies does not really engage with materiality, and even worse, archaeology, the discipline par excellence concerned with things, has not really been interested in material culture at all for a long time but with things as proxies for something else (e.g. social status, ideology). Olsen's critique is both compelling and engaging, but there are aspects to his rhetoric in the defence of things which are arguably counterproductive. In particular, one might observe a tension between his call for making things symmetrical to people and emphasizing the autonomy and difference of things. Although the argument for symmetry is relatively sound, drawing heavily as it does on the actor-network theory of Bruno Latour, Michael Callon, and John Law, the argument for autonomy is pure rhetoric and begs the question, What are things? Indeed, what Olsen himself means by materiality is ultimately left somewhat vague – and perhaps this was never really his agenda, which rather concerns the incorporation of actor-network theory into archaeological thinking. Nonetheless, his work, and particularly his recent book, certainly stands as one of the best extended reflections on the issue.

Eva Domanska expressed a similar call for a return to things but articulated the problem more explicitly in relation to the problem raised earlier: how to find a way beyond the dichotomy of a physical, positivistic description of things, on the one hand, and on the other hand, a semiotic approach to material culture as text, symbol, or metaphor (Domanska 2006a: 173; see also Domanska 2006b: 338). Like Olsen, Domanska draws on the agency theories of Bruno Latour but also the material hermeneutics of Don Ihde, whereas her key point borrows from the anthropologist Gísli Pálsson's metaphors of human-environment relations (Pálsson 1996) and applies them to the human-thing relationship. Under Domanska's appropriation, Pálsson's concepts of orientalism, paternalism, and communalism, respectively, denote attitudes of mastery, stewardship, and equality between humans and things. Thus, under orientalism, things are mere tools, whereas under paternalism, they take on human qualities; she suggests that the biographical approach to objects is one of the latest and most popular manifestations of this paternalism, anthropomorphizing objects in terms of human life cycles. The idea of a communalist materiality draws on Latour and the notion of symmetry with the swapping of properties between humans and things rather than things solely taking on human attributes (also see Latour on pragmatogonies; Latour 1994; but see Latour 1992: 159–60). However, this presupposes that there are properties of things which are different to those of humans and begs the question, What are they? This is never explained, so once again, we are perforce returned to an implicit notion of materiality predicated on physicality.

What both Olsen and Domanska share in their call for a return to things is an ambiguity about materiality – on the one hand, invoking an autonomous and tacit physicality to things (which remains unarticulated), and on the other hand, stressing the symmetrical role of things in their interaction with people. The same ambiguity cropped up with the responses around Andrew Jones's attempt to link the current discourse on materiality with archaeometry and the more down-to-earth business of materials-based analysis (Jones 2004). Jones's proposal for the concept of materiality as a vital bridge between archaeological theory and the archaeological sciences was well intentioned, but he too easily conjoined a vulgar or brute notion of physicality with the social concept of materiality, without considering the differences (see e.g. Julian Thomas's response to Jones: Thomas 2005a). It is the social concept of materiality which has perhaps received the most contemporary attention, in particular because of the widespread influence of Bruno Latour and his colleagues, with their actor-network theory. Specifically, the theory argues that agency needs to be decentred from the human subject and distributed among a network of people and things, a collective; these ideas, and especially the writings of Latour, have been circulating in archaeology since the late 1990s (e.g. Boast 1997: 187–9; Shanks 1998; Graves-Brown 2000; Pearson & Shanks 2001: 47–50; Jones 2002: 176–81; Knappett 2002, 2005; Knappett & Malafouris 2008). Some of this interest has crystallized around a self-styled movement called symmetrical archaeology (Olsen 2007; Shanks 2007; Webmoor 2007; Witmore 2006, 2007). However, similar developments have occurred through different trajectories – indeed, Hodder's original notion of an active material culture which he proposed in the 1980s set the stage for thinking about objects in more symmetrical ways, and it has been important to Colin Renfrew's notion of material entanglement (Renfrew 2001; see also DeMarrais et al. 2004; Hodder 2011). Other influences include the work of the anthropologist Alfred Gell, whose ideas of object agency (Gell 1998) have been taken up by archaeologists such as Andrew Jones (Jones 2005, 2007).

Most of this work, however, with the exception of symmetrical archaeology, falls within what Domanska called a paternalistic approach to objects, in which objects take on human or social qualities in an asymmetrical fashion (Miller 2005: 13; Meskell 2004: 57; Hicks 2007: 251). The reason is perhaps quite simple: a truly symmetrical archaeology demands nothing less than a complete reconfiguration of archaeology and, in fact, of disciplinary knowledge and boundaries tout court, because it is about reassembling the whole division of the human and natural sciences (Latour 1993). Such demands do not come easily, if they are even plausible at all. Latour's arguments for reassembling the social are compelling. He argues that there is no abstract or supraentity called society or the social, but rather that it is the product of particular interactions between such networks, and it is these networks and how they may or may not connect up that should concern sociologists, anthropologists, and archaeologists (Latour 2005). This bottom-up approach is an explicit attempt to reverse the whole Durkheimian trend which has dominated the social sciences, to flatten it, a point echoed by Miller in his reference to the tyranny of the subject in anthropology (Miller 2005: 36–7) and that is echoed by symmetrical archaeologists (also see Hicks 2007: 251–3). Indeed, for Miller, the concept of materiality is being deployed to reconfigure the very structure of the social sciences (see also Henare, Holbrood, & Wastell 2007). The paradox is, however, how can it do this when discussions of object agency seem to either fall back on a concept of the social or else tacitly invoke a physical definition of materiality? Recent attempts to tackle this paradox remain somewhat unsatisfactory, as I demonstrate.

Miller, from very early on, advocated a revival of the externalization thesis, specifically the Hegelian and Marxist version of objectification (cf. Miller 1987, part 1, and Miller 2005: 7–10). The important difference, however, between objectification and externalization is that it is not simply the externalization of human consciousness, imposed on an external material. It is this, but it is also more – in the process of externalization, the object is reinternalized to alter consciousness, insofar as it provides consciousness with a mirror of itself. The subject makes the object, but the object also makes the subject, in dialectical fashion. Many archaeologists have adopted Miller's theory of objectification in discussions of materiality (e.g. Meskell 2005: 5; Tilley 2004: 218), although only Miller has given it detailed treatment (but see Tilley 2006). Both Ingold and Thomas have, however, criticized this thesis for retaining a dichotomy between mind and matter, culture and nature (Thomas 2007: 18–20; Ingold 2005: 123–4; 2007: 14). In response, they talk about the transformation of materials in the world, and Ingold in particular is very critical of the concept of materiality altogether, because it obstructs attention to the more relevant, material properties of things (Ingold 2007: 1–3; see also Ingold 2010). Indeed, Ingold explicitly critiques the notion of externalization as derived from Marx as being a patently false representation of human labour (Ingold 2007: 5). For Ingold, these material properties include generative forces, a recognition which is far more significant than simply ascribing them agency like magic dust (ibid.: 12). Many of the responses to Ingold's paper 'Materials against Materiality' returned the same charge of dualisms and indeed argued that the concept of materiality is important precisely to avoid a relapse into a physical view of materiality which his concept of material properties seems to presuppose (Tilley 2007; Knappett 2007; Miller 2007). Ingold's material properties ultimately rest on the vulgar, physical definition of materiality.

In some ways, the protagonists of this debate share very similar attitudes and goals – to overcome the obvious dualisms of mind and matter or nature and culture, to assert that people and things mix and make each other. Yet at the same time, both sides accuse the other of sustaining rather than overcoming these dichotomies, and their differences can appear to be based largely on personal allegiances or dislikes for a certain philosopher (i.e. Marx versus Heidegger) rather than grounded in a point of substance. At the risk of oversimplifying, the differences may come down to whether one sees a dualism as a productive tension in the manner of a dialectics, or an obstructive dichotomy in the manner of René Descartes. In this context, the recent injection of French approaches to technology and material culture offers what is perhaps not so much a middle ground as an example of an approach to materiality which is simply not hung up at all on such dichotomies (Naji & Douny 2009; Coupaye & Douny 2009). The Francophone tradition of the anthropology of techniques, stemming from the seminal work by Mauss (1973 [1936]) and later Leroi-Gourhan (1993), focuses primarily on the performances or practices which involve human bodies and objects, rather than materiality per se – or rather, it is about materiality in the making, rather than materiality as a given or stable substance with physical and/or social properties. It captures something of both the phenomenological approach, which emphasizes the relation between embodiment and materiality, and the Marxist, dialectical approach, in which people and things bring each other into being. Conventional work in this field, however, has tended to narrow its focus, both by restricting the study of techniques to just certain types of social activity (usually involving the production of objects) and by focusing solely on the transformation of the objects. Several scholars in this tradition have recently been arguing for extending the field to all kinds of practices, from agriculture to magic (Naji & Douny 2009; Coupaye 2009; Coupaye & Douny 2009). Under the influence of Jean-Pierre Warnier and his praxeological approach (Warnier 2001, 2009), there is also a stress on understanding how such techniques also act (back) on subjects as well as objects. In many ways, this could be seen as a return to Mauss's original definition of techniques as any action which is both effective and traditional (Mauss 1973: 75) – effective because it has to make a difference in the real world, and traditional because it has to form some part of an inherited social and/or cultural system as opposed to a completely individual or idiosyncratic act.

The increasing visibility and popularity of the Francophone approach to technology in the Anglophone tradition has also coincided (perhaps not coincidentally) with a resurgence of Schiffer's behavioural archaeology. Of course, Schiffer and colleagues have been working and developing their approach since the mid-1970s, but its most prominent face has always been formation theory. Yet this was only ever one aspect to behavioural archaeology, another being the relation between material culture and human behaviour; indeed, they have always advocated that the basic premise of behavioural archaeology is about the relationship between people and things, irrespective of time and place. It is only in the past decade or so that Schiffer has developed this aspect in more detail, especially in two recent coauthored books (Schiffer & Miller 1999; Skibo & Schiffer 2008). It is clear that from these works Schiffer has developed a more sophisticated concept of behaviour which goes beyond the simple notion of correlates with material culture; moreover, explicit connections are made to wider developments in material culture studies, especially the similarity between his behavioural chains and the Francophone operational sequences (Skibo & Schiffer 2008: 9–10). Indeed, it is interesting how Schiffer calls his approach a performance-based theory. Moreover, Schiffer and behavioural archaeologists are not the only ones to make connections with the Francophone tradition, but others working on technology, such as Marcia-Anne Dobres, have also helped bridge the gap (Dobres 2000).

This focus on performance, both by behavioural archaeologists and the French school, helps us see that what really matters is perhaps not materiality but materialization, a process in which objects and people are made and unmade, in which they have no stable essences but are contextually and historically contingent. Nicole Boivin has explored such intersections on the long term, drawing on the mutually constitutive relations between material culture and human biological evolution (Boivin 2008). Seeing materialization as a process, whether long or short term, however, still begs the question regarding the immaterial; or, What is it that is being materialized? Does this not throw us back to the externalization thesis, in which the immaterial is conceived in terms of the ideational, spiritual, or mental? Not necessarily. Buchli has recently argued that the immaterial can be perceived in quite different ways; in particular, one can bypass the whole mental-material dualism by reframing the issue in terms of immanence and transcendence (Buchli 2010). Buchli draws on the contrast between two forms of Christian presencing of the immaterial of the divine: icons and idols. With icons, the presence of the divine works by reference to a transcendent prototype, which is not copresent with the icon; destroy the icon and the divinity remains unharmed. With idols, in contrast, divinity is immanent and copresent with the object; destroy the idol and destroy (part of) the god. Applying Buchli's argument to material culture in general, one can suggest that the problem with the externalization thesis and the notion of the immaterial as the mental is that it stems from a transcendentalist view of the material-immaterial relation: it posits the immaterial as existing in some transcendental realm (as prototype).

Conversely, reading the immaterial in terms of immanence rather than transcendence leads to a very different ontology of materiality and materialization; ultimately, and ironically perhaps, materialization is not about matter at all but about form or organization (DeLanda 1997). What is materialized is not something which lies above or outside the material (i.e. ideas, beliefs) but simply qualities always already inherent in matter itself but not actualized. This is the Whiteheadean distinction between the potential (eternal objects) and the actual (actual entities and/or occasions), or the Deleuzian distinction between the virtual and the actual. To illustrate this, consider almost any object around you, such as a brass screw. The brass has certain properties defined by the metal alloys of which it is composed and the specific production processes which formed the screw. It is an actual object; however, before copper and zinc were alloyed together, before precision moulds for metal casting were made, the brass screw was simply a bundle of unrelated potentialities. I am not saying that before brass screws became actual objects, they were potential or virtual objects, existing in some kind of Platonic world of ideal forms; this would be a transcendental argument. Rather, the various qualities of those already-existing elements which, when combined, make brass screws were virtual qualities until this actual combination. The point is that material reality is teeming with virtual or potential qualities or properties which never get actualized. Just think of all the potential relationships with other human beings you could but never will have, and this captures closely what I mean. In this sense, objects always hold something in reserve; they are always both virtual and actual entities, simultaneously; for both Whitehead and Deleuze, this is how novelty is possible. It is how new things can come into the world.

Framing it in this way sidesteps the paradox of social versus physical definitions of materiality, as we now have a set of terms which applies to any kind of entity – people and trees, buildings or water. Moreover, the very concept of materiality perhaps becomes more of a burden than a benefit because of its historical associations with the mental (or indeed deeper, Aristotelian associations with substance ontology), as Ingold has previously suggested (Ingold 2007). Materiality is, therefore, fundamentally a relational process, not a type of substance, and what really matters is the relations between entities, as well as what kinds of entities there are. Indeed, in many ways this is the more central point of the arguments made by scholars drawing on actor-network theory, such as Olsen or Knappett (Knappett 2005; Olsen 2010); although both talk about materiality, their discussions actually supersede this term and do not really get embroiled in discussions about definitions of materiality or things. In switching the focus to entities and their relations – and in such a way that does not presuppose a given ontology (e.g. mental and material entities and/or substances), our understanding of material culture and the archaeological record has the potential to lead us in new and exciting directions, as I argue in the following chapter.

—5—

Archaeological Entities

I N THE PREVIOUS CHAPTERS, I examined three broad ways in which archaeologists have defined or perceived the archaeological record – as the remains we encounter and the archive we produce, as the formation of deposits and assemblages, and as material culture. My argument is that one of the key problems with contemporary theory is that it addresses each of these facets independently; in effect, we have a set of diverse and lively theories about fieldwork and data collection, formation processes, and materiality, but none of these theories seems to be talking to the others. This kind of fragmentation has created serious problems for archaeological stories, notably expressed in what I have called a new interpretive dilemma, in which our explanations often hover between vacuity and incommensurability. This is not meant as a judgement of all archaeological stories, but it is suggested to be a real and common enough problem to warrant consideration. In this and the subsequent chapter, I explore ways in which we can connect these diverse facets of the archaeological record and thus forestall precisely this kind of dilemma. I should make it clear, however, that this is not some attempt at a grand or unified theory for archaeology; nor is it a rebuke of theoretical pluralism. Rather, my critique is directed at fragmentation, whereby the connections between theories or realms of archaeology have become so detached as to be effectively severed. The case is quite simple: if we cannot connect our practices of excavation, survey, or artifact analysis with some broader theory, perhaps introduced from an outside discipline, then something is surely wrong. These connections may be long and circuitous or short and direct, but they must surely be traceable. One way to ensure this traceability is to map out a broad terrain among the three discourses on the archaeological record. In this chapter, therefore, I attempt to draw connections between the archaeological record as formation theory sees it and in terms of the discourse on materiality and material culture (Chapters 3 and 4). In the following chapter, I link this synthesis to the third aspect, the remains and/or archive (Chapter 2).

If we recall the discussion of palimpsests at the end of Chapter 3, the crucial element was the tension between processes of erasure and inscription; if we now juxtapose this process to that of materiality, then we get the dynamic concept of materialization, and more specifically, we can see the processes of inscription and erasure alternatively as processes of materialization and dematerialization. Objects (as palimpsests) enfold these twin forces into their very constitution. I spend most of this chapter attempting to elaborate on this simple idea; however, the first, and perhaps most critical, point to make is that in realigning the concept of materiality with formation theory in this way, it shifts our whole focus towards objects or things as entities, that is, singular, individuated beings. Almost all prior discussion on materiality, especially as it is articulated in archaeology (and related disciplines) and concerns material culture, could be said to focus on the properties of things rather than on things as entities. Whether materiality is defined by physical attributes or by sensory qualities, this presupposes a view of objects in terms its properties; the issue of the object qua object, that is, as a singular entity is held in suspension. Yet by invoking the concept of materialization instead of materiality, we immediately switch our attention to this other aspect of the object – how it comes or ceases to be a singular entity. It also provides a direct bridge to formation theory, which arguably is also about processes of becoming rather than the already made. For that reason, this chapter begins by asking a very simple question: what kind of entities do archaeologists encounter?

Archaeology and the Problem of Realism

IF WE ASK OURSELVES what it is that archaeologists write and talk about, when they explain or interpret the archaeological record, our answers would vary wildly, as any one narrative or account mixes up a range of entities or objects: pottery sherds, buildings, people, typologies, households, ideologies, seeds, economies, chiefdoms, climate, societies – the list is endless. Sometimes these accounts are even framed within archentities, such as capitalism or evolution. Yet as Sperber pointed out some time ago, the ontological status of many of these entities is usually left undefined (Sperber 1992: 57). A large part of this is about processes of abstraction, moving from bits of pottery to the collapse of states, and in this sense, inevitably, many of the entities are not specifically archaeological but cited by anthropologists, sociologists, and historians. Such widespread use would alone largely account for the lack of discussion in archaeology. Nonetheless, as Stephen Shennan put it rather succinctly some time ago:

> [O]ne of the problems with much existing social archaeology is that it has tried to write a history of very generalized social institutions, made up of vague roles, when it has evidence in general not of roles but of practices.
>
> (Shennan 1993: 55)

But even here, Shennan may be jumping too fast; what *are* practices? The implied question is, What exactly is the archaeological record evidence *of*? Indeed, Sperber suggests that we need to distinguish between facts or evidence and the reality that such evidence refers to; archaeology may collect and study vestiges, but it is not about such vestiges (Sperber 1992: 56). But is this correct? Perhaps the problem lies precisely in the fact of making a distinction between the world of 'evidence' and the world of 'evidence of' – between potsherds and seeds on the one hand, and abstract social entities like class and religion on the other hand.

Leslie White raised this issue many years ago in his review of Kroeber and Kluckhohn's book on the culture concept; criticizing the authors for their constructivist view on the concept of culture as an

abstraction, White strenuously argued for the reality of culture or cultural phenomena against what he perceived as an opposing trend:

> *[Kroeber and Kluckhohn] have expressed a prominent – perhaps the*
> *dominant – trend in conceptions of culture during the past*
> *twenty-five years, and they have done it effectively and well. This*
> *trend is away from the conception of culture as objective, observable*
> *things and events in the external world toward the conception of*
> *culture as intangible abstractions. We deplore this trend because we*
> *believe that it is veering away from a point of view, a theoretical*
> *standpoint that has become well established and has proved itself to*
> *be fruitful in the tradition that is science: the subject matter of any*
> *science is a class of observable things and events, not abstractions.*
>
> (White 1954: 467)

Since White wrote those lines, the trend he identified has only continued in the direction he feared. Indeed, on the whole, the question of the
ontological status of abstract archaeological entities is never raised (but
see Gibbon 1989: 167–71). Indeed, perhaps the only time such a question has explicitly surfaced in archaeology is in the typological debates
of the 1950s about the meaning of types (Wylie 2002: 42–56). The
issue here was polarized by the positions of Brew and Ford on the one
hand, who argued that types were constructs of the archaeologist (Brew
1946; Ford 1954), and on the other hand by Spaulding, who insisted
they were real, empirical phenomena which related in some way to the
actions or ideas of the people who made the objects (Spaulding 1953).
Dunnell characterized this opposition in terms of etic and emic units –
emic units being those derived from the phenomena, and etic units
being those imposed on it (Dunnell 1986: 177). Yet even this debate
did not really directly address the issue of what kind of ontological
status types have, because the debate was largely an epistemological
rather than an ontological issue. Indeed, when the ontological issue
did surface, it was largely discussed in terms of mental templates. That
is, types as real phenomena (emic units) were not construed as objects
but as expressions of mental representations and/or concepts of people
in the past, such as folk taxonomies or what Irving Rouse referred to
as modes (e.g. Childe 1956a: 10; Chang 1967: 71–88; Rouse 1960).
However, as Dunnell points out, another interpretation is that types

are simply recurring structures generated by behaviour (Dunnell 1986: 177). But then this begs the question of the ontological status of such structures.

It is useful to situate this question of the ontological status of archaeological entities within broader discussions about scientific realism. The question of realism in the philosophy of science largely derives from disputes about the nature of theoretical entities which are strictly unobservable except through their effects – objects such as quarks or genes (e.g. Maxwell 1962). The debate arose in the wake of logical positivism, which effectively excluded such entities from scientific knowledge because of their lack of observability; as a result, they became seen in various different ways as fictions or constructs which help to explain observable reality (see e.g. Gibbon 1989: 18–20). This antirealist view of such entities was countered by the emergence of realist theories in the 1960s and 1970s which argued for the reality of objects such as quarks and genes (e.g. Bhaskar 1975; Gibbon 1989: 143–59). Antirealism made a comeback through the prominent and debated work of Bas van Fraassen in the 1980s (van Fraassen 1980). Antirealists are erring on the side of caution because they know their history of science: in the past, scientists have proposed all kinds of theoretical entities, such as ether and phlogiston, which modern science regard as unreal. The same might one day be said about genes and quarks. In response, realists argue that to deny such entities any reality is to unleash the potential for full-blown constructivism, as the very distinction between observational and theoretical entities is impossible to maintain in any absolute sense. This latter point in particular is pivotal, because as Maxwell pointed out in his original seminal article, it is impossible to establish any a priori grounds for distinguishing the observable from unobservable, as this boundary can empirically change – just consider the invention of the microscope.

This summary simplifies a much more complex topic, for which it is important to distinguish between different forms of realism and also nonrealist or instrumentalist approaches as well as antirealism (for a summary of this debate, see Wylie 1986, reprinted in Wylie 2002). For the purposes of this chapter, however, the important point is the relationship between observability and realism. One of the first – of few – attempts to explore this issue in archaeology was a paper by John Fritz titled 'Archaeological Systems for Indirect Observation of the Past', which linked it to logical positivist arguments about the structure of archaeological knowledge (Fritz 1972). Fritz recognized that archaeologists, along with many other scientists, were trying to understand what he called remote phenomena – that is, phenomena not directly observable. These include things such as subatomic particles, the id, processes occurring over long stretches of time, and of course past events (Fritz 1972: 136). If the goal of archaeology, as Fritz saw it, was to understand the prehistoric past, his question was simple: if we cannot observe it, how can we understand it? Drawing on comparisons with other sciences which face the same problem, such as nuclear physics, Fritz argued that we understand it by means of instruments, which mediate our observation. Just as physicists rely on bubble chambers to 'see' electrons, so archaeologists rely on the archaeological record to 'see' the past. Fritz identifies an important problem, but I believe his solution got off to a wrong start straightaway; he argued that the archaeological record was an instrument in the sense that our conceptual terminology helps us read it, and it was thus this conceptual terminology that needed the attention. The bulk of Fritz's paper is then concerned with outlining such a terminology in line with logical positivist thinking. It is ironic, in fact, that Fritz did not even consider the actual instruments archaeologists use – from trowels to microscopes – in his discussion, because this would have taken his argument on an altogether more interesting path, as I discuss in more detail in Chapter 6.

More recently, the philosopher Peter Kosso has taken up the issue of realism in the broader context of archaeology and history (Kosso 1992, 2001). All historical sciences posit processes and objects which are strictly speaking unobservable because they have perished or ceased to be – living bodies, erosion, or behaviours are all inferred from the morphological and contextual characteristics of bones, fossils, rocks, and soil. In fact, Kosso has argued that, in a sense, all observation is of past events because there is always a time delay between the event and our perception of it; moreover, he suggests that the pastness or presentness of an event is actually irrelevant – what matters is the information obtained from any observation, whether it is of material traces, documentary testimony, or living people (Kosso 1992, 2001). Kosso is in effect suspending the issue of realism in relation to observation and focusing purely on the epistemological features – indeed, he explicitly says as much (Kosso 1992: 26). Thus, for Kosso, archaeologists observe the past as much as physicists observe electrons – that is, they don't, or at least not directly so but only through the traces or effects they produce (also see Fritz 1972). Kosso's paper is an attempt to argue for symmetry or parity between historical and nonhistorical sciences in terms of their empirical status; from an epistemological standpoint he makes a strong case. However, in eliding the issue of realism, he conflates at least two very different senses of observability. Moving bodies, erosion processes, or behaviours are all observable in principle – just not in fact. The same is not true of quarks and genes, which are purely theoretical entities and thus unobservable in principle. There may be parity in terms of observable effect but surely not in terms of unobservable cause. Even accepting Maxwell's original argument about the inability to distinguish the observable from unobservable on a priori grounds – which Kosso does (Kosso 1992: 26) – does not necessarily mean that there is no meaningful distinction to be made between historical and contemporary phenomena.

Although philosophers have adopted many different positions on the issue of realism, for many it is something of a red herring. Ian Hacking has suggested that the whole debate about scientific realism which revolves around observability is doomed to irresolution, simply because it is founded on a representational theory of science – for there will always be multiple representations of reality, even if they are not equally plausible (Hacking 1983). Hacking's alternative is to think of scientific realism in terms of intervention not representation – that is, what counts as real is what we can affect or what affects us (Hacking 1983: 146). This view of realism thus argues that electrons or quarks are real because we can do things with them and they can do things to other things – even if we cannot directly see them. This recalls Samuel Johnson's famous retort to Bishop Berkeley's idealism by kicking a stone (Hill & Powell 1934: 1:471). What made the stone real was that Johnson could move it with his foot or that the stone could cause a pain in his toes; one can see Johnson's act as a statement of an interventionist over a representational theory of realism (even if he did not intend it in that way). A comparable approach has also emerged from feminist philosophies of science, particularly from Karen Barad, whose approach stems from an extension of Judith Butler's concepts of materialization and performativity into questions of technoscience

(Butler 1993). Barad proposes a theory of agential realism which also attempts to avoid representationalist arguments in favour of the mutually constitutive nature of objects and our instruments of observation and/or intervention through the concept of intraaction (Barad 1998, 2003, 2007).

Such positions therefore do not worry that electrons or quarks might eventually be dismissed, like phlogiston or the ether; the fact is, they work for us now, and if they are dismissed, it will be because they cease to work. This notion of what works as what counts shifts our whole perspective towards the central importance of scientific practice as a material performance and how this affects what counts as real. This is something I pursue in detail in the following chapter, in which in extending the issue of observability to devices such as telescopes and bubble chambers, the issue of realism is subordinated to concrete practices around which science operates. Indeed, this is the point of departure for science and technology studies (STS), out of which actor-network theory largely emerged (Lynch & Woolgar 1990). In many ways STS is not really concerned with realism at all; arguably, it is a form of constructivism, although Latour would argue that constructivism is realism, and vice versa (Latour 2003); importantly, such constructivism needs to be distinguished from social constructivism as practiced by sociologists of scientific knowledge. So STS constructivism, at least as elaborated by Latour, is where reality is constructed collaboratively by a diverse set of actants – individual people, machines, samples, buildings – not by our culturally or socially informed worldview. Indeed, social constructivism replaces only one mysterious term (e.g. nature, reality) with another (e.g. society); it begs this question – what is the social and how is it constructed?

This question leads us to another side of the realism debate that is perhaps more problematic and one which applies not just to archaeology but to all social sciences. Conventionally, issues of scientific realism are regarded as largely relevant only to certain sciences, primarily physics – most other sciences, including biology, geology, and archaeology do not face this problem, as they do not need to posit theoretical entities in the first place. They simply deal with the observable world of trees, rocks, and pottery (although of course there is some crossover when it comes to molecular biology and genetics, for example). In part, this reflects a bias towards a reductionist ontology, yet one could equally question the existence of supraentities such as cultures and societies. These are no more observable than atoms – they are theoretical entities but posited at an aggregate level of existence rather than a molecular one. What is the ontological status of a culture or society, or indeed of many of the other abstract concepts we use to talk about social phenomena such as chiefdom or class, the economy, or masculinity? Most of us would probably argue that such terms are representational or theoretical abstractions, ways of accounting for certain recurrent phenomena, and of course this is the justification of most similar entities in social theory – they are methodological rather than substantive concepts, and to treat them as somehow real is to commit the cardinal error of reification or hypostatization. To reify is, literally, to turn something into an object. But then this begs the question: if they are not objects, what kind of entities are they? Is it all right to just call them abstractions, concepts, representations, and if so, does this commit us to a Cartesian dualism of mental and material entities? What is their ontological status, and what relation do they have to objects?

Part of my aim in this chapter is to attempt some sort of answer to these questions, to explore what kind of entities archaeologists implicitly invoke. Rather than just jump in to this can of worms without pause, let me say from the start that I do not begin by questioning the ontological status of those entities which archaeologists call objects. In fact, I deliberately take a rather naive stance and just assume that our commonsense understanding of bits of bone, iron nails, and glass bottles as objects is pretty much solid and good to go. If someone were to ask archaeologists whether such things exist, most would probably answer in the affirmative without even thinking. Me too. So let us leave aside all these familiar objects and instead focus on those types of entity for which the question of ontological status is more equivocal. I should say in advance, however, that my discussion of equivocal entities ends up referencing these unequivocal entities we call objects and, in the process, transforms our conception of them too. Ultimately, my goal is to try to link all discussed entities to the broader concept of materialization as described at the opening of this chapter. So what are these equivocal entities? Given my previous discussion of realism and observability, two clearly stand out: past events and social aggregates. Both are regularly used in archaeological discourse, and in some cases, a single term might incorporate both entities – consider the concept of social evolution, which arguably incorporates both social aggregates and past events. The discussion that follows initially keeps the two aspects separate and attempts to explore both in some detail, starting with archaeological events.

Archaeological Events

THE ARCHAEOLOGICAL record is haunted by absences (Lucas 2010c). Archaeologists are only too aware that much of the material culture from the past has not survived into the present because of processes of decay or destruction. Indeed, as was explored in Chapters 2 and 3, such concerns form a key part of archaeological methodology, from source criticism to formation theory. However, there is perhaps one absence that seems to haunt us the most: people as living, breathing beings. Their remains often survive, of course, but a skeleton is not the same as a living being. The envy – tacit or open – that archaeologists feel for ethnographers, whose subjects are alive and who can be engaged with, is an ever-present reminder of this absence and is encapsulated in that well-worn phrase defining the goals of archaeology: to get at the Indian behind the artifact (Braidwood 1958: 734). Kent Flannery's classic response to this offered archaeologists something of a sop to comfort their envy: our goal was really to get at the system behind both the Indian and the artifact (Flannery 1967: 120). And of course in a way he was right; arguably, even ethnographers are interested not really in people but rather in kinship systems, religious beliefs, and so on.

Part of this is also about privileging the human subject; archaeologists, like ethnographers, sociologists, and historians, are ultimately interested in people, even if we also have a penchant for potsherds. Ruth Tringham's critique of archaeological narratives populated by faceless blobs can be seen as a counterriposte to Flannery (Tringham 1991). It is debatable whether archaeology will ever drop this privileging of people, despite recent calls for a posthumanocentric archaeology (e.g. Normark 2010); however, this is a complex issue, which I return to in the final chapter. Nonetheless, because humans and things are so intermingled (as discussed in the previous chapter), arguably, the focus on the absence of people is really a red herring. What is missing is not the human subject, but the animation that links people, objects, animals, buildings, and landscapes. In short, what archaeologists really envy ethnographers for is their access not to people but to life. We deal with the dead. Although decayed objects constitute an important category of the de facto unobservables of the archaeological record – that is objects which are observable in principle, just not in fact – the most important aspect of this class of unobservables is events, not objects (Lucas 2008, 2010c).

The question arises then: what is an event, especially as it conceived in archaeology? It is actually difficult to find any detailed or sustained discussion on the nature of archaeological events in the literature, except in relation to another, more dominant concept such as process or structure (for rare exceptions, see Chang 1967: 105–9; Brooks 1982; see also Beck et al. 2007; Bolender 2010; Lucas 2008). Try finding the word in the indices of archaeological theory books, and you will be disappointed. The fact is that the concept of event has become severely diminished and, more often than not, stands almost as an empty term. Vernacular usage of the word 'event' in the archaeological literature tends to be extremely varied in its scope; the agricultural revolution, the Maya collapse, or a specific burial might all be called events, although they clearly unfold over different durations and pertain to quite different interpretive contexts. However, perhaps precisely because of this semantic poverty, it becomes easier to redefine the concept. Let us then review the concept as it has appeared in the literature to see how it has gained such a status, before going on to revitalize it.

One of the hallmarks of the new archaeology was its concern with finding general processes operating in prehistory in contrast to the more particularistic approach of traditional history and its reconstruction of singular events. Indeed, such a theme was ultimately to define the emergence of processual archaeology in distinction to culture-historical archaeology. Perhaps the classic statement of this distinction is by Lewis Binford in a paper titled 'Some Comments on Historical versus Processual Archaeology' from 1968, in which he challenges the Sabloff-Willey paradigm of historical-developmental interpretation (Binford 1968c). At the root of this disagreement is Binford's critique of the notion that historical events somehow constitute basic facts, which can be reconstructed independent of processual interpretation. Binford argues that any sequence of historical events presupposes causal relations and therefore processual explanations. Historical events are therefore not independent of historical processes but, in fact, subordinate to them. In short, the particularity of events becomes connected to an epistemology of naive empiricism or inductivism, in which event is to process as fact is to theory. Although Binford is not replacing events with process, he is subordinating them and effectively stripping the event of any significant explanatory power. This is the first stage in the diminution of the concept. The second occurs under postprocessualism.

In reaction to cross-cultural generalization, postprocessualism tried to bring back some of the historical particularism which processual archaeology ignored. However, it achieved this not by returning to the traditional historical notion of the singular event but by emphasizing the role of human action and agency theories (Dobres and Robb 2000). Agency has thus come to supplant any positive role the concept of event might have in this arena. Nonetheless, a key element of the postprocessual reaction was a revival of interest in archaeology as history, part of which was simply a continuation of the closer relation that existed between archaeology and history in European archaeology (Hodder 1987). Yet this was not a return to traditional history but one influenced by changes in historical theory since the 1930s, most particularly the French *Annales* school (Last 1995). Part of this shift in historical theory was not dissimilar to the arguments about process and event just outlined; the *Annales* historians were trying to get away from traditional descriptive or event-based history toward understanding more general social and historical processes. However, in doing so, the notion of event became reconstituted as short-term history rather than something opposed to this new history.

In Hodder's seminal discussion of the relevance of *Annales* history to archaeology, there is a sense that events could retain some interpretive potential; he refers to Braudel's definition of an important event as one which has consequences, and of chains of events to identify the relationship between these events and medium- and long-term history (Hodder 1987: 6). Yet because of a scalar model of time, this relationship is quickly collapsed into an opposition between structure and event. Indeed, in general, the concept of event was always ambiguous in *Annales* history with regard to the medium- and long-term scales, and Braudel even suggested banishing the word 'event' because of its former connotations, replacing it with 'short-term history' (Braudel 1980: 27).

In archaeology, the event as short-term history has come to be more or less synonymous with archaeological 'ethnographies' – narratives of everyday practices, which recur over the short term (Harding 2005). As such, the meaning of the word 'event' in much contemporary archaeology is unfortunate, if not downright misleading. Event is now frequently shorthand for small-scale structures as opposed to medium- and long-term structures; if against the concept of process it was stripped of any explanatory power, against structure it becomes completely assimilated into the scalar model of time as a generalized concept and loses almost all sense of particularity.

One of the problems inherited from these positions – perhaps the key problem – is the relationship between two ontologies, which inhabit two temporal planes: the event as a particular occurrence on the one hand, and structure as an enduring set of practices or beliefs on the other hand (and in this respect, it echoes issues raised in the following section regarding the relationship between the individual and society). The particular problem I highlight concerns the articulation of these temporal planes; how do a structure and event relate, temporally? The usual response would no doubt be that structures are made of practices or routines, which in turn are made up of individual events; in other words, structures are simply recurring events, and thus they can be larger or smaller scale depending on the extent of recurrence. This, for example, is the basis of Chang's discussion and distinction between events and activities; events he described as 'unique, empirical happenings', whereas activities are abstract categories of similar events in which a pattern can be recognized (Chang 1967: 105–9). But there is a problem; what about unique events which cannot be subsumed under activities? How do they relate to recurrent events; indeed, how does one define a unique as distinct from recurrent event?

Brooks's discussion of events from 1982 offers the complete opposite approach; he identifies an event as any specific activity or task such as butchering an animal or a court trial (Brooks 1982: 68). His way of then aggregating events is not to follow Chang by positing recurrent events but to literally aggregate them together according to their temporal proximity; thus, episodes are all the events that occur within any given day on a site, whereas a series is the totality of all episodes that occurs on such a site. Brooks's scheme appears at first sight to be totally particularistic; however, he recognizes that events and episodes can be structured and recurrent, but he accounts for this by traversing his event hierarchy with a corresponding hierarchy from individuals to collectives. Brooks's scheme is somewhat confused, as many of the commentaries that followed his paper pointed out, and part of this relates to his lack of discussion between unique and recurrent events. Indeed, the problem or lacuna in both Chang's and Brooks's discussions is this failure to address the relation between these two notions of event – the processual event (or rather the traditional historical event) as a particular occurrence and the postprocessual event as recurring occurrences of relatively short duration.

In a recent paper, Beck et al. (2007) bravely attempt to deal with this relationship, after a certain manner. Drawing on the work of the historian William Sewell, they suggest that an event is a sequence of particular occurrences that transform a structure by reconfiguring the material resources and mental schemas that constitute such structures (Beck et al. 2007). Through four case studies they present the potential of an eventful analysis for archaeology, and although the event (as a sequence of occurrences) can clearly occur over long time spans, events are generally of short duration compared to structures. In some ways, such a perspective combines the concept of structure as convention-ally used with a more traditional notion of event. This approach was extended in the context of a conference in which numerous archaeolo-gists engaged (or not) with Sewell's ideas to rethink the nature of events in archaeological explanation (Bolender 2010). Although important points are raised in this paper and the conference proceedings, there remains the critical shortcoming of easy abstraction; that is, although the event is defined as a cascade of particular occurrences, the details of this cascade are elided, and the concept of event becomes an all-too-easy shorthand term. In effect, all the problems of linking event and structure remain but are reproduced through the opposition of occur-rence and event. In focusing on the cascade of occurrences as a whole (the event) in relation to structure, the authors actually cut out the most important insights of path dependency, namely historical sequence (see e.g. Griffin 1993; Mahoney 2000).

The problem here, and indeed with all conceptions of the archaeo-logical event, is that when it comes down to it, an event defined from a historical or sociological perspective does not really work well with conventional archaeological objects. Abstractions such as structure or practice can be made to fit with archaeological data because they are so generalized, but the concept of event is, by definition, highly particular. Yet if we want to understand the archaeological record historically, in terms of continuity and change, we need some kind of equivalent to the event. The problem is that we tend to see archaeological events in terms of our everyday or conventional understanding of the event, and thus any archaeological event is almost always an aggregation by this measure. Moreover, there is the added problem of whether the events used in narratives actually bear any comparison to events in reality; the historian David Carr argued that with the reconceptualization of narrative history in the 1980s through the work of Louis Mink, Hayden White, and Paul Ricoeur, among others, a basic discontinuity was perceived between real events and historical events (Carr 1986). Because the events in historical narratives were inflected with a narrative structure, they could not be compared with events as they really happen; this of course made the distinction between history and fiction blurred, if not collapsed altogether. But it also effectively severed any link between events in reality and events as they appear in narratives – an issue which Carr attempted to redress by arguing for the reality of a narrative structure to events (Carr 1991; see also Passmore 1987). This has not really been tackled at all in archaeology, except obliquely in a couple of papers by Hodder (1993, 1995). What are the 'real' events of the archaeological record?

One of the more difficult issues with interpreting the archaeological record in terms of past events as we conventionally understand them is the aggregate nature of the record – no matter how refined our methodology, no matter how much we try to dissect the archaeological record into constitutive elements, it will always remain a palimpsest of residues of such events (see Chapter 3; see also Bailey 2007). Even taking an apparently easy example of a single event in the archaeological record, such as the cutting of a grave pit or backfilling it, can be broken down into a sequence of multiple events of shovelling, which are unlikely to be discernible. Whether or not we treat the multiple shovelling actions as a single event depends on how we view them in the aggregate: for example, if it was important to the person digging the grave to start digging from a particular end, then the progression or order of digging is meaningful, and therefore to treat the grave cut as a single event ignores this. If you think this if far fetched, then think about what constitutes an event the next time you go on to a site to excavate. In short, the arch-aeological record comprises palimpsests of higher or lower resolution in relation to an event, as conventionally understood. Moreover, even when we have high-resolution palimpsests, we still frequently aggregate them ourselves into larger temporal blocks or phases to make them comparable – simply because the resolution of palimpsests can vary so much. The problem appears intractable and indeed is, so long as we do not question what an event is, or even reflect more seriously on its relation to objects. In the following section I unpack this event-object relation, and rather than think about how objects can be interpreted in terms of the event, I think about how an event could be interpreted in terms of objects.

Events as Objects

The relation between objects and events is conventionally an asym-metrical one insofar as the dominant metaphysics in Western thought has privileged objects as the fundamental building block of reality. Although event-based or process philosophies have as old a pedigree as atomistic ones, on the whole, philosophy and science have tended to privilege objects over events. A third approach is to consider them equal and being two very different types of entities or particulars which are both necessary to understand reality. Davidson, for example, has argued that events can be individuated in the same way as objects, and there is no reason not to accept them as a basic ontological cat-egory similar but different to objects (Davidson 1969). Indeed, prob-lems only ensue when one subsumes one of the entities under the other: an object-based ontology has the problem of accounting for change or time, whereas an event-based ontology always faces the problem of dealing with persistence or recurrence. Yet all of these views presup-pose that objects and events can be distinguished at all – a fact which is by no means incontestable (Mayo 1961; Dretske 1967; Quinton 1979; Hacker 1982; Casati & Varzi 2008). The philosopher Quine, for example, argued that objects and events are effectively the same – both occupy a heterogeneous chunk of space-time; they differ only in terms of their duration (Quine 1960: 171; 1970: 30). In contrast, it is possible to imagine an eventless object (stationary ball) or an objectless event (e.g. clap of thunder), so surely the two are distin-guishable?

This is obviously a complex issue, but it does seem that the distinction between object and event is somewhat fluid itself and that although we can point to some entities and say, 'This is an object' and to others, 'That is an event' without much difficulty, there are also classes of phenomena which are much more ambiguous (e.g. clouds, soap bubbles, shadows). One vitally significant aspect to the distinction between objects and events revolves around their respective relations to space and time. First consider objects and space; it has been argued that objects occupy space in an exclusive or proprietary manner (i.e. two objects cannot exist in the same region of space at the same time), whereas more than one event can occur in the same space-time chunk (Quinton 1979: 201–2). Being impenetrable, objects demarcate and occupy exclusively a three-dimensional region of space; in one sense, objects could even be said to define spatial difference insofar as space is not considered an empty container. Indeed, if it is impossible to perceive an objectless space, objects must therefore define the possibility of space. Now consider events and time; events signal a change in the state of affairs – if there is no perceptible change, one can hardly point to an event. This captures our everyday sense of the word, of an event as a happening or occurrence (Dretske 1967: 481–2; Shipley 2008). As mutable, events thus occupy contiguous (but not necessarily exclusive) moments in time; they mark change or temporal difference unlike objects which tend to persist in the same state. Indeed, insofar as time is not an empty container for events or an eventless time is inconceivable, events then define the possibility of time.

On the surface, these appear to be satisfactory ways of distinguishing between objects and events; yet the problem is that one can always invoke counterexamples. In the case of an object's proprietary relation to space, this breaks down when considering more fluid entities, such as liquids and gases which do interpenetrate, as when I add milk to my coffee. One could exclude these entities from the category of objects, but then it raises a new question: what are they? Moreover, what about the smell emitted from a more solid object such as a mint leaf – its smell surely interpenetrates with other objects, such as my fingers when I rub the leaf between them. The only way to rescue the impenetrability of objects here is to invoke the Cartesian-Lockean distinction between primary and secondary qualities of objects, whereby objects are solely defined by their primary qualities (i.e. spatial extension). But then this simply becomes a circular argument. With events and change the relation also breaks down, because even with phenomena for which nothing happens, time still passes – a stationary ball does not mean stationary time. Indeed, the very notion of endurance or persistence of a stable state implies time and therefore, paradoxically, change. Moreover, any event marking a change presupposes prior and posterior states or conditions of nonchange: the ball moving changes from a stationary to a mobile object – and usually back to a stationary one again. Without this, one would not be able to demarcate the limits of change or, thus, the limits of an event. Indeed, consider the case of clouds again, which were so problematic for objects; they are equally problematic for events but for a different reason: on a windy day, they are constantly changing and thus make it impossible to mark the beginning and end of the event. In such cases, one might talk of processes rather than events.

Objects and events thus seem to resist any easy definition or demarcation and are clearly inextricably entwined with space and time; indeed, just as one conjoins space and time into a unified entity (space-time), then one also ought to conjoin object and event. As such, it can be useful to consider the more event-based or process ontologies, as they offer the best antidote to the dominant object-based ontology, and in this respect the key figure is the philosopher Alfred North Whitehead. First in his lectures of 1919 on the *Concept of Nature* and later elaborated in his major work *Process and Reality*, Whitehead argued against a materialist theory of nature, by which he meant an atomistic, object-centred theory rather than one which foregrounded the passage of nature, as he called it – the fact that the world is in a constant state of flux or becoming rather than composed of static elements (Whitehead 1978; 2004). He talked about the Great Pyramid of Giza as an event but gave a more detailed illustration of his ideas through another Egyptian monument, Cleopatra's Needle, which now lies on the Embankment of the River Thames in London (Whitehead 2004: 166–72). Whitehead saw this obelisk as a continual happening or occurrence; not only has it moved location – first from Heliopolis to Alexandria in 12 B.C., then from Alexandria to London in 1878, it is constantly changing on a microscale in terms of accumulated soot and grime and the erosion of surface particles and on atomic scales in terms of the interchange of molecules. Even though we ordinarily recognize an object such as this

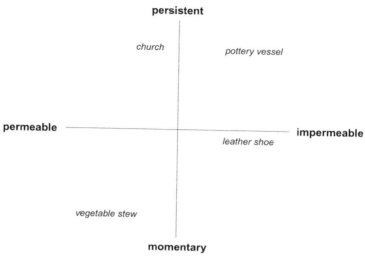

Figure 12. Grid of forces defining objects and/or events; note that this also flattens any ontological distinction between primary and secondary qualities (i.e. objective and subjective).

obelisk as a stable entity (what Whitehead called an enduring object), it is nonetheless a particular type of network (what Whitehead called a nexus and, more specifically, a society) of more basic, momentary events (which Whitehead called actual entities or actual occasions).

Whitehead's ontology is complex, and it would take me too far away from my argument to dwell on it here. The important point is to retain the idea of the eventlike nature of objects and the significance of seeing objects as stable networks of events – or to choose a more archaeological term, as 'assemblages', with 'stability' being the critical term, as we shall see. Thus, objects are assemblages, and assemblages are objects; the distinction between them, insofar as it can be made, is not one of kind but one of degree. One might think of them as ideal points on a grid defined by qualities of permeability and persistence – that is, how impermeable they are to material reconfiguration on the one hand, and how enduring they are on the other hand (Figure 12). An artifact such as a pottery vessel may have a short use-life before it is broken, but it is difficult to modify without completely changing what it is; a building, in contrast, can be repaired, fixed, altered, and stand for centuries, yet still function as a building. Both pots and buildings are, nonetheless, objects as well as assemblages. Objects as assemblages are thus something more like a machine or an organism than the conventional idea of assemblage in archaeology – a concept I discuss in more detail in a later section of this chapter – an organization of matter which operates as an autonomous or semiautonomous entity but one which variously permits flows of material in and out. Such assemblages are in a sense alive or animated, even if many of their parts are conventionally considered inanimate; a notion of extended animacy has, for example, been claimed for assemblages such as termites' nests, and the same equally applies to buildings or other cyborgs (see e.g. Knappett 2005: 16; Turner 2000). Such a description evokes an older theoretical language, that of systems theory and cybernetics. It may seem ironic that, today, one should be invoking systems theory as an influence, but there is a fundamental difference between the systems theory employed in archaeology of the 1970s and that used here. In the 1970s, cultures were systems, whereas ideologies or technologies were subsystems. These cultural systems are abstractions, reifications of social phenomena; the systems I am talking about are concrete, material assemblages made of stone and earth, flesh and bone. Having discussed events, let us move on to the second problematic issue: archaeological abstractions.

Archaeological Abstractions

ARCHAEOLOGISTS reference abstract entities almost as much – if not more so – than the concrete ones; indeed, the more archaeologists incorporate theoretical developments in related fields such as anthropology, the greater prominence these abstract entities take on in our discourse. This was cited as one of the key problems of the new interpretive dilemma I discussed in Chapter 1 and could be restated as a lack of ontological continuity between the entities we routinely use in archaeology and those prevalent in general social theory. As Johnson suggests in the particular case of the concept of agency,

The overwhelming majority of archaeologists continue to divide the past and its material remains into cultures, phases and types. All three of these words appear commonsensical, to the extent that they appear to be simple and jargon-free. However, all three are anything

but commonsensical. In particular, all three militate against the
visibility of agency in the archaeological record, in particular
through their construction of that 'record' in terms of entities
characterized by similarity rather than variability – in other words,
in terms of entities where individual agency is less rather than more
immediately apparent.

(Johnson 2006: 123)

In other words, the reality depicted by our archaeological concepts like culture or type does not fit with the reality implied in concepts like agency – there is some parallax or displacement. Whether or not we accept this in the particular case of agency, I believe such parallax is more prevalent than we care to imagine. The question is, What do we do about it? I suspect that many archaeologists might suggest that we need to readjust our archaeological terms to fit those of social theory, that entities like types and cultures are simply too cumbersome to be effective and in fact are downright constraining. They served a useful purpose back in the day when we were trying to construct chronologies and so on, but they are theoretical anachronisms, belonging to another age of archaeological reason, like phlogiston or the ether for physics. There is no doubt some truth to this – these traditional archaeological entities do need critical and careful handling, and as Johnson says, they are anything but common sense, carrying all kinds of theoretical implications. However, the same goes for concepts taken from social theory; indeed, maybe the bigger problem is not the ontological implications of our archaeological entities but those relating to our conventional descriptions of society and the social. Before we start questioning our own concepts, perhaps we need to question the social first of all.

Society and the Individual

The former British prime minister Margaret Thatcher once said that there is no such thing as society. In fact, questioning the reality of social phenomena such as society is not new but has been a constant, albeit muted, theme in the social sciences since the beginning of the twentieth century and can be traced back to the father of social science, Émile Durkheim. Durkheim stressed the importance of studying society in terms of social phenomena or concepts; this may seem like a tautology, but Durkheim was reacting to a dominant position in eighteenth- and nineteenth-century thought in which interpretations of society were reduced to the actions of individuals, in which collective action was considered simply the sum of individual actions. Like Spencer and Comte before him, for Durkheim society needed to be understood in terms of social phenomena, not individual psychology, because a society was more than the sum of its parts, and he often drew on metaphors from other sciences to illustrate this emergent property, such as organisms or metallic alloys (Durkheim [1895] 1964: xlviii; [1898] 1953: 26). That Durkheim considered society a kind of object is borne out in the language he uses to describe social phenomena; he suggests that society has a reality separate and distinct from individuals – he talks of a social substrate or society sui generis (Durkheim 1964: xlix; 1953: 26). It has been argued that such phrases should not be taken literally, or that they just reflect Durkheim's lack of clarity on this issue (Lukes 2006: 9; see also Gross 2006: 47–8). Yet if one takes Durkheim's argument consistently, the ontological consequence is clear: social phenomena are real.

Whatever Durkheim's actual views on the ontological status of social phenomena, most sociologists and anthropologists have tended to resist seeing social phenomena as real in the same sense as pottery or people are real and to castigate any such claims as reification. Rather, social reality remains embedded in what is observable, namely individuals and their actions, not in some supraindividual entity like society. Weber, for example, was emphatic in rejecting any social or collective reality beyond individuals, basing social studies on the actions and relations of individuals (Weber 1978: 13–15), a focus which most social theorists maintained throughout the twentieth century. Yet at the same time, explaining the actions and relations of individuals in social terms meant invoking concepts which clearly exceeded the individual – such as institutions or social structures, even if these were usually defined as representations held by individuals. In doing so, the ghost of Durkheim's social substrate lurked in the background, and a split into two realities, the individual and the social, was a constant danger. Indeed, such a threat was one of the prime motivations for the development of practice theory in the 1970s and 1980s, which sought to create a middle term between the individual and society, thus preventing their ontological divergence (Bourdieu 1977; Giddens 1984; Porpora 1989). There have been various philosophical attempts to elaborate on the nature of social phenomena, from Roy Bhaskar's critical realism to the more recent social ontology movement inspired by the work of John Searle (Bhaskar 1979; Collier 1994; Searle 1995, 2006; Weissman 1999; Lawson et al. 2007). All these approaches essentially revolve around the same, central problem: the explanation of social phenomena with an ontology that accepts their existence only through the actions of individuals. It is, as the philosopher Searle puts it, a hidden or invisible ontology (Searle 1995: 4–5).

The paradox is actually quite explicit in Durkheim's original definition of social facts, put forward in his *Rules of Sociological Method* ([1895] 1964). There, he defined the concept of social facts according to two criteria: first, social facts are things, by which Durkheim meant not necessarily material objects but any externally observable phenomena; second, social facts are social, insofar as they have an existence different to that of psychological facts (Durkheim 1964). In a sense, like many of his contemporaries in other fields, Durkheim was attempting to get back to the phenomena themselves using new, empirically tested concepts. However, there is a contradiction between Durkheim's two aspects of social facts, namely the quality of thingness he imputes to phenomena which are not really observable. Consider a social fact such as an institution like the church – it is surely observable through its buildings, religious objects, and priests, as well as the various events in which such objects come together. But in what sense is the church itself observable as a social fact? This is the paradox of social facts – in being social, in the sense Durkheim and indeed the social sciences in general take the term, they are not really observable at all. Of course by the same token, electrons are not observable either, except through the tracks they leave in bubble or cloud chambers, and it is precisely on that basis that some, like Bhaskar, have argued for the reality of the social (Bhaskar 1979: 57). Yet in many ways, the issue of realism in the social sciences is much starker than the natural sciences; there, any number of theoretical entities have and will be proposed to explain certain phenomena. In contrast, with the social sciences it seems to boil down to one basic dichotomy: individuals and society. On the whole, scholars have generally denied the reality of society as some kind of separate entity but rather have argued for some kind of quasi status wherein it is dependent on individuals for existence, yet still somehow separate from individuals.

For some, the whole problem of the realism of social phenomena (and the society-individual dualism) has been led down a blind alley; Durkheim's original problem – and one we still try to tackle – is how to explain human aggregate phenomena. In this context, the recent revival of interest in the work of Gabriel Tarde has provided a different alternative to Durkheim's solution of this problem and, concurrently, a new, counterfactual ancestor for the social sciences (Toews 2003; Borch 2005; Barry & Thrift 2007; Vargas et al. 2008; Candea 2010; Latour 2002a, 2005). Under this revision of social theory, Durkheim's error was to propose invisible abstract phenomena (e.g. society, social structures) to account for visible aggregate phenomena (e.g. interpersonal relations). In contrast, Tarde's approach explained such aggregation through the concept of repetition and, more specifically, imitation (Tarde 1899; 1903). Although Tarde had some influence on American sociology in the early twentieth century, specifically on the microinteractionist tradition which emanated from the Chicago school of sociology with figures like Cooley and Mead in the 1920s (Leys 1993; Kinnunen 1996), he was more or less forgotten by mainstream social theory. The recent revival of interest in Tarde is linked to the contemporary popularity of actor-network theory (ANT), which is avowedly anti-Durkheimian and shares much closer affinities to the microinteractionist tradition. However, there remain critical differences between this tradition and ANT, the most fundamental one being the issue of what counts as a social actor.

There is no need to go into detail about ANT, as it has been covered endlessly in the contemporary literature, not least by archaeologists (see Chapter 4). In brief, the two key concepts are the actant and the collective. Moreover, ANT focuses on the nature of what it calls collectives or networks and sees them as fluid entities which form and disperse according to circumstances (Callon & Law 1997). These collectives are formed from individual actants, which include anything from speed bumps to scallops, from Pasteur to pots; the critical point is that there is no privileging of people. In particular, ANT's expanded perspective on actants, which includes the material world beyond people and the associated dismantling of the very divide between human and nonhuman, in many ways resolves the problem of aggregation in a radically new, yet startlingly obvious way. It is Latour who has articulated this best through the idea of the missing mass; just as in physicists'

accounts of the universe there is a problem of dark matter or missing mass, the same goes for sociologists accounts of society (Latour
1992). Latour argues that objects make up this missing mass, and more
important, if we reintroduce this missing mass we no longer have need
for abstract entities like social structure. These missing objects will do
the same work. This is quite revelatory because for the first time we can
avoid the whole dualistic ontology of individual-society and rethink the
landscape of social science. Latour has thus proposed a flat ontology
to replace the dual ontology of individuals and society, because now
all entities stand on an equal plane – people, buildings, pottery, pigs
(Latour 2005). Such an approach shares much common ground with
the recent object-oriented ontologies which have been emerging under
the banner of speculative realism (Harman 2002, 2005; Mackay 2007;
Bryant, Srinicek, & Harman 2011).

For some, such an approach is not just anti-Durkheimian but also
antisocial, insofar as the very use of the term 'social' is somewhat
suspect (Latour 2005; see also Webmoor & Witmore 2008; Dolwick
2008). However, alternatively one can see it simply as a way of rethinking the social, which is the position I adopt later in this book. For now,
though, the immediate question is this: what does this mean for our
conventional archaeological entities such as types and cultures? I argue
that by rethinking the social in terms of networks or collectives of various entities from cars to houses, from plates to people, we are already
more than halfway to creating ontological continuity with our archaeological entities. No longer do we have to struggle to find social
abstractions like religion, personhood, or class reflected in the archaeological record; we have already levelled the ontological field so that
all we have to do is trace the connections between concrete entities as
they appear in the archaeological record. To elaborate on this point
and to make the link between archaeological entities and the ANT
notion of collective, I here examine a concept that has wide currency
in archaeological methodology but has, on the whole, received almost
no theoretical attention: the assemblage.

The Archaeological Assemblage

The concept of assemblage in archaeology is in many ways a very loose
term, used in various ways, but two of its most common meanings
are a collection of objects associated on the basis of their depositional

or spatial find-context (e.g. midden assemblage) and a collection of one type of object found within a site or area (e.g. pottery assemblage), often also referred to as an industry (e.g. Joukowsky 1980: 279; Carver 2009: 224; also see Joyce & Pollard 2010). These two meanings seem quite distinct, yet they do cross over, as we shall see. Indeed, what I want to do in this section is see whether we can better define what an archaeological assemblage is, and in such a way as to maintain coherence while giving the concept more theoretical depth. To this end, it helps to remember the very meaning of the word, that is, an assembling or gathering together of things. But first I want to draw out the various connotations of the term as it is used in archaeology, so let me begin with this primary distinction between a depositional and a typological assemblage.

The concept of depositional assemblage is often regarded as synonymous with the notion of context. For example, here is Gordon Childe: 'The archaeological context should disclose *association*. When a group of types are found together under circumstances suggesting contemporary use they are said to be *associated*. Mere physical juxtaposition does not guarantee association' (Childe 1956a: 31, emphasis in original). Although Childe is using the word 'context' rather than 'assemblage', his definition is clearly similar to the concept of a depositional assemblage. The term 'context', of course, has wider connotations (for a review of the concept of context and its changing meanings, see Papaconstantinou 2006), but the important aspect as brought out in Childe's definition is not necessarily the link to a single deposit or layer but that an assemblage is a collection of things as a meaningful association rather than some arbitrary juxtaposition. For Childe, examples of association included artifacts trodden into a house floor or a collection of grave goods, whereas stone tools found in river gravels constituted an example of physical juxtaposition or, adopting Braidwood's term, 'aggregation' (Childe 1956a: 31–2). Since the advent of formation theory, such simple statements are of course no longer as easy to make, and the question of how far even a floor assemblage is really an association as opposed to an aggregate is open to question (see Chapter 3). Nonetheless, this distinction has played an important part in archaeological method and theory.

However, there is another characteristic to note in Childe's definition, and that is the phrase 'group of types'; in other words, an assemblage is not simply a collection of individual objects but of objects as types of things. Childe is probably referencing the pivotal concept of find combination as developed in Scandinavia in the nineteenth century, which looked at recurring combinations of types as a means of dating through occurrence seriation (see Chapter 3). Of course, find combination need not be exclusively about dating; as a meaningful association of types it could be interpreted in multiple ways according to the particular objects and/or types and context in question (e.g. a particular grave assemblage could be read in terms of gender identity). Given that find combinations as groups of types incorporate typologies, one has to be careful to distinguish between a group of types and a typology per se; indeed, the distinction between the two lies at the centre of a debate in the 1970s in Scandinavian archaeology between Mats Malmer and Bo Gräslund (Malmer 1976; Gräslund 1976). Typology is of course something given more prominence in the other major definition of an assemblage, as mentioned earlier. Such typological assemblages, however, are usually characterized in more specific terms of a single type or class of object; thus, one talks of ceramic assemblages, lithic assemblages, or faunal assemblages. Such assemblages are defined by a very broad classification of things (into pottery, stone tools, bones), and although normally we would not use the word 'typology' to refer to such classifications, as a general and generic term, using 'typology' in this context should not cause too much confusion.

Yet a typological assemblage, though it would appear to be very different to a depositional assemblage, still requires some spatial parameters defining the limits of the population (of types), and usually those parameters are defined ultimately on depositional terms. For example, one does not take just a random group of pottery or animal bones and study this; the collection is constrained by provenance, which can mean anything from a single (usually large) deposit to a whole site or even a region, defined by a date range (e.g. the assemblage of Iron Age tweezers from the Cambridge region). Just as the depositional concept of assemblage references find combination and typology, so the typological concept of assemblage references deposition or spatiotemporal association (Figure 13). Thus, our archaeological concept of assemblage always combines two elements, and the difference between depositional and typological assemblages is largely about giving one of these two elements greater prominence. The question I now pose is this: how do we theorize this and link it to the ANT notion of collectives as discussed in the previous section?

Let us recall the basic meaning of an assemblage – as an assembling or gathering of things; the question can be rephrased as, How do we see deposits and types in terms of assembling processes? Let us start with the easier one – deposits. Deposits are often viewed as envelopes or containers for their finds; this can be a limiting perspective (see Chapter 3), but only if one views the deposit as an abstract container rather than part of a concrete process which gathers together soil, potsherds, flint tools, and bone splinters. It is important to see deposition in terms of formation theory and, in particular, to focus on the nature and agencies of the assembling process. In many ways, the important depositional assemblages are not necessarily individual layers but rather broader contexts of deposition, which act as containers such as graves and buildings. Such spaces divide up the spatial continuum into centres of gravity in which other entities assemble and, as such, act as containers for such entities, allowing some objects in and prohibiting others. They facilitate assembly through containment. What about types, though – how do they constitute assembly processes? Most archaeologists would probably call types, constructs, or representations of the archaeologist as somehow vaguely reflective of past norms, structures of practice, or mental templates. How are these assemblages in the true sense of the word? On the one hand, a typological assemblage, such as a collection of pottery from a site, is a true assemblage in the sense that the archaeologist sorts and separates fragments of pottery from other objects and subdivides them from each other. The resultant bags and boxes of pottery are concrete, physical assemblages, even if they did not start like that. In a sense, what archaeologists usually do is convert depositional assemblages to typological ones in the course of their work. This is something I take up in more detail in Chapter 6. However, even if we think of types as somehow referring to real entities in the past, there is a sense in which they can still be considered assemblages.

What we have to remember is that typologies are based on relations of similarity between objects, and that such similarity is not fortuitous but directly linked to concrete practices of production in the past. In short, typologies are fundamentally connected to issues surrounding the reproduction of objects. A type is simply shorthand for a serial object. The conventional way to see such reproduction is in terms of some

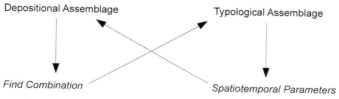

Figure 13. The two basic meanings of the archaeological assemblage and their mutually interdependent nature.

abstract archetype, formerly a mental template but these days most likely a set of social rules or grammar. According to conventional practice theory, such reproduction occurs through social structures, which outline the parameters of the social phenomenon in question; moreover, each object reproduced simultaneously reproduces this structure, just as it is also produced by it. Thus in making a pot, the potter draws on a set of rules which he or she puts into action and, in doing so, reinforces those rules. This practice-theory view of social structure is not that different to the older normative theory which posited mental templates, except that the notion of a set of rules or structure is said to be recursive in relation to practice. Either way, reproduction is made possible through an abstraction, so that the type is conceived as a relation of the general to the particular. Is there another way to see this, though? What if we dispense with the archetype – how does one object come to resemble another?

If we adopt the position of the Francophone school of operational sequences and in particular Leroi-Gourhan's original ideas of how materiality emerges through the interaction of embodied action on matter (see Chapter 4), then reproduction is not generated from within a human subject by some set of internalized rules (or mental template) but is actually dependent on the external configuration of the human body and the objects used in any particular manufacture. Reproduction depends not on rules but on memory, and such memory is distributed between all the elements involved in production. For example, it occasionally happens that someone asks me how to do such and such with a particular computer program; when I think of how to do it, I often cannot remember – I have to actually sit down at a computer and go through it myself. In this way, memory is distributed among my fingers, the keyboard, and the screen. Types, then, need to be seen as serial objects produced through the iteration of technique, where technique is understood as the interaction of gesture and matter. It is this iteration of technique which links each object of a type to another, in a process of enchainment. Types thus constitute sets of objects or an assemblage, enchained together by virtue of a process of iteration. Incidentally, the similarity to Tarde's concept of imitation in this context is not without significance.

One of the reasons we slip easily into the language of abstractions and archetypes like mental templates or social rules is because, although we can clearly see the evidence of these multiple acts of technique in the archaeological record, we cannot perceive the order of each act; a set of types is effectively a palimpsest insofar as it represents a sequence of connected object-events whose relation cannot be dissected but only inferred. Thus, we may have a collection of one hundred pots of one type, and we can say that each of these is a repetition of another – but we have no way of knowing the order of iteration or the nature of the enchainment, let alone how complete our series is. It is this inability to see the serial nature of types in the archaeological record that reinforces our inclination to treat types in terms of an abstract or supraentity (e.g. mental template, set of rules). This chain remains invisible, collapsed into a palimpsest with many links missing, but it is nonetheless still a chain. The key issue for typology is how closely the iteration is conducted, that is, how much variability is allowed between serial objects; although there will be gaps in our series, this does not prevent us from exploring the extent of resemblance. The actual conditions governing this will no doubt vary, but that is not of immediate concern here – rather, it is seeing the creation of types as a product of a serial practice.

To sum up: the archaeological concept of assemblage incorporates two different meanings, but each needs the other: deposition on the one hand and typology on the other hand. I argued that we need to draw out the proper meaning of assemblage as a gathering or assembling of things if we are to link it to the ANT notion of collectives, and to this end, I suggested that we see deposition and typology as two different but complimentary acts of assembling: containment and enchainment, respectively. In the next section, I deepen these two concepts by showing how they can be tied in to a more general theory of assemblage as a way to articulate the nature of the social, and thus complete the link to the ANT concept of collectives.

A New Taxonomy of Archaeological Entities; or, Archaeology as the Science of New Objects

One of the questions about collectives or assemblages is, When does a network of objects or actors constitute a new entity as opposed to just an endless network? Is society simply an open-ended web of objects like nails, people, and cars, or are there intermediate entities which carve up the social into more discrete and stable chunks? Just as on the atomic level, there is not homogeneity but differential combinations of atoms which partition reality into a chair, table, floor, and computer, can we not argue the same at the social level? This is not to imply that such entities have the same properties as chairs and tables – they may be less durable, more permeable, but still the same basic issue is involved: stability of association. I find it ironic that in focusing on stability, we come back to Pitt Rivers's discussion of material culture and the importance stabilization played in his evolutionary theory (see Chapter 4), although the discussion that follows is inevitably somewhat different. In particular, for Pitt Rivers, stabilization was not a problematic concept but rather simply a by-product of being an object; conversely, for us, the critical issue revolves precisely around the problem of stabilization – that is, how do objects or assemblages (or collectives or networks) stabilize?

This is a question that has been taken up by Manuel DeLanda, who has developed a concept of assemblage theory after Deleuze (DeLanda 2006). I am not the first to draw on the work of DeLanda (see e.g. Normark 2010), or indeed Deleuze (e.g. Shanks 1992), but I would like to develop their ideas in the context of my prior discussion of archaeological assemblages. DeLanda's assemblage theory of society attempts to explain how collective entities (e.g. institutions, tribes, nations) can exist in a way that they are not reducible to their parts but also foreground historical fluidity as the basis for such synthetic entities rather than essentialist (i.e. typological) arguments. Assemblages are defined by relations of exteriority – that is, not so much by their internal configuration but by their relations to their environment, that is, other bodies and assemblages (DeLanda 2006: 10). As such, the component parts of an assemblage have a certain autonomy insofar as they can move between assemblages. The stability of any assemblage is determined by twinned processes of territorialization and deterritorialization on the one hand, and by coding and/or decoding on the other hand.

Table 5. *The Archaeological Concept of Assemblage Articulated through the Concepts of Enchainment and Containment*

Enchainment (Coding)		Containment (Territorialization)
	Assembling as iteration	Assembling as gathering
Recurrent association	Recurrent citation (typology	Centres of gravity
(find combination)	and/or serial object)	(buildings, spaces)

For example, a building acting as a meeting place helps stabilize an assemblage such as a religious ceremony (e.g. Sunday service) through territorialization. Similarly, the use of language and texts (e.g. prayers, hymn books) also helps stabilize this assemblage through coding. In effect, coding and territorialization act to rigidify or ossify the relations of a network to create stability and thus new entities at an aggregate level.

How do we make this work with the archaeological concept of assemblage? If we translate coding and territorialization into the twin terms underlying the archaeological assemblage as discussed in the previous section, what we are essentially dealing with is the enchainment between objects on the one hand (coding), and on the other hand, containment – that is, the creation of fixed and circumscribed spaces which act as firewalls and centres of gravity for repelling and/or pulling objects together (territorialization). Enchainment has definite resonance with the concept as used by Chapman in his fragmentation thesis (see Chapter 3), although here I divest it of any intrinsic associations with personhood or even fragmentation (see also Brittain & Harris 2010); alternatively, both concepts can be seen as linking to Latour's concepts of circulating reference and centres of calculation, respectively (Latour 1987). Nonetheless, I develop both terms in rather different ways here (Table 5). I look at enchainment first.

How do we understand the stabilizing force of enchainment? Fundamentally, objects can be enchained only through repetition – that is, when their association invokes a prior object or event. Such repetition can take one of two forms. It can either be a recurrent association, such as weekly Sunday gatherings in a church where the same elements (e.g. same priest, same congregation, same building) are brought together. Or, it can be a recurrent citation in which the elements differ but each assemblage invokes the other through similarity, such as three different gatherings in three different churches on the same Sunday. In both cases, the enchainments are fairly ephemeral as individual events (though they need not be), but their structure or pattern may be long lasting. From an essentialist or typological point of view, the difference between the two repetitive processes is irrelevant because the focus is fixed on the structural similarities of the various assemblages. Yet for assemblage theory, the difference is important because they reflect very different processes of enchainment; the first is all about routinization, the other, about citation. The idea of routinization is well known from practice theory (e.g. Giddens 1984), but citation may need a brief elaboration.

The concept of citation in archaeology largely comes through recent work on memory practices (e.g. Mills & Walker 2008; see also Chapter 3). Andrew Jones has brought this out very clearly and powerfully in his studies of prehistoric ceramics, where decorative motifs normally applied on one type of pot (Beaker) are cited, that is, copied on another (Grooved ware; Jones 2007: 135–40). However, the concept of citation can be extended much more widely to include a whole range of archaeological phenomena, such as skeuomorphs, where the form of one object is copied in a different medium (e.g. ceramic versions of metal pots or textiles; see Ortman 2000; see also Tilley 1999). In fact, I would argue that citation even applies to two identical or near identical objects – that in short, it actually underlies what we traditionally call types, as discussed earlier under the notion of the serial object. In a way, a potter who makes a storage jar which looks the same as the one he made yesterday is citing that previous jar, or indeed all previous jars he has either made himself or seen. It might be argued that extending the concept of citation this far loses some of its force; this is partly true, which is why we need to be careful to distinguish both the degree of citation and its frequency. Citation itself does not guarantee stable enchainments between things; only if the citation is sufficiently recurrent and sufficiently extensive will it then act to stabilize networks, although this is always a question of degrees.

Let us briefly turn to the other process of stabilization, containment, or the creation of centres of gravity. This is where more permanent or durable assemblages act as a container or theatre for more ephemeral assemblages; an example would be the church used in those weekly Sunday congregations, but all buildings or constructed spaces at whatever scale perform this function. Here, the church, itself the product of a recurrent citation (i.e. insofar as it materially references other buildings we call churches), also acts as a centre of gravity for more ephemeral collectives such as funerals, weddings, christenings, and Sunday services. Its very durability but also its larger scale work towards the territorialization of these gatherings, thereby acting to anchor them in a fixed and stable space.

By paying attention to these twin processes of enchainment and containment, we can begin to understand how assemblages are stabilized and thus how new entities can emerge within the social. For it is when and where both of these processes of stabilization intersect that one can perhaps start to talk about new kinds of entities: the church as both the building and the more ephemeral gatherings which occur within it. At the same time, it is precisely because the ephemeral gatherings are ephemeral, disperse, and move on that the church itself is connected to other spaces; the wedding party moving to the community hall for the party, the guests dispersing to their homes, the newlyweds to their honeymoon destination. What is perhaps distinctive about social entities as against other entities (e.g. chairs or tables) is their relative permeability. Not that they are completely so – only certain types of gatherings normally occur in churches; and although they may not resemble more solid entities like chairs, they do bear much closer resemblance to organic entities, like the human body, which also permits (and prohibits) flows of materials in and out (Figure 14).

What is interesting about these new kinds of entities is how they also often exist on different temporal and spatial scales; if we can accept that physics can posit molecular entities not visible to the naked eye but only through mediating devices, then surely archaeology can posit aggregate entities similarly invisible except through other kinds of devices. Svetlana Alpers has made this point in connection with Dutch landscape panoramas and maps, which both present to the eye things which it would ordinarily not be able to see (Alpers 1989: 133). Just like the microscope, the map enables us to perceive new kinds of entities (e.g. cities) as wholes rather than as perspectival parts. In adopting the more generalized technology of map making, archaeologists can see things they could not otherwise have seen. The same is also true of calendrical systems when integrated with dating methods – they offer

Figure 14. Buildings as organisms: the 'autopsy' of an eighteenth-century turf and stone complex in Iceland. Composed of organs and various circulatory systems, this image highlights the drainage system for the circulation of ground water beneath floors.

a temporal horizon beyond our ordinary experience so we can track the histories of entities which develop at much slower tempos than we are capable of perceiving. Time perspectivists (and others) have made a merit out of this insofar as they claim that the archaeological record is precisely configured to offer up such longer-term horizons and thus slower-paced processes (see Chapter 3). My only critique of this argument is that it often strives to look for generalized processes operating at different time scales, whereas I suggest that the important point is to look for more particularized slow entities – and indeed, they are usually right there in front of us (e.g. a building or structure that has endured centuries or even millennia). In this context, the notion of persistent place used by time perspectivists is perhaps the most powerful and relevant (e.g. Schlanger 1992). The remaining question is how to link this back more specifically to the archaeological record; we can certainly try to understand the things we dig up or examine in terms of stabilizing networks, but that is only half the story; what defines the archaeological record is not simply enchainment or territorialization but equally dispersal and deterritorialization. What kinds of processes are involved in destabilizing networks, and what are the implications of this for understanding the archaeological record?

Towards a Theory of the Residue

IN DISCUSSING the example of the church earlier as a process of territorialization, I alluded to the fact that it was also the product of enchainment. Another way of phrasing this is to call the church the residue of a prior, more ephemeral assemblage: the event of construction, in which people, machines, stone, glass, carts, and horses all came together for a certain period, which may be years, of course, albeit episodically (see Edensor 2011 for a nice example of a similar approach taken in the study of a real church). This assembly, however, eventually disperses – the masons go to work on another building, the horses return to the farm, leftover materials go to other projects, and so on. What is left of this ephemeral assemblage is primarily the church itself – plus whatever construction debris may lie buried around it. Yet as a residue, it is much longer lasting than the assemblage itself. By the same token, an object such as a pottery vessel is also the residue of an assemblage; if we revisit our pot in the potter's shed, then the assemblage refers to the process, which brings together the potter's hands, clay, water, sand, tools, wheel, and so on – often in a centre of gravity, the potter's work shed. The final pot – as an object – is by implication the residue of this assemblage in the same way as the church is. Assemblages are almost always ephemeral, and most of the elements which combine in them depart and recombine elsewhere: the potter's hands go to eat lunch, the tools go back to the bench, the remnant scraps of wet clay are tossed outside and washed away in the first rains or recombined with a new paste – all that remains is the pot itself. Almost all, if not all, objects are then strictly speaking residues of prior assemblages. Moreover, all such residues are inevitably reincorporated into new assemblages and may act as parts in enchainment or containment processes. The church acts as a container, territorializing congregational networks, whereas the pot acts within multiple, recurrent association enchainments as part of diverse assemblies, including wedding dinners. Clearly, this definition of a residue does not conform to our ordinary sense of the term, especially in archaeology – yet it is not that alien either. In this final section of this chapter, I explore this connection between objects as residues and our conventional notion of residues, through the paired processes of enchainment and dispersal, and containment and exposure.

Memory and the Archaeological Record

If we recall the discussion of palimpsests at the end of Chapter 3, the crucial element was the tension between processes of erasure and inscription. The archaeological record lies between these virtual extremes of total preservation and total erasure, which always remain nothing more than virtual. Yet perhaps the same applies to assemblages and material reality in general; these processes of inscription and erasure can be seen equally in terms of materialization and dematerialization. Enchainment and territorialization are simply two sides of materialization or inscription and will always be in tension with their opposite force. It is always a question of degrees of (de)materialization. It is this concept of materialization that enables us to conjoin what was previously separate: the ontology of things (i.e. materiality) and their biographies (formation theory). The important question for archaeologists is this: to what extent do changes in materialization preserve the traces of previous organizations? I argue that the material world is, at any given time, an archive of this process of (de)materialization.

To explore this notion, I link these processes to the concept of memory, taking as my starting point Geoffrey Bowker's analysis of the geological record in terms of memory (Bowker 2006). Bowker's study focuses on the pivotal work of Lyell, whose three-volume *Principles of Geology*, first published between 1830 and 1833, was an attempt to present a picture of earth history in terms of regular cycles of destruction and construction. One of the consequences of these processes was that, at any one point on the planet, a full sequence of events would never be present – there would always be gaps. To his contemporaries, these gaps were interpreted as evidence of catastrophism (i.e. severe and sudden changes over the face of the earth); to Lyell these were just an inevitable effect of the twin processes of inscription and erasure and said more about the preservation or memory process than the actual tempo of earth history. For Lyell, this history was gradual and incremental, not catastrophic. Bowker has suggested that Lyell saw the geological record in terms of the earth creating its own archive – only imperfectly so (Bowker 2006: 55–6). He draws our attention to Lyell's use of the analogy of census taking to illustrate the imperfection of the geological record – that depending on how far apart in time each census is, the corresponding archive as successive records of population statistics will show gradual or revolutionary changes (Lyell 1833: 31).

Lyell's observation is fundamentally the same as that of the contemporary problem of time averaging (see Chapter 3). What is intriguing in Bowker's portrayal, however, is the notion of the geological record as a kind of autoarchive; certainly, Lyell was also reacting to the theological interpretations of earth history by many of his colleagues, which invoked the hand of God and made analogies between the 'book of nature' and the Bible. For Lyell, the book of nature had no author other than itself – and in this sense, the geological record was an autoarchive (Bowker 2006: 55). What if we extend this idea to the archaeological record? It might seem somewhat superfluous, but let us consider it seriously for a moment. Instead of God, archaeologists usually attribute authorship of this record to past people (or culture – and sometimes nature; consider here Schiffer's c- and n-transforms). In one sense, this is fine – after all, the archaeological record is conventionally characterized as a combination of human and natural elements, so citing human and natural agents as causes is another way of saying that the archaeological record is self-creating. However, the problem lies perhaps not so much in the 'auto' part of autoarchiving as in the 'archiving' part; the conventional way to view the archaeological record is as a set of residues, traces, or effects. It immediately sets up an opposition between cause and effect, past and present, event and object – or more generally, between dynamic and systemic, and static and archaeological contexts. The point about an archive is that it reaches out to the future as much as it is a record of the past.

How do we begin to reconceptualize the archaeological record as an archive? Of course, one meaning of the archaeological record is precisely that – the archive we create; but this is understood in terms of our own, archaeological operation and the residues *it* produces (e.g. drawings, photographs, samples, finds). I talk more about this in Chapter 6; for now, I address the more obscure issue of how the archaeological record as stratified deposits (including finds) might be viewed as an archive prior to our intervention. One of the few archaeologists to explicitly recognize the archiving nature of the archaeological record is Laurent Olivier, who likens archaeological remains to memory (Olivier 2008). Olivier's book is a rich excursus into the idea of archaeology as memory, and in particular he draws on the concept of palimpsest to emphasize how the archaeological record is like a memory-object (e.g. souvenir, keepsake, memento) insofar as it articulates a tension between preservation and loss, and erasure (Olivier 2008: 200). Olivier highlights what he considers the fundamental paradox of our discipline: archaeologists can study only what survives from the past, but what survives does so only because it has changed (ibid.: 267). Thus, the archaeological record should be construed not as evidence or testimony (*témoins*) of the past itself but as signs or symptoms (*signes*) of a memory constituted in time through repetition and transformation (ibid.: 272). In many ways, this is the most radical point of Olivier's book – conventionally, archaeologists bemoan the incompleteness of the archaeological record, yet it is precisely this loss which enables us to make sense of the past (ibid.: 274).

But is all this likening of the archaeological record to memory not just metaphorical? How does it actually help us to do archaeology differently, as Olivier suggests in his book? To answer these questions, it is useful to draw out the connection between memory and palimpsest in such a way that it highlights the fragile notion that memory is somehow something that only humans or sentient beings possess – because ultimately, this is the critical obstacle to any suggestion that the archaeological record is somehow an autoarchive. Ironically, one of the most common metaphors of memory provides a perfect illustration: that of the imprint. Paul Ricoeur has reminded us of the Socratic view of memory, which linked the image (*eikon*) with the imprint (*tupos*), drawing on the metaphor of a seal impression on a block of wax (Ricoeur 2004: 13). Freud provided a more up-to-date version of this metaphor in his 1925 discussion of the mystic writing pad; this was a device that enabled one to both erase previous impressions to make way for new ones and to preserve the original impressions through the doubled surface of a wax slab under waxed paper (Freud 1957). Such definitions could equally stand for the concept of palimpsest as I have articulated it in this book. What is interesting in these metaphors is how memory is characterized through very material processes, yet perhaps what is even more provocative is that maybe these are not metaphors at all, but actual examples of memory, but of a different kind: we see them as metaphors only because of the ontological split between mind and matter.

The notion that a trace can be defined as a material memory highlights the importance of how the past is preserved in, or is contemporary with, the present – in a truly Bergsonian sense (Bergson [1908]

1991). An imprint on a block of wax or a footprint in the sand are not signs of an event (even though one can see them that way); they are actual physical remnants of the event itself, of someone writing or of an animal walking across the desert. The hominid footprints found at Laetoli in Tanzania are the extended ripples of an event that happened 3.6 million years ago, into our present. In this sense, time is not a series or succession of moments, but a continuum on which the past is stretched into the present. This is exactly how Bergson character-ized memory (Bergson 1991). For Bergson, the relation among past, present, and future could not be characterized in a serial manner but needed to be seen in terms of a heterogeneous continuum, or what he called duration (*durée*). Consequently, the past is preserved in the present, and it was this quality which also guaranteed the possibil-ity of memory; without it, memory would be indistinguishable from imagination. Indeed, memory (or pure memory as Bergson called it, to distinguish it from recollection or habit memory) was precisely this temporal continuum. A similar argument was made, but from a very different perspective, by Edmund Husserl, the founder of phenomen-ology who developed a special concept of memory (retention) to explain the fluxlike or continuous nature of experience (Husserl 1966; also see Lucas 2005: 22–4).

What is interesting is that the problem which both Bergson and Husserl tried to resolve – namely the preservation of the past into the present – is essentially the same as the paradox of the archaeo-logical record: that it is fundamentally a contemporary phenomenon, yet simultaneously of the past. Moreover, both resolved this problem by appealing to a concept of memory, albeit in very different senses. Can we then use the concept of memory also to resolve the paradox of the archaeological record? This is what Olivier has suggested, but I am not sure he offers a concrete proposal of how this would actually appear. Certainly, archaeology has drawn a great deal on memory studies in the past few years (Bradley 1998, 2002; Gosden 1994; van Dyke & Alcock 2003; Mills & Walker 2008; Boric 2009; Jones 2007), but almost all of this literature actually acknowledges a very different intellectual pedigree, which is usually traced back to Maurice Halbwachs's work on collective memory (Halbwachs 1980, 1992). Adopting Durkheim's social ontology against what he saw as Bergsonian psychologism, Halb-wachs proposed the notion of a collective framework of memory. What is pivotal to Halbwachs notion of collective memory, however, is that it is essentially the reconstruction of the past in the present (not its preservation, as with Bergson), and it is this which has dominated memory studies in recent times. In short, Halbwachs elided from Bergson the very aspect of memory that was critical to his philosophy of time: duration. Indeed, one could argue that Halbwachs reversed the whole trope of memory from being about the past persisting in the present to it being re-created in the present. Consequently, most contemporary archaeological studies on memory are of little help in this issue because of their essentially Durkheimian approach to memory.

The failure of this tradition is brought out in a recent revival of Halbwachs distinction between living and dead memory, taken up by Pierre Nora in his opposition of memory and history (Halbwachs 1980; Nora 1989). Living memory is memory which still plays an active and emotional part in the present; dead memory, in contrast, has been severed from the concerns of the present and exists as detached knowledge about the past. Nora takes up Halbwachs's distinction and translates it into a deep, contemporary schism between memory and history in which history embodies Halbwachs concept of dead memory, whereas memory is a mere shadow of its true self, reduced to acts of archiving and preserving the past but devoid of any real purpose except the fear of forgetting. Contemporary memory thus revolves around the construction of sites of memory (*lieux de mémoire*), objects, things, events, or places at which the rupture between past and present is evident, yet not complete. These sites of memory contrast with environments of memory (*milieux de mémoire*) in which the past is continuous with the present, and no sense of rupture is experienced.

Halbwachs's and Nora's views on history, archaeology, and memory are vitally important, but they more or less bypass the possibility of total or absolute forgetting (see Ricoeur 2004). Indeed, Nora even intimates as much when he suggests that most archaeological remains might appear unable even to act as sites of memory, simply because the rupture with the past is so complete (Nora 1989: 20–1). Nora's concept of *lieux de mémoire* captures the ambiguity about this rupture, but in the case of a Mesolithic flint scatter, there is surely no ambiguity: forgetting is total. Or is it? The issue here concerns the status of materiality vis-à-vis memory, for one could argue that the very survival of such traces in the present suggests that forgetting is not total. The issue, rather, is how, as archaeologists, do we deal with such ambiguity? The problem lies in the detachment of collective memory from materiality, in the sense that the material traces of the past have been preserved into the present, but all social memory has gone. We can treat the archaeological record as if it were a memory archive, but how does this help us reconnect forgotten collective memory to forgotten materiality in cases when only the latter can be unforgotten (i.e. unconcealed)? In a sense, the Durkheimian notion of collective or social memory developed by Halbwachs and underwriting most contemporary discourse is actually the cause of the problem insofar as it presupposes the separation in the first place. Memory is not something divided between the collective and the individual, or between the mental and the material; memory is a feature of any entity (see Bowker 2006). For archaeologists, the issue is about how to see their entities in terms of memory; what we need, in fact, is a theory of residuality.

Residuality and Archaeological Entities

Archaeologists may study residues, but what exactly are residues? I have argued that most objects, such as churches or pots, can be seen as residues of prior assemblages. Like our everyday notion of the residue, they are the leftovers, the remnants of something absent or gone; at the same time, this does not quite capture the full meaning of what we think of when we think of residues. Why not? I suppose part of our concept of the residue also carries with it connotations of abjection or casting off – the unwanted, the excess – like the construction debris created in the building of the church. But the residue also seems to apply to objects as much as it is them – the ruined foundations of the church as the residue of a former, standing church. But this is to forget that the church is also an assemblage itself as much as an object – or a key part of multiple assemblages insofar as it is a territorialization for weddings, funerals, masses, and so on. So it is indeed a residue in multiple ways, not just one. As archaeologists, we try to understand the various assemblages of which it is a residue or remainder.

How do we understand this relation of the residue to the assemblage? Basically, it is about what kind and how many assemblages an object is a residue of. This is not an easy question, and for many residues, we may be able to offer only highly generalized statements. There is no doubt that archaeologists have become very good at trying to reconstruct assemblages from fragments, but as we all know, such reconstructions are always partial, simply because the vast majority of assemblages leave no material residue. This is not to say that objects from such assemblages do not survive (e.g. broken crockery or food scraps in the landfill), but the objects are usually implicated in hundreds, if not thousands, of assemblages prior to their deposition, and to pretend that we can obtain a full sequence is naive in the extreme. In short, we must not conflate surviving elements of an assemblage with the material residuality of an assemblage itself. In the one case, we are talking simply about things, in the other, organization of things. In this sense, what we need to remind ourselves of is the notion of the residue containing a memory of the assemblage. If we think about the archaeological record in terms of the residue of assemblages, we must consider such residues as possessing a memory of the assemblage itself, insofar as the organization of the residue captures, however faintly, the organization of the parent. It is the residue of this organization that is being sought, not simply the elements or objects which were part of it.

Under what conditions is memory preserved? Consider the example of the grave as the residue of a funeral. A funerary rite involves a collection of objects (e.g. bodies, grave goods, a coffin) that during most of the rite are variously mobile, as in orbit around a virtual centre (Figure 15). At the end of the rite, some, but not necessarily all, of the elements converge and stabilize at this centre point (the grave), whereas the others disperse to conjoin other mobile assemblages. The grave thus retains some memory of this assemblage. Now compare the case of a pot with that of a grave. Like a grave, the pot itself is not an assemblage per se, but the residue of one, as argued earlier. But there is a difference between a pot and a grave. Unlike the component parts or objects which make up the grave, which can still easily be separated, the component parts of the pot – clay, sand, water – cannot. Indeed, the whole point is that they have transformed into a new substance, ceramic. The same is not true for the grave. What are the implications of this? Simply put, we should ask, When the grave is dispersed, do any of its components retain any memory of having once been part of the grave? Very unlikely, except perhaps for any items that might be exclusively associated with a grave – such as a coffin. The pot, though, is different; smash it into two or twenty pieces and each sherd will still retain a memory of the whole it once was. We might say that pots

Assemblage as Object/Event

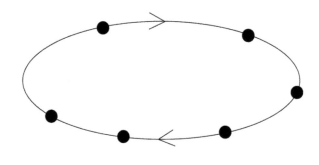

Dispersal and Stabilization

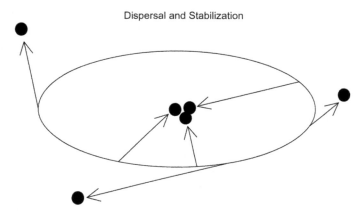

Figure 15. Diagrammatic representation of how assemblages stabilize and disperse.

are more fractal than graves insofar as any part is also the whole in microcosm – albeit a reduced whole.

But this polarizes the issue too much, because what is really at stake is this part-whole relation. Indeed, the smaller the potsherd, the blurrier (usually but not necessarily always) is the whole which it evokes. We find a small sherd, and we may recognize it as porcelain, but from what kind of vessel is hard to say. Similarly, if all that remains of our church is the construction debris, we can say, on the basis of fragments of ashlar stone, glass, and nails, that here was a building – just not what kind of building. The fundamental property in terms of residuality is, I argue, that of irreversibility: the extent to which parts of assemblage bear the

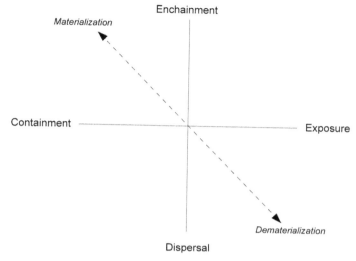

Figure 16. Grid of forces of assembly and disassembly in terms of the processes of enchainment and/or dispersal and containment and/or exposure; materialization is enhanced as enchainment and containment work together, whereas dematerialization is accelerated as assemblages are dispersed or their firewalls breached.

imprint of this assemblage, even after disbandment. Thus, no matter what subsequent assemblages an object enters into, it still carries these traces with it. Once you combine clay and water and fire, the result, a relatively stable and irreversible change, has occurred which, even after breakage, retains the traces of this materialization. Once you combine stone, timber, and glass to construct a church, these elements – even though they do not invoke the whole in the same way as a potsherd does a pot – are still relatively specialized matter towards a certain kind of assemblage. That is, their specific materialization evokes a variously specific whole of which they are parts. Modern machinery takes this to an extreme, as when small parts may be highly specialized for very individual objects – from one small part, you can re-create the whole.

But this is only half the story, because the issue is not solely about how materialization preserves memory but equally about how dematerialization – or rather lack of it – also acts as a preservative. Consider the example of the grave again; unlike pottery vessels, these appear much more reversible from a purely internal or intrinsic perspective; disassemble a grave and it can, by and large, be separated into the same parts that made it up (e.g. body, grave goods, pit). Yet graves remain (relatively) stable for centuries, if not millennia, aside from the decay that accompanies some of their elements. Why? The only answer can be the absence or weakness of dispersive forces which would otherwise threaten to undo this assemblage. In effect, the very fact that the grave is buried or entombed specifically protects it from such forces – it puts the assemblage in quarantine (or partial quarantine at least, as other forces such as microbes and chemicals still attack it). In fact, every entity is quarantined in some form or another – one might say that such quarantining is the condition of creating stability in an otherwise continuous flux of assemblages. It is what makes objects possible. As every forensic scientist knows, the sooner a crime scene is contained, the better, simply because dispersive forces are always at work. The crime scene investigator, by controlling the flows of materials and forces in and out of a locale, quarantines the scene. Seeing the quality of resid-uality thus depends on the stability of assemblages, and this stability in turn partly depends on the creation of firewalls around assemblages, cutting their links to other assemblages (i.e. the environment), and points towards a critical continuity between the past and the present in terms of the archaeological record (Figure 16). The archaeological intervention effectively breaks this firewall, disperses previously stable entities like graves, and reconnects the parts into a whole new set of assemblages. It is to this topic that I turn in the following chapter.

6

Archaeological Interventions

I N THE PREVIOUS CHAPTER, I explored the nature of archaeological entities and touched on the issue of scientific realism. Because no entities would seem to be observer independent, whether theoretical entities like electrons or observable entities like pots, the debate is somewhat sterile. More significant, though, not only are entities observer dependent, but also there are strong grounds for accepting that they are actually constituted through the very practices of science; Karen Barad called this agential realism (Barad 2007). Latour would call it constructivism – but constructivism understood in a very special sense (Latour 2003). It is not that we make up reality; rather, reality is constructed through the very interactions of scientists, their equipment, and various bits of matter. Indeed, as Latour puts it, the more or better constructed, the more real. I think we can make the same arguments for archaeology.

Let me give an example; to late-nineteenth- and early-twentieth-century British archaeologists, it was believed that prehistoric houses consisted of pits dug into the ground. These so-called pit dwellings were observed and reported on in many excavations and exhibited a variety of forms, whereas their identification seemed heavily supported by classical sources (Evans 1989b: 438). The recognition of post-built structures, though not unknown, was not widely appreciated until after a German archaeologist, Gerhard Bersu, a refugee to Britain on the advent of the Second World War, brought German methods of quasi-open-area excavation to a British Iron Age site. Bersu's excavation methods – that is, his mode of intervention, resulted in a gestalt change in the perception of prehistoric settlements. Subsequently, post-built structures became widely acknowledged, but more important, the features previously interpreted as pit dwellings for the previous century became something else – quarry pits, rubbish pits, natural hollows, and so on. This is a good example of how archaeological reality can change in relation to intervention; pit dwellings worked for a long time, but as soon as archaeologists changed their mode of intervention, they ceased to work.

There are surely differences between electrons and pit dwellings; for example, one could argue that at least with pit dwellings, there is an observable object which remains constant; it is just the designation that has changed. But this just brings us back to a representational theory of realism; it is more productive to focus on the relation between intervention and the creation of objects. In this respect, it is interesting to consider Maxwell's closing remarks to his paper on realism in which he suggests that one of the most exciting aspects of science has been the emergence of strikingly new kinds of entities (Maxwell 1962: 27). In the same vein, let us claim the same about archaeology; we discover new kinds of entities (e.g. chambered tombs, prehistoric settlements, palstaves, Clovis points), which are filling our museums and store rooms at an exponential rate (Lucas 2001a: 212). Moreover, the labour involved in their discovery also generates a whole range of associated products: notebooks, drawings, photographs, books, and so on. Archaeology is a material practice, or rather a materializing practice, and seeing it this way helps us to understand the link between the issues discussed in the previous chapter concerning archaeological entities and those discussed in Chapter 2 on the archive. This is the aim of this chapter: to attempt to draw together the synthesis forged in Chapter 5 between materiality and formation theory, with the third facet of the archaeological record, the archaeological operation, to suture what has been a fragmented concept. There are many ways to characterize the archaeological operation or process, and I review these by way of an introduction. However, the approach that is taken later is different in two ways: first, most such accounts present the operation as a linear process (e.g. from data collection to interpretation). This misrepresents the multisited nature of archaeological practice as a network of inter-acting domains, with no necessary start or end point. Second, most approaches tend to adopt a reductively conceptual or representational stance – that is, they portray the archaeological process as if it were a purely intellectual exercise rather than a material practice. This is by no means true of all accounts, but it largely remains the dominant and conventional account. This chapter thus offers an operational defini-tion of archaeological practice along these lines, but first, in keeping with the structure of this book, I briefly explore the received views on the matter.

Received Views of the Archaeological Operation

AS DISCUSSED IN Chapter 2, one sees little explicit discussion of method in archaeology prior to the end of the nineteenth and early twentieth centuries; when it is mentioned, it is usually in terms of a very simple opposition of the collection of facts and the presentation of theory to account for such facts. Flinders Petrie, writing in 1904, in what was perhaps the first book on archaeological method written in English, reaffirmed the idea that archaeology was 'the latest born of the sciences' (Petrie 1904: vii) and lamented the general lack of organization to archaeological work; he suggested a very simple, two-step procedure for a systematic archaeology:

> *(1) the complete definition of facts by means of a corpus of all known varieties of objects, in terms of which every object can be defined; and (2) the arrangement of material in its order of development by statistical methods and comparison, which bring out the original sequence of construction.*
>
> *(Petrie 1904: 122–3)*

Beyond that was the role of historical imagination, which Petrie likened to the legal procedure of assessing evidence in relation to interpretation (see Chapter 2; Petrie 1904, chapter 13; Petrie 1906). What is ironic, however, is that the major part of Petrie's book is about excavation techniques, and in a sense, one can read into the whole text an implicit view of the archaeological operation as three staged:

1. The collection and presentation of facts by excavation and recording (chapters 1–10)
2. Their organization, which involved both the development of a corpus and arrangement into chronological sequence (chapter 12)
3. Their interpretation in historical terms (chapter 13)

An explicit three-staged approach was indeed outlined by Randall-MacIver, who frequently and approvingly referenced Petrie in his paper 'Archaeology as a Science' (Randall-MacIver 1933: 8):

1. Collection and recording in the field
2. Housing, conservation, and exhibition
3. Comparative study and publication

It is therefore somewhat odd that Petrie singled out the middle step in his call for a systematic method in archaeology, especially as most of his book was concerned with a systematic approach to excavation and recording. Part of the reason may be the legacy of nineteenth-century thinking in which it was the work performed on collections rather than the work involved in gathering collections that was of prime importance (see Chapter 2). Indeed, it was Petrie and books like his *Methods and Aims in Archaeology* that were helping to shift the focus towards an interest in fieldwork methods in Britain – but this took a long time. Thus, Crawford's *Man and his Past* devotes only one short chapter to excavation, whereas his methods chapter is all about association and classification (Crawford 1921), and the same general lack of interest in excavation can be found in Childe's general works (e.g. Childe 1956a, 1956b). It was not until the third quarter of the twentieth century that books about excavation and data collection started to appear more regularly in British archaeology, as already discussed in Chapter 2.

Yet what seems to happen at the same time is a fragmentation or splintering of discourse in relation to the archaeological operation; on the one hand, there is an accumulation of fieldwork manuals which deal with data collection, and on the other hand, an accumulation of

theoretical texts which largely focus on data organization and interpretation (see Chapter 2). The two genres rarely reference or speak
to each other. One sees this particularly clearly in North America.
Although statements on field method can be found as far back as the
nineteenth century, the first proper textbook was Heizer's *Guide to
Archaeological Field Methods*, published in 1949, which has since run
through multiple editions and has been joined by multiple competi-
tors (Heizer 1949; Heizer & Graham 1968; Joukowsky 1980; Hester,
Shafer, & Feder 1997). A year earlier, Walter Taylor published his famous *Study of Archaeology*, which more or less ignored excavation and
focused solely on interpretive problems around collections. Taylor saw
the archaeological operation in terms of a grand vision of the human
sciences which harked back to the nineteenth century; in the context
of discussing the relationship of archaeology to history and anthropology, he adopted and modified a four-stage model for the historical and
nonexperimental sciences proposed by Berr and Febvre in the 1930s
(Berr & Febvre 1957). Taylor thus suggested that there were five steps
in the procedure of the human sciences (Taylor 1983: 32–8):

1. Definition of a problem in terms of a conceptual scheme
2. Gathering, analysis, and criticism of empirical data
3. Ordering of these data in chronological sequence
4. Search for and establishment of reciprocal relationships within this
   series (i.e. integration and synthesis or historical reconstruction)
5. Understanding the nature of culture in a cross-cultural, comparative manner

He argued that steps 1–3 were shared by all three disciplines, archaeology, history, and anthropology (as ethnography); step 4 was shared
only by history and anthropology (which at this level he called historiography and ethnology); step 5, the sole preserve of anthropology. This
is clearly a nineteenth-century vision in which culture (and anthropology) acts as the universal concept uniting all social sciences (see Chapter
4), but what is worse, of course, is that it relegated archaeology to a
menial status in this hierarchy: 'Archaeology *per se* is no more than a
method and a set of specialized techniques for the gathering of cultural
information. The archaeologist, as archaeologist, is really nothing but
a technician' (Taylor 1983: 43).

Taylor, of course, was not saying that archaeologists should leave the job of interpretation up to historians and anthropologists but that their particular skills as archaeologists were relevant only in the first three steps of the interpretive process; after that, their training in historical and anthropological interpretation kicked in, an interpretation which ought to be applicable to any kind of data once they had been processed, whether historical, ethnological, or archaeological. Taylor's vision was echoed by many in North America during this period, most notably Gordon Willey and Philip Phillips, who, borrowing a phrase from Maitland, affirmed that archaeology is anthropology or it is nothing – or at least American archaeology (Willey & Phillips 1958: 2). Moreover, they simplified Taylor's procedural scheme even further by presenting a convergent model for anthropology and archaeology, yet one based on similar operational levels (Willey & Phillips 1958: 4). They suggested that the operation of all sciences could be reduced to three stages: observation, description, and explanation. At the observational level, archaeology and anthropology were obviously the most distinct, resting on different empirical data, but as they approached the explanatory level, they became closer and closer.

Yet models of the archaeological process oscillated between those who reduced it to a minimum sequence, as did Willey and Phillips, and those who wanted to stretch it out, as Swartz proposed in 1967. Swartz suggested a seven-stage operational sequence based on broad (yet unstated) precedents in both scientific and historical methods (Swartz 1967: 487):

1. Preparation – background knowledge and research design
2. Acquisition – collection of data through fieldwork
3. Analysis – placing of data in a space-time framework through classification and contextual association
4. Interpretation – understanding the production and use of artifacts based on association and/or analogy
5. Integration – reconstruction of past lifeways and synthesis into cultural taxonomies
6. Comparison – identification of cross-cultural regularities
7. Abstraction – formulation of general laws about culture

Swartz's paper, rarely referenced, is actually a paradigm of clarity, and even if not original, it manages to condense and incorporate much of

North American theory up to that time – with the notable exception of avoiding any references to Binford or the emergence of new archaeology. Swartz's main point in the paper, however, is to emphasize the conceptual order of these stages insofar as each step is dependent on the prior one; he also suggests that steps 5 and 6 are parallel rather than sequential insofar as both depend on step 4 and both lead to step 7. In this sense, they represent alternative paths to the ultimate goal of archaeology (step 7: general laws).

What is interesting about Willey and Phillips's scheme, and the derivative version proposed by Swartz, is the importance put on developing a body of concepts consistent with these stages; as they put it in the opening lines of *Method and Theory in American Archaeology*,

> *It has been said that archaeology, while providing data and generalizations in such fields as history and general anthropology, lacks a systematic body of concepts and premises constituting* archaeological theory. *According to this view, the archaeologist must borrow his theoretical underpinning from the field of study his work happens to serve, or do without... Acceptable fieldwork can perhaps be done in a theoretical vacuum, but integration and interpretation without theory are inconceivable.*
>
> *(Willey & Phillips 1958: 1)*

The notion of developing an explicit, archaeological theory was to be echoed later by Binford in relation to his middle-range theory, but the notion that fieldwork could be performed in a theoretical vacuum is very telling and speaks to the rift between data collection and data interpretation. Thus, most of Willey and Phillips's attention was devoted to creating concepts which operated at their middle and top level of procedure: culture-historical integration and synthesis (Phillips & Willey 1953; Willey & Phillips 1955; Willey & Phillips 1958). In this they developed their famous basic units of component, phase, tradition, and horizon (largely drawing on and modifying existing taxonomic schemes in North America), as well as the synthetic terms which applied to developmental cultural sequences (lithic, archaic, formative, classic, and postclassic). Yet it is precisely the bottom level of fieldwork, which they regarded as unproblematic and/or atheoretical, which is my focus in this chapter: to examine our concepts at this level in an operational manner.

The first hint at changes to this view came with the new archaeology, which started to place greater emphasis on reflexivity in field methods – primarily in terms of sampling theory (Binford 1964; Watson, LeBlanc, & Redman 1971: 114–26; Mueller 1975). The focus on sampling is not accidental but was linked to new epistemologies of archaeological interpretation involving the testing of hypotheses using statistical methods (see Chapter 2); as such, it was critical to control the quality of data. However, the link between the overall archaeological operation and the new scientific epistemology was made most explicit in Fritz and Plog's revisions to Swartz's seven-stage operational sequence to make it conform to a deductive-nomological model of archaeological explanation (Fritz & Plog 1970: 410–11):

1. Acquisition of an hypothesis
2. Formulation of test implications
3. Formulation of research strategy
4. Acquisition of data (i.e. fieldwork)
5. Analysis of data
6. Testing of hypothesis
7. Evaluation of research

This model was to be subsequently criticized by Binford for being inapplicable to the archaeological record, although as he himself realized, it nonetheless had a wide influence on the way many archaeologists thought they ought to proceed (Binford 1983: 14–15).

However, although these shifts in archaeological practice speak of a real concern to incorporate theory into fieldwork, its effect was not so much to a forge re-union of theory and fieldwork as to engender a proliferation of theory according to the different stages of the archaeological operation (Table 6). Thus, David Clarke proposed five levels of archaeological theory, the last three of which related to the three stages of the archaeological process: retrieval theory, analytical theory, and interpretive theory (Clarke 1972: 16–17; see also Clarke 1978: 12–13; Sullivan 1978). Much the same division was proposed by Schiffer many years later when he divided archaeological theory broadly into three domains – social, reconstruction, and methodological theory, with the latter relating to the archaeological process and further subdivided into three subtheories relating to the recovery, analysis, and

Table 6. *Different Proposed Schemes for Dividing Archaeological Theory from the 1970s and 1980s (after Clarke 1972, Sullivan 1978, and Schiffer 1988)*

Clarke (1972)	Sullivan (1978)	Schiffer (1988)
Predepositional and depositional theory	Formation theory	Reconstruction theory
Postdepositional theory		
Retrieval theory	Recovery theory	Recovery theory
Analytical theory	Analytic theory	
Interpretive theory		Social theory

inferences made of archaeological data (Schiffer 1988). Despite the difference in publication dates, both Clarke and Schiffer effectively reduce fieldwork theory to issues of sampling (Clarke 1972: 16; Schiffer 1988: 474–5) and thus show no real theoretical development since Binford's 1964 paper on research design (Binford 1964). The 'real' theoretical attention remained focused on the analytical and inferential levels (e.g. Clarke 1978), as it did with Willey and Phillips in the 1950s – and it has remained so until relatively recently.

If Binford opened the door to theorizing fieldwork, it was a door which most archaeologists with an interest in theory subsequently chose to ignore, including Binford himself. Part of this, as already mentioned, related to the particular epistemological model which many archaeologists were operating under in the later twentieth century, which, despite the recognition that fieldwork was theoretically implicated, still equated fieldwork with data collection or description, in opposition to explanation or interpretation (Hodder 1997). As the view about the relationship between theory and data changed during the 1980s and they came to be seen as interdependent rather than independent of each other (see Chapter 2; Gibbon 1989; Kelley & Hanen 1988; Hodder 1986; Wylie 1992b), it was only a matter of time before fieldwork was no longer seen as separated from interpretation. The shift can be detected as early as the late 1980s and early 1990s (Carver 1989, 1990; Tilley 1989; Hodder 1989b; Richards 1995), but it was not until the turn of the millennium that one sees a critical mass of literature emerging – largely from a postprocessualist perspective – which returns to the theorization of fieldwork (e.g. Andrews, Barrett, & Lewis 2000; Chadwick 2003; Hamilton & Whitehouse 2006; Hodder 1997, 1999,

2000; Bender, Hamilton, & Tilley 1997, 2007; Edgeworth 2003, 2006; Jones 2002; Lucas 2001a).

Implicit of course in all this recent theorizing of fieldwork is the idea that the different stages of the archaeological process are not so distinct. One of the earliest manifestations of this occurs in Watson, LeBlanc, and Redman's recognition that the actual archaeological process does not necessarily have to follow the conceptual or logical process of explanation: 'In logical terms, the order of genesis of problems, hypotheses, and the data pertinent to them is immaterial... what is important is not the temporal order of their generation or presentation, but their conceptual relations' (Watson, LeBlanc, & Redman 1971: 14–15). Thus, they make a distinction between the practical sequence of the archaeological operation and the logical or conceptual sequence, and although in many cases, the two do mirror each other, there is no intrinsic reason for this to be so. However, the idea of a conceptual order remained a dominating influence in archaeology and one which still persists today. Hodder's hermeneutic approach to the archaeological process provides one of the more explicit reworkings of the traditional linear and segmented approach and is best exemplified in his presentation of an interpretation of the Neolithic causewayed enclosure at Haddenham (Hodder 1992: 213–40; 1999: 34–40). Although obviously interlinked and expressive of a broader unity, Hodder's presentation of the hermeneutic spiral incorporates the traditional division of fieldwork, analysis, and interpretation, but what he adds is a fourth sphere – the broader, background sets of knowledge which inform our understandings of sites such as Neolithic enclosures (Figure 17). This broader background is there both prior to fieldwork and subsequent to interpretation, and indeed one hopes that one's own particular fieldwork and interpretation will have made a difference to this broader context by the end of the process. One way to see this is therefore as a circle, replacing the old linear model, but Hodder's use of the spiral is deliberate because he wants to emphasize the movement or change which occurs through the articulation of specific studies and general knowledge. What is a little ironic, though, is how similar in structure this is to Clarke's flow model of the archaeological process decades earlier, which Hodder actually reproduces in his book *The Archaeological Process* (1999: 4). This is not to deny important differences – doubtless Clarke's model explicitly separated data and theory as

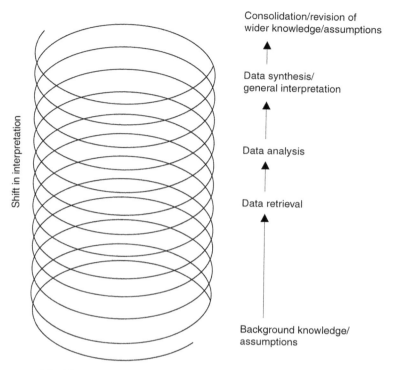

Consolidation/revision of
wider knowledge/assumptions

Data synthesis/
general interpretation

Data analysis

Data retrieval

Background knowledge/
assumptions

Shift in interpretation

Figure 17. Hodder's version of the archaeological operation: the hermeneutic spiral (adapted from Hodder 1992).

distinct stages in the process, whereas Hodder is clear that the relation between data and theory are interwoven at all stages. But the separation of stages in themselves remains intact, as does the general notion that they are part of a repetitive and dynamic process.

This structure can also be seen in Andrew Jones highly engaging study of scientific practice in archaeology, where he highlights the effect of fragmentation produced by this process (Jones 2002: 39–49). Like Hodder, Jones argues that interpretation occurs at all stages of the archaeological process, and he underlines the importance of reintegrating the fragmentation of practices which have been developing in archaeology the past century as a result of the diversity of specialisms (see also Lucas 2001a: 65–74). However, the concept of linearity remains implicit and begs this question: does this accurately describe what we do? Of course, to some extent it does – we excavate, we process, we write up the results. But this oversimplifies what is a much more complex network of practices, and it does so precisely because underlying it is a conceptual rather than a practical view of the archaeological process. What I mean is that the archaeological process is considered principally in terms of a process of reasoning, inference, and interpretation rather than a set of practices. This does not mean practice is ignored, as is clear, for example, in both Hodder and Jones, but only that it is subordinated to the intellectual process. Regardless of the philosophical differences between Clarke and Hodder – and they are significant – both conceive of the archaeological process as an intellectual endeavour which, even if expressed through practice, does not take as its starting point practice itself.

The first changes to this view emerged from Hodder's former students Shanks and Tilley; although the emphasis on archaeology as a practice is evident in their early joint work (e.g. Shanks & Tilley 1987), it is only in their subsequent separate publications that a more practice-based approach to the archaeological operation emerges. One of the first was Tilley's paper 'Excavation as Theatre', published in 1989, in which he likens fieldwork to a dramatic performance, inverting the relation of script to performance in terms of excavation and site report (Tilley 1989: 278). Tilley's description of excavation as the active production of material remains marks a critical turning point but remains very general in its discussion. Tilley subsequently explored such themes in greater depth in collaboration with Barbara Bender and Sue Hamilton as part of their project on prehistoric landscapes in southwestern England (Bender et al. 1997, 2007). Michael Shanks took a slightly different route and has foregrounded the notion of archaeology as a craft, which he articulated in publications from the early 1990s, especially his book *Experiencing the Past* (Shanks 1992). However, the idea was most succinctly drawn out in a joint paper with Randall McGuire, originally presented at a Society for American Archaeology meeting in 1991 but published only five years later as 'The Craft of Archaeology' (Shanks & McGuire 1996). In this paper they argue that archaeology be seen as 'a mode of cultural production or technology' (Shanks & McGuire 1996: 76). The stimulus of the paper was to view archaeology as a socially embedded practice (hence a 'craft') rather than an abstract, intellectual exercise, a view which was influenced by a growing body of work in the sociology and philosophy of science, specifically that associated with science and technology studies (ibid.: 79; Lynch & Woolgar 1990).

Although the invocation of archaeology as a craft has some resonance with earlier views about the working methods of humanist disciplines, such as Wright Mills's work on the sociological imagination (Mills 1970: 215–48; see also Ingold 2008: 83–6) or Collingwood's on historical imagination (Collingwood 1946: 231–49), Shanks's concept is much broader in scope. Following Gero (1985), Shanks and McGuire criticized the implicit hierarchy of academic valuation which is superimposed on the traditional model of the archaeological process, whereby the work (and those people working) on the bottom stages (i.e. fieldwork, analysis) is valued less than the work at the top (i.e. theory, synthesis):

In this scientific mode of commodity production the higher levels of analysis each appropriate the products of the lower in their practice so that the theorist is accorded greater renown than the prehistorian, the field director a higher position than the laboratory assistant, and the synthesizer more attention than the faunal analyst. We divide the practice of archaeology into those of us who manage and sit on committees, synthesize, generalize, and theorize and those of us who sort, dig, and identify.

(*Shanks & McGuire 1996: 82*)

In contrast, Shanks and McGuire proposed seeing archaeological practice as nonlinear and nonhierarchical, and rather composed of a range of different activities which are simultaneously both theoretical and practical: 'there is no single correct route to the final product – the archaeological work. There is no hierarchy of archaeological practices, from washing sherds to theory building" (ibid.: 83). Shanks has pursued such ideas in even more unorthodox directions recently through the notion of performance (Pearson & Shanks 2001; Shanks 2004).

Shanks's work can be considered part of a broader movement to recognize the sociopolitical nature of archaeology, one in which knowledge production must be seen in terms of contemporary situated practices. Similar developments emerged in North America from feminist and gender perspectives, especially in the work of Joan Gero. Against a background of highlighting the sociopolitical context of archaeology, Gero and her colleague Goodwin conducted research on the gendered construction of knowledge at a Palaeo-Indian site in Argentina

(Gero 1996; Goodwin 1994; but see Politis 2001; also see Moser 2007). For Gero, one of the key issues to arise from this and subsequent work was the issue of ambiguity and certainty (see also Gero 2007). The development of all these ideas about the archaeological operation as cultural production is extremely important, and many of the same studies which influenced them also play a key role in my own argument. In particular, the emphasis on the nonlinear nature of archaeological practice on the one hand, and its social nature on the other hand, are both vital. However, my interest in the archaeological operation originally stemmed from a different and third angle: the materiality of archaeological practice and how archaeological discourse is constituted through this (Lucas 2001a, chapter 6; 2001b). All three of these concerns are interconnected, and it is my purpose in the remainder of this chapter to elaborate on their intersections. To do that, it is useful to start by summarizing the philosophical background to such an approach.

Rethinking the Archaeological Operation

THERE IS NO DOUBT than one could characterize much of archaeological epistemology since the late 1980s as under the influence of a constructivist turn – that is, that archaeological knowledge is not just discovered but made; that it is not simply about internal issues of evidence and testing but equally about external issues such as the social and political conditions under which knowledge is created (e.g. Shanks & Tilley 1987: 186–208; Hodder 1984; Wylie 1992a, 1996). Such a turn was common across the social sciences and humanities, and one of the key elements was precisely a focus on disciplinary knowledge as a form of practice rather than simply an intellectual operation. Michel de Certeau (1988) provides us with an important early perspective influenced by French theoretical work on history, especially that by Michel Foucault in *The Archaeology of Knowledge* (Foucault [1969] 2002). Foucault's main concern in this work was to examine the nature of discourse in history and at the same time to provide a theoretical basis to his earlier works. In general, however, Foucault's book was an attempt to map out what he saw as an epistemological mutation which history was undergoing at the time, from one in which historians construed documents as sources to write history to one in which they worked with documents as monuments – by which history becomes a form of memory work (Foucault 2002: 7–8). De Certeau takes up these ideas in his important paper 'The Historiographical Operation', which was originally published in 1974; in it, he expands the notion of the historiographic operation to incorporate the relation among three elements: the place or social institutions in which history is conducted, the analytical procedures used, and the products: texts (de Certeau 1988: 57). De Certeau's approach was remarkably ahead of its time insofar as it embraces a very broad notion of historical practice, beyond the restrictions of a purely epistemological perspective. Of particular importance is his emphasis on the importance of seeing documents – the historian's primary data – as constructed through the constitution of archives and how the form of archives affects historical work (ibid.: 72–7).

De Certeau's discussion of the historiographic operation is extremely important but has been somewhat overshadowed by the work of Bruno Latour on the scientific operation. Latour's studies on 'science in action', along with those of numerous other scholars, has resulted in a much more detailed and extended genre of writing about the practice of science than exists for history – although many of the insights are easily transferable. Such research on the scientific operation can be considered part of a general development in the history and philosophy of science called postpositivism, which emerged in the 1960s and is especially marked by Thomas Kuhn's seminal study *The Structure of Scientific Revolutions* (Kuhn 1962). During the 1970s, various approaches developed which are often labelled broadly as 'constructivist', although they vary in important ways; however, the common element lay in detaching the philosophy of science from epistemological issues – or at least problematizing them further – by relocating them within how science is actually practiced. It is largely in how practice was conceived that the differences lay, from conventional sociological and historical approaches of the Edinburgh school of the sociology of knowledge (e.g. Bloor 1976; Shapin & Schaffer 1985) to the more detailed ethnographic and microscale studies (Latour & Woolgar 1986; Latour 1987; Knorr 1981; Knorr-Cetina 1999; Lynch 1985; for an extremely good overview, see Golinski 1998; see also Shapin 1982, 1995). A wealth of literature exists about multiple aspects of scientific practice (e.g. locales, inscriptions, instruments) and from varying philosophical positions, but Latour's now-classic book *Science in Action* provides perhaps the clearest and most synthesizing source to date (Latour 1987).

Taking these insights, we can see that fieldwork is not so much data collection as the intervention in a locale or space – the field – through the mobilization of various elements (e.g. people, trowels, cars, tapes, money) which create and sustain that intervention for as long as necessary, or possible. However, this explains only half of the matter, because fieldwork does not just involve intervention; it also involves the production of artifacts, in the broad sense of objects produced as a consequence and through the practice of fieldwork (e.g. drawings, samples, photographs, finds). These objects constitute what we might call the archive. This happens through a process of materialization insofar as new material assemblages are created in the process (see e.g. Lucas 2001a, chapter 6; 2001b). Such created assemblages or archives are themselves mobile, which means that they can be carried over into other sites or locales, such as museums or lecture halls, and work towards their creation or maintenance. Fieldwork is thus implicated in a whole array of locales outside the field – government ministries, heritage bodies, archaeological organizations, local authorities, and banks – which totally disrupts any clear divisions between an inside of archaeology as a scientific discipline and an outside of society.

Two things I should emphasize: first, this view of archaeological fieldwork departs from earlier work in focusing on the material constitution of the field and archaeological evidence, as opposed to epistemological issues such as that encapsulated in the debate over description and interpretation. In this, I can make no claim to originality. Indeed, the work of Matt Edgeworth deserves special mention; originally conducted as part of doctoral research completed in 1991, his analysis of an archaeological excavation is refreshing and remains almost unrivalled, even today. Published only recently, it is a superb analysis of the archaeological operation from a material perspective and quite ahead of its time (Edgeworth 2003). Although it suffers from some rather blatant dichotomizing (despite an explicit attempt to avoid such), among other things, the book still offers one of the best and sustained analyses of how archaeological facts are produced in the field, from a participant-observer on an excavation of a Bronze Age site in Britain. More recent work in the same vein, but theoretically more sophisticated, includes that by Tom Yarrow, who has looked at the mutually constitutive relationship between people and things on excavations (Yarrow 2003, 2006, 2008; see also papers in Edgeworth 2006), and work by Tim Webmoor and Chris Witmore on the transformative practices between the archaeological record and its archives (Webmoor 2005; Witmore 2004, 2009).

The second point to stress is that I am not arguing that archaeological evidence is constructed – at least in the sense it might be normally understood. We do not invent or create our data; it is not a fiction of our minds or a social construction. However, neither is it just given. It is produced through the material interaction of an assemblage of bodies and/or objects which are mobilized by our interventions in or on the ground. The notion of the archive, as I use it here, thus makes no separation between potsherds and site plans, soil samples and photographs, but rather mixes up categories which conventionally we might keep apart (i.e. actual remains and our records). In the following section, I develop these ideas in more detail. I begin by exploring the archaeological record in terms of intervention, more specifically as a mode of production. In a later section, I address the product – the archive – and consider its function as a mobile assemblage which can circulate itself in other sites. Together, they form what one might call part of the archaeological economy.

Archaeological Modes of Production in the Field

ONE OF THE OFT-CITED pleasures of archaeology as an academic discipline is that part of it involves physical work; whether this is shovelling out a segment of prehistoric ditch or walking the landscape, fieldwork is an act of intervention that differs quite profoundly from practices involved in the nonfield or even nonexperimental sciences, which tend to be desk bound. However, my intention here is not to overemphasize differences among disciplines but to focus on the specific nature of archaeological fieldwork as a material intervention. In particular, I explore how archaeological intervention, as a mobilization of objects and bodies, mediates between the site and the archive. One of the obvious things to point out here is that the nature of the objects assembled on any site will affect the nature of intervention; different technologies produce different sites. Planning a site using an electronic station, for example, vitiates the need for grid pegs, which in turn completely alters our perception of space on the site. Similarly, the advent of routine use of photography demanded a whole new set of aesthetics which affected the location of spoil and the neatness of trench edges, as well as inaugurated the practice of cleaning before the photo shoot (Chadha 2002; Witmore 2009: 529–30). However, equally if not more important than technology per se is how the technology is mobilized to create a site; a site dug using the North American unit-level approach and one dug using single-context methods may use identical sets of tools but mobilize them in very different ways to create very different-looking sites – and correspondingly very different-looking archives.

Indeed, the material form a site takes could be said to be produced as much by the archive (reversing the conventional chain of causation) as the other way around. It is interesting to consider, for example, how excavation methods at Pompeii and Herculaneum in the nineteenth century were influenced by the axonometric drawings produced by Weber in the eighteenth century. Excavations at Pompeii between the 1730s and 1750s were conducted by tunnelling through the ash rather than by full-scale clearance; the results were often very confusing, especially to visitors who gained no real sense of the buildings. Walking around Pompeii and Herculaneum today, where buildings and streets have been completely cleared, is an entirely different experience. What is interesting is the role the archive may have played in this transition. The Swiss engineer Karl Jakob Weber was hired to work on both sites in the 1750s, and although Weber improved the excavation methods, he still employed tunnelling; more influential were his high standard plans, which were also the first examples in archaeology of the use of axonometric projection, a technique borrowed from architects and military engineers, who had been using it since the early sixteenth century (Parslow 1995: 168–70). However, such views were never visible in the remains themselves but only through Weber's architectural drawings; yet once such drawings existed, they added to the need to see the actual buildings in the same way, and thus helped to change excavation methods from tunnelling to open-area clearance, pioneered by Fiorelli in the 1860s.

Both sites and archives are thus created simultaneously through acts of intervention. There is nothing 'natural' about a cross-section of a pit; or a one-metre slot through a ditch line; or even, for that matter, a site stripped of its topsoil. It would have never looked like that except through our intervention. A field notebook arranged by excavation squares and dates looks very different to a file of context sheets, and each relates to very different and specific modes of intervention. However, I am not so much interested in the differences between specific traditions of intervention as in the general process of how intervention mediates between the site and the archive. I suggest that we see this in terms of two related and very material processes: disaggregation and assembling.

Viewing fieldwork, and specifically excavation, as disaggregation has some resonance with a view of scientific procedure as reductionist; just as the chemist breaks up a substance into atomic elements to understand the whole, so archaeologists break up the site to understand it as a whole. There are many different ways to break apart an entity – from using a mechanical excavator to using a toothpick. We can shovel out the dirt, or we can sieve it, we can remove it en masse, or we can remove it in spits or metre squares. There are many variations and possibilities when it comes to breaking apart an entity, and the ways in which we do it will clearly have an implication for the way we subsequently characterize its content. This is a major concern in issues of stratigraphy and sampling methodology. However, a common critique of this reductionism is the lack of integration at the end – that often, once the parts have been separated out, that is enough. So the typical excavation report has different sections on stratigraphy, finds, animal bones, plant remains, soils, and so on, and integration may be either nonexistent or at a minimal level such as chronology (Jones 2002: 40–50). A common way to see this is as a constant dialectic or hermeneutic between analysis and synthesis, the need to break something apart to see how it works, and in contrast, not to lose sight of the fact that the parts belong together as a whole, and for it to have any meaning, it is only insofar as the parts relate to one another.

This contemporary vision of the archaeological process fits in with postpositivist epistemologies, in which instead of fieldwork or lab work being constituted by neutral or objective data collection which is only subsequently subjected to interpretive analysis and synthesis, they are both equally interpretive but at a different level. However, this tends to elide the important function of material fragmentation and reassembly as a constitutive part of fieldwork; again, to see it not in epistemological terms but in ontological ones. Fieldwork is fundamentally about the dual processes of material disaggregation and assembly. The material acts of separating objects and/or grouping objects after disaggregation involves creating new assemblages – of pottery or bone, of photographs and drawings (Figure 18). The archive incorporates both found and made objects, potsherds and drawings, but what matters here is not so much to distinguish between these as to see that both are mobilized to create a new assemblage or set of assemblages, which can be transported from the field to elsewhere – Latour's immutable mobiles (Latour 1987: 227; 1990: 26). Phrased another way, as I have discussed in an earlier work, the archive makes the analysis of a site iterable – through the archive or publication, we can revisit the site over and over again (Lucas 2001a: 212–14). Iterability and mobility are two of the key characteristics which define the archive. Let me now elaborate on these themes of disaggregation and assembly, taking each process in turn.

Disaggregation

What is it that archaeologists do in the field, materially speaking? This obviously depends on the nature of the fieldwork, for some interventions leave little material effect on sites, such as various forms of topographic or remote survey. In such cases, intervention is primarily about assembling (see next section). However, other types of fieldwork materially alter the nature of the place – whether minimally as in surface collection of artifacts or maximally as in total excavation. In such cases, intervention is largely about material displacement – or more specifically, disaggregation, followed by displacement and partial reaggregation. If you think about it, what we do on an excavation is break down a continuous mass of matter into smaller chunks; we encounter a site at its surface, and it presents itself as one solid, yet heterogeneous entity. The very first act is to circumscribe this material continuum by defining an area of intervention: the limits of excavation; subsequent acts further circumscribe and remove smaller segments of this area, usually according to perceived differences in the soil (e.g. different layers). Critically, moreover, after each act of disaggregation, the remaining material continuum changes its form and offers new possibilities of circumscription; in this way, new layers or objects are thus continually emerging but in ways partially determined by the order of disaggregation. Indeed, the archaeologist often needs to disaggregate

Figure 18. The assembling process: sorting finds as they come out of the ground from a postmedieval site in Iceland (photo courtesy of the author).

the background and/or field around an object (i.e. deposit) or remove another deposit to make this object emerge.

This raises an important aspect of archaeological intervention: movement. One can think of movement in different ways – at one level, it might simply be the tempo or speed at which fieldwork is conducted. For example, one of the advantages of long-term but seasonal projects over short-term, one-off projects is the greater ability the former has for postexcavation analysis to feed back into excavation strategies insofar as the time between seasons is used to study material and critically reflect on the results and direction of fieldwork. This is not impossible on more contracted projects, but because of the accelerated pace of work, it is often much harder. Johnson makes a similar point about the British tradition of landscape survey and how returning to the same places over and over again creates a unique form of intervention quite different to excavation (Johnson 2007). Another aspect of movement is its extent; thus, landscape-based projects involve much more mobile interventions than a single-site excavation, which is almost sedentary by comparison, and indeed often can reveal a very different perspective on sites (e.g. Bradley 2003). More generally, of course, survey and excavation fieldwork practices involve very different forms of intervention and often divide archaeologists into almost antagonistic groups (e.g. Bender et al. 2007: 247–8, 253–7). A third aspect of movement is directionality – this is critical in both survey and excavation, but in quite different ways. Tilley's survey work has shown how the direction of movement can create very different experiences of the same landscape and reveal different details. On excavations, stratigraphy is obviously a key determinant of directionality in the process of intervention, but many sites (especially plough-zone sites) offer a lot more freedom in terms of the order of excavation, as features are arrayed primarily horizontally. Edgeworth provides some interesting examples again of how comprehension of some parts of a site were dependent on excavating other parts first, even if there was no stratigraphic reason to dig one before the other (Edgeworth 2003).

Although these three aspects of movement (speed, extent, direction) are important to understanding the nature of archaeological interventions, both in survey and in excavation, they are a digression from the main topic of this section: disaggregation. The point I return to is how disaggregation is inextricably entwined with the delineation and identification of discrete objects from the material continuum of a site. If circumscription and disaggregation are bound in a recursive process during excavation, the same is also true of another act, that of separation. In disaggregating a deposit, it is reduced into smaller or larger parts, according to the means used – mechanical excavators, spades, trowels, or sieves. All of these break up the soil in different ways and affect the conjoined act of separation. For during this process of disaggregation, separation simultaneously occurs as the majority of the material mass is relocated to a spoil heap, whereas some constituents – finds or samples – are bagged and tagged. Finds (if initially bagged together) and samples then go through another stage of disaggregation as different materials (ceramics, bones, lithics) or individual fragments are separated, whereas soil samples are broken apart in a flotation machine into flots and residues. In this way, excavation as intervention can be considered a serial practice of disaggregation, but one in which, critically, disaggregation is mediated by acts of circumscription and separation which define the objects produced in excavation.

It is these acts of circumscription and separation which are important because they provide the necessary link between the site and the archive – they enable the transference of parts or properties from the one to the other. In the process of disaggregating a solid mass of soil, in the separation of spoil from finds and samples, parts of the site become parts of the archive; in disaggregating a layer, in circumscribing its boundaries and in crumbling portions between ones fingers, its properties, such as dimensions and texture, are transferred onto paper through drawings and words. In short, disaggregation is simultaneously the beginning of an act of assembly – the assembling of the archive.

Assembly

The conventional image of the field archive is that it is a record – a representation of what we observe in the field; its significance lies in the fact that it is taken to be a copy of the physical remains encountered. Conventional archaeological discourse characterizes this copy in terms of objectivity and accuracy – the closer the archive comes to reproducing the original (i.e. the site), the better. The archive strives to be like the original – that is its main goal (hence the archive objective; Roskams 2001: 35). This goal often leads to a proliferation of the archive – its ever-growing size – as new technologies of recording offer new possibilities of the copy. However, there are two problems with this notion. The first is intrinsic to the very concept of the copy; because the archive is seen as a copy, it always carries the burden of trying to be like the original, yet at the same time, by definition, it never can be identical to it; it will thus always be seen as supplemental to the original, secondary and deficient (Derrida 1996). The second concerns the issue of semantic ascent (Quine 1960: 271–6; Gooding 1990; Baird 2004); that is, how do we cross the ontological divide between the world and talking about the world – between the soil, bones, and stone tools and our drawings and descriptions of them? This is essentially the problem of representation. The archive is seemingly of a totally different nature to what it purports to copy – the one a set of inscriptions intended to be read, the other a collection of physical objects. Both problems can be avoided if we rethink the concept of the archive less as a representation or copy and more as a process of translation or transference.

The term 'translation' is not without its problems, too, as we tend to think of it as a purely linguistic process, and it evokes the opposition of original and copy. However, following Roman Jakobson, I argue that 'translation' can be construed in three different ways: intralinguistic, interlinguistic, and intersemiotic (Jakobson 1959). The first refers to rewording something in the same language, the second to rewording in a different language (the conventional meaning of translation), and the third to resignifying in a different sign system altogether – as in translating a novel into a film. It is this last meaning of translation that comes closest to my use of 'translation' here. Moreover, the term 'translation' is also used in geometry to refer to a certain type of symmetrical movement or displacement, and this, too, captures something of the shift of properties between the site and the archive that occurs during intervention. Indeed, this is perhaps the important issue here – more than semantic ascent, the archive as a reproduction is about how the properties of one object (e.g. a posthole) are reproduced or transferred to the other (a drawing of a posthole). Thus, the shift from site to archive should not really be viewed as a shift from the material to the conceptual or representational realm at all, but as a translation of material properties from one material form into another. Such a serial view of the production of archaeological knowledge makes the problem of semantic ascent redundant, as has been well argued by sociologists of science (e.g. Latour & Woolgar 1986; Lynch & Woolgar 1990: 5–6). This is perhaps the major flaw in Edgeworth's otherwise groundbreaking study in which he draws a sharp boundary between what he calls material transactions and acts of inscription (Edgeworth 2003). The archive is just as material as the site itself, from the bags of finds to the folders of recording sheets or even digitally stored data; it is just a different form of materiality.

To rethink the archive as a translation in the sense outlined here also unsettles the conventional asymmetry between original and copy, which both terms (i.e. archive and translation) also imply. For what happens in the process of translation is not unidirectional but bidirectional: the archive is not simply in a passive role with respect to the site but actually acts back on the site itself. This process expresses an idea of the active copy, which one sees in Walter Benjamin's discussion of mechanical reproduction in relation to art and Michael Taussig's notion of mimesis (Benjamin 1992: 211–44; Taussig 1993). Consider a section drawing; conventionally, it is said to represent a cross-section of a deposit or series of deposits. But to draw a section, we must first prepare a vertical face in the ground. In fact, the reason we cut the ground in this particular way is precisely because we are already predisposed to read the soil as if it were a drawing. In short, the way we sculpt a site, the way we intervene with it, is set up precisely for the manner in which we read it in translation. In other words, we want the site to take on the material form of the archive as closely as possible – and not the other way around, as orthodoxy would have it. The archive is not simply a passive copy of what we see in the ground – but we make the ground into a material form according to the material form of our archive (Figure 19). The same can be seen in numerous other examples, such as the grid pegs laid out like a piece of graph paper across the site or the marking out of the edges of a layer with a trowel, as if it were a pencil on paper.

What this example further highlights is the central importance of the tools, equipment, and devices used to mediate between the site and the archive during intervention. Their role in discussions of scientific practice is widely acknowledged (e.g. Gooding 1990; Baird 2004; Lefèvre 2004; Knorr-Cetina 1999; van Helden & Hankins 1994). In one way, such instruments and equipment can be considered various interchangeable prosthetics of the human body, constituting what we might call the archaeological cyborg (cf. Haraway 1991; Clarke 2003). The archaeological fieldworker is never just a person but always a person with or as part of a larger assemblage of other things – measuring tapes, pencils, cameras, trowels, and so on. Archaeological intervention such as fieldwork is possible only because it mobilizes and assembles a series of bodies and objects together, which together produce translations of the site into the archive. Needless to say, these are not archaeological innovations but ones borrowed and adapted from other fields, especially map making and technical drawings. Indeed, most of the processes of translation that archaeologists routinely use today are so taken for granted that they appear obvious and unproblematic, whereas in fact they probably had a contentious early career. As Latour would describe it, they have been black boxed – that is, we no longer need to worry about how or why they work, we just use them (Latour 1987; see also Pinch 1985: 29–30). More contemporary examples of novel translation devices which remain un-blackboxed are the experimental projects in the phenomenological tradition, such as the wooden frames used to record views from Bronze Age

Cutting the trench through
the boundary

Preparing a flat surface

Scored lines in the soil

The field drawing

The final drawing

Figure 19. The translation process: mobilizing properties from one material medium to another – an archaeological section through a medieval turf-built boundary wall in Iceland.

Figure 20. Translation devices. *Top:* Archaeological planning frame in use, which requires the illustrator to be mobile (photo courtesy of the author). *Bottom:* Artist's perspective frame (*griglia*) in use, which requires the illustrator to be immobile (woodcut from Albrecht Dürer's *Painters Manual* of 1525).

house door openings (Bender et al. 1997, 2007) or the cowbells used to record soundscapes in prehistoric enclosures (Hamilton & Whitehouse 2006).

But let us return to more conventional translation devices, and in this respect, it is important to emphasize the dominance the visual field has. Indeed, the privileging of vision over the other senses, of a scopic discourse, is closely linked to the development of cartographic reason in the sixteenth and seventeenth centuries (Pickles 2003; Lefèvre 2004), and it is thus no wonder that it is visual translation devices that remain the most black boxed. In drawing archaeological plans and sections, the material culture of fieldwork is a vitally important part in constituting the record, the archive, of translating what is in the ground into an inscription. In conventional methods, the grid we lay out on the site, the physical pegs we bang into the ground, provide the basic key to the translation process – they act to homogenize the space, to effectively transform the space on the site into a Cartesian grid. Once the site has these grid pegs in, we even begin to start moving around the site in a different way, we experience it in a different way, as part of a prelude to translating the site onto paper. The grid makes the site and a gridded piece of paper equal, commensurable – it makes it possible for us to inhabit the site as if it were a large piece of paper. The grid pegs therefore are a primary key in this translation process; measuring tapes used to plan off the grid can be considered merely temporary extensions of the grid. A planning frame performs the same operation in miniature, and as a device shares similarities to the fifteenth-century *griglia* used in perspective drawing, one of four perspectographs described by Albrecht Dürer (Figure 20). However, there is one vital difference between Dürer's *griglia* and the archaeological planning frame, and that lies in its manner of use; in the former, the illustrator remains stationary to make use of the grid as a perspectival guide, thus producing an Albertian projection which has a vanishing point (Alpers 1989: 138). In the latter, by contrast, the illustrator has to be mobile to produce a Ptolemaic projection with a distance point, which assumes that the observer is both nowhere and everywhere. The introduction of electronic surveying equipment in the 1990s to a large extent reorganized the conventional archaeological cyborg – now the human body is the prosthetic, the attachment required to push a button, whereas the new translating machine does all the rest of the work that grid pegs, tapes, pencil, paper, and the human body used to.

Concurrent with the birth of professional archaeology in the late nineteenth century was the birth of a new translating machine of visual inscription: the camera. The camera performs a completely different type of translation to cartography; if mapping is about vision and space, photography is much more about vision and time. What characterizes the translation of photography, whether stills or video, is not a spatial isomorphy between site and archive but a temporal one – the photograph translates the site at a particular moment or moments in time. This makes the photograph particularly resonant insofar as it captures the ephemerality of the moment. Elizabeth Edwards has talked about the use of photography in anthropology and how it was seen as a way of capturing something which will not be there much longer. Photography was a key tool in salvage ethnography, and she quotes Malinowski's lament that anthropology's object was disappearing at is very moment of recognition (Edwards 2001). The camera and photographic image clearly take on a double resonance in this context. There may be a deep affinity here with the use of photographs in archaeology to capture the ephemerality of fieldwork and its destructive or transformative effect on archaeological remains.

There is no doubt that visual translation through cartography and photography constitutes a major part of the archaeological archive; however, visual translation is also performed through text, through writing. The site diary or unit form which records things like the colour of a deposit relies on producing a textual translation for a visual quality; often this is done simply by drawing on vernacular language, but many archaeologists, especially soil specialists, use a prosthetic such as a Munsell colour chart to aid this translation (see Goodwin 2000). Similar prosthetics are used to characterize other visual qualities such as the extent and nature of inclusions. But textual translation also incorporates nonvisual senses, most particularly touch: the hardness of a deposit or its particle composition is primarily recorded through touch, and again, we often use prosthetics to aid this process. Much less commonly, the others senses of smell, taste, and sound are employed – indeed, these are usually relegated to informal notes or conversation rather than part of a conventional coding. The dominance of a scopic discourse in archaeological translation is fairly clear – almost all our machines are constructed to record visual phenomena, and with new digital technologies this dominance has only been underlined further. It is only recent work in phenomenology which has started to change that, but inevitably the translating devices in such contexts tend to be simple and unsophisticated compared to visual prosthetics (e.g. Hamilton & Whitehouse 2006). However, more generally, the scope for new digital technologies to change the way we engage with the field is becoming increasingly a focus of interest and discussion (e.g. Ryzewski 2009; Charest 2009; Morgan 2009; Shanks 2009; Witmore 2006).

To summarize, the archive prefigures or constitutes the nature of fieldwork so that inscription is already determining in advance the way in which fieldwork is conducted because of the specific nature of the inscribing devices. In this way, the whole process of archaeological intervention is highly ambivalent: not only is the archive produced through fieldwork; it also simultaneously constitutes the nature of fieldwork as a particular type of material engagement. In doing so, it makes the very distinction between the site and the archive fluid and ambiguous, and any distinction really emerges only once the archive leaves the site. Indeed, it is precisely what is portable or mobile that actually defines the archive; once an archive does exist as an independent assemblage, discourse develops around it, not around the site. Archaeological discourse is primarily about plans, photographs, notes, statistics – about the copy, not the original. This has become so ingrained that we do not even notice it any more. To some extent, this is increasingly being realized in the way that the preservation of archives is now considered almost as important a problem as the preservation of sites: archives themselves are becoming monuments and part of cultural heritage, as seen in the U.K. Archaeological Data Service (www.ads. ahds.ac.uk) or the U.S. Digital Archaeological Record (www.tdar.org; Kintigh 2006; Richards 2002, 2008).

Circulating References

THE DISCUSSION in the previous section about fieldwork as a mode of production could be reproduced, with some minor changes for other locales or sites of archaeological work, especially laboratories or finds rooms. However, in discussing locales or spaces of archaeological production, it is easy to slip into an obvious dichotomy between the field and 'home' (e.g. Lucas 2001a: 12–13). However, as Witmore has pointed out, this simplifies what is a more multiple and heterogeneous space (Witmore 2004, 2007); indeed within just the field, there are multiple variations which structure the nature of the field differently, such as the difference between excavation and survey (Bradley 2003), academic and commercial fieldwork (Bradley 2006), amateur and professional or training and research excavations (Everill 2007).

Moreover, these categorizations can easily overlap at the same locale, thus negating any exclusivity implied by the dichotomous way in which I have just presented them. Thus, the field itself is not a homogeneous site, any more than 'home', which includes laboratories, universities, commercial organizations, museums, libraries, and so on. This is not to reject any attempt to classify such sites – the examples given clearly exist and have stabilized as recurrent theatres of operation because of specific historical practices. Moreover, despite their differences, similarities between different fields are to a large extent maintained by the various excavation and survey manuals and contexts of learning and teaching which make the field more like a mobile laboratory. Indeed, whatever the different nature of remains at any site, archaeologists try to reproduce the same set of material conditions for their interventions: site huts, trowels, spades, buckets, surveying tools, and so on. These constitute the mobile laboratory, and in that sense excavation is contra conventional wisdom, a repeatable experiment.

The issue is how such locales (e.g. laboratories, archaeology departments, museums, conference halls) act as channels for the circulation of artifacts or assemblages produced in the field. Indeed, the iterative manner in which such objects circulate through sites actually helps to solidify and stabilize both sites and artifacts and assemblages (Latour 1987, 1999). This is what Latour refers to as circulating reference, which follows not so much a linear path as an expanding network. In this section, I discuss the initial postfield life of the archive: what happens to it between the field and its circulation in academia and other contexts? To some extent, a bifurcation occurs with the archive, as it can enter two different disciplinary streams: museums and archaeology. One might be tempted to say that the 'found' component of the archive (i.e. finds) enters museums, whereas the 'made' component (i.e. records) stays in archaeology, but this is an oversimplification. Archaeologists still study and use the finds, and records can sometimes be the subjects of museum displays. Rather than reduce this to some simple dichotomy, it is better to keep in sight the networked nature of these sites and objects; archaeology is shorthand for a certain route through these sites as much as it is implicated in their construction. I do not focus on museums here but on archaeology as an academic discipline.

Archaeology as Literary Production

I think it is important to recognize that much of archaeology is about producing texts, by which I mean any relatively self-contained 'object' which incorporates written words and images of all kinds (e.g. photographs, line drawings, graphs) and in whatever form (whether conventional print or digital media). Of course, in stretching the definition of a text this way, I am in danger of eliding significant variability in the range of archaeological products, especially the potent distinction between words and images and the largely implicit valuation that attends to each in academic discourse (see e.g. Cochrane and Russell 2007). But I need a term to denote this broad category of archaeological product as distinct from the artifacts, soil samples, and building remains which normally define archaeological activity, and as such, I am considering texts as material products (e.g. a book, journal, slideshow) rather than linguistic entities (i.e. words). If you think about what constitutes the greatest part of archaeological activity, it is about producing texts, from lecture notes to conference papers, from field notes to monographs. Indeed, whatever the value placed on practical experience, in the academy textual production forms the primary basis for student education and academic accreditation. One way of looking at such texts is to see what kind of work they perform in archaeological theatres of operation – classrooms, conference halls, heritage offices, and even the field (for such approaches to images, see Shanks & Webmoor 2010; Perry 2009). This is a rich field of investigation and one which is simply an extension of how I looked at the materiality of fieldwork in the previous section, looking at how tapes and surveying tools, trowels, and pencils perform in the constitution of sites or the field. Moreover, this would require more extensive treatment than I can do justice to here, so instead I consider the nature of this literary production more generally in terms of the construction of archaeological knowledge.

The dominating function of literary production is true not just of archaeology but also perhaps of all academic disciplines; however, it was not always like this. In the seventeenth century there was a key distinction in the emerging experimental sciences between trials and demonstrations; trials were conducted in private and were performed repeatedly and under varying conditions, whereas demonstrations were the perfected experiments, those given in public and reported on in the minutes of meetings (Shapin 1988). Demonstrations were the seventeenth-century precursor to publication, which eventually emerged as the dominant means of persuasion and end product of scientific practice (Shapin 1984). A similar case can be argued for nineteenth-century archaeology, in which the key moment in archaeological society meetings was not the reading of papers but the field trips to sites. Such field trips were the equivalent of demonstrations in the experimental sciences, in which archaeologists could observe and discuss the findings directly. During the early twentieth century, as site reports became increasingly more important in the authorization of knowledge, they also became more and more depersonalized as the third person tone was adopted (Hodder 1989b).

As Shapin has argued in the context of experimental science, the publication of fieldwork or experiments acts as a virtual witness (Shapin 1984); if one is unable to attend experimental demonstrations or field trips and site visits – a fact which must have become increasingly common as the size of the scientific community grew – then a published text acts as a testimonial to the event. Indeed, it is the act of witnessing that was central to establishing the credibility of the experimental sciences in the seventeenth century, a feature which in many ways united the status of evidence in both the natural sciences and history and can even be traced back to jurisprudence (see Chapter 2). Published reports thus acted as proxy witnesses, which is also why in the early days of scientific reporting the narrative was very much in the first person (Dear 1985). The use of the third person was generally reserved for those parts of the account which touched on the setting up of the apparatus and was also largely associated with the work of technicians and assistants to the experimenter. It is thus interesting to see how published reports shifted from predominantly first- to third-person narratives over the course of the nineteenth century. Why this occurs can be seen in relation to similar shifts in the visual component of scientific texts and emergence of objectivity as an epistemic virtue (Daston & Galison 1992, 1997).

As Daston and Galison have argued, objectivity came to be defined in a post-Kantian sense as the absence of subjectivity; the issue in being objective was primarily about how to remove oneself from the equation and was thus linked to the cultivation of a new type of scientific self or subject. In the context of scientific reporting or recording – in this case, visual representations – this meant the production of images in which human input was minimized and the output automated as much as possible; it is no coincidence that such a development emerged alongside that of photography. Yet it also affected scientific drawings, so that instead of an idealized image or collage being used to depict a plant or animal for example, a range of specimens were increasingly favoured, thus showing the diversity of types and leading to a common nineteenth-century literary product, the atlas. The obvious counterpart of this new epistemic virtue of objectivity in textual representation is the elision of first-person narratives in favour of the third person. However, such an ideal of objectivity was always under severe strain. Daston and Galison argued that two responses ultimately crystallized in the late nineteenth and early twentieth centuries: to attempt to reduce the subjective element even further, chiefly by relying on more mathematical and graphic forms of representation, or to accept subjectivity and control it through what they call trained judgement. The latter in particular became very important in relation to the contemporary institutionalization of the sciences in universities and led to standardized and collective forms of pedagogy.

The tensions between the ideal of objectivity and the acceptance of the subjective element increasingly emerged as an explicit concern in archaeological texts from the early to mid-twentieth century, although it is perhaps a more common element from the later part of that century. More particularly, the tension between, say, field diaries and standardized recording on pro forma sheets in the case of texts, or that between artistry and graphic convention in the case of site plans and artifact illustrations, attests to the continued tension felt between the ideal of objectivity and the role of the subject. Consider, for example, the tension often described in manuals about how to draw sections, specifically whether or not to draw any solid lines indicating distinctions between layers (Adkins & Adkins 1989: 82, 125). A common solution is and was to have two section drawings: a naturalistic one portraying what the archaeologist saw and an interpretive one showing the archaeologist's interpretation. Such distinctions between descriptive and interpretive illustrations are a common feature of archaeological monographs, and they mirror the common distinction in unit sheets between physical description and interpretation. Expressed in the growth of methods manuals, the notion of trained judgement constitutes an important part of the cultivation of the archaeological self and was indeed explicitly commented on in early texts. Babington's *Introductory Lecture on Archaeology* to the University of Cambridge in 1865 devoted several pages to the qualities necessary for an archaeologist (Babington 1865: 63–8), whereas Petrie's *Methods and Aims* and Droop's *Archaeological Excavation* devote a whole chapter to the topic (Petrie 1904; Droop 1915). However, from the mid-twentieth century, when such manuals became a common feature, explicit or extended discussion of such qualities receded, to be replaced by more detailed instructions of procedure which the reader was supposed to learn and reproduce. Thus, typical modern manuals include chapters or sections on different methods of trenching according to the type of site, how to plan, how to draw sections, how to photograph, and so on, often with extreme detail with regard to technique (see e.g. Barker 1982; Carver 2009). Even though such instructions are given in earlier manuals, they take on a much more central role in subsequent texts. Objectivity was ingrained in the very style of pedagogy.

Such epistemic virtues are now inscribed in archaeological organizations like the British Institute of Field Archaeologists, the European Association of Archaeologists, and the U.S. Register of Professional Archaeologists, which all have codes of conduct and standards of practice. The emphasis is on ethical and responsible behaviour and tends to follow the conventional structure of the archaeological operation as discussed earlier in this chapter – proper research designs, proper standards of recording, obligations to ensure proper storage of material and dissemination of results. More detailed guides to good practice are enshrined in field and other manuals, university courses, and so on. However, such ethical demands do not exist solely in these abstract texts; they are also ingrained in practice and especially in the tools and other objects mobilized in the field: it is not only agency that is distributed between nonhuman entities but also morality (Bennett 2010). The seminal paper on this issue was Langdon Winner's 'Do Artifacts Have Politics?', which generated a lot of argument, not least because it became so widely quoted (Winner 1980; Joerges 1999a, 1999b; Woolgar & Cooper 1999). More recently, Latour provides several classic examples of how objects embody ethical and legal demands, such as self-closing doors, seat belts, and speed bumps (Latour 1992; also see Latour 2002b). In each of these examples, specific actions have been taken away from humans and delegated to objects. Thus, closing a door after oneself is an act which is delegated to a piston and spring mechanism; what is important, though, is the reason for such delegation: it counters the unreliability of human users to close the door after opening it. The reasons you want the door closed are various but might include preventing heat from escaping out of a room or building, reducing noise from outside, and so on, which in turn save money or create a quiet environment. The chain of effects relating to such actions is thus inevitably tied in to certain moral codes – such as quietness in a library. The self-closing door is thus not simply a functional device but a moral one, too; a moral behaviour is delegated to the door, which means that its design and construction can be viewed as what Verbeek has called 'ethics by other means' (Verbeek 2006: 369). It is not hard to think of archaeological examples. Consider a pro forma recording sheet with a series of prompts; this is not just about creating standardized records but also about creating a moral archaeologist by defining the range and nature of the archaeologist's choice in making records.

Objectivity thus needs to be viewed not so much as an epistemological position as an epistemic virtue; it is an ethical issue before it is an epistemological one. As such, it contributes to the valuation of literary production because it occupies the space between observing the world and writing about it or representing it; if one side of this equation is missing, the value of the other side automatically drops. We all know that old quip about archaeologists who write but don't dig, but equally bad are those archaeologists who dig but do not write (e.g. unpublished sites). Indeed, if anything, the latter is often considered worse than the former; in the former, it tends to be seen as a bad reflection only on the archaeologist concerned, whereas in the latter, the whole discipline of archaeology seems to suffer for this deficiency. In this sense, the asymmetry clearly marks out a direction for the archaeological operation. The whole archaeological process is characterized as a movement towards textualization – from intervention to archive, from archive to publication – with a valuation based on the degree of textualization. Another way to see this is as a progression towards discursive closure: from field notes and/or archive to published monograph, where field notes are very much working texts, drafts – incomplete – whereas publication is conventionally considered the final word. Of course, history shows that publications are often not the final word, and sites can be reinterpreted – especially if one goes back to the incomplete texts (i.e. the archive). But then this perhaps just shows that the progression is reversible – that what we are dealing with is more of a pendulum process between archive and publication than a simple progression. Nevertheless, the structure of the discourse remains one set around the terms of incomplete and complete.

This can be further explored by looking at three areas in which a tension is felt over a transgression of this structure. First, there is the demand to produce a coherent narrative while still in the field – as an interim report, for the press, for exhibitions; these often give us an uneasy feeling, because we have not had a chance to go through all the information; we have not analysed all the finds; we have not completed the process. We are doing something which should be at the end. A second and related point is the need to explain or show to nonarchaeologists the process of fieldwork while in the field and the resentment this often incurs. It is as if people should not be seeing archaeology in action, as if they have no right to be there: their proper place is in the museum or the bookshop, they should see archaeology only at the end, once we have produced our narrative and completed the process. They are too early. Even when public tours are organized, when the behind-the-scenes is promoted, it is usually carefully controlled with fences, pathways, signs, and so on. Finally, there is the problem of unpublished projects – consider all the sites that remain unwritten or confined to hard-to-obtain grey reports, or that take decades to publish. We feel that archaeology is losing out, that at worst, the site maybe should never have been excavated in the first place. In all three cases, the tensions are brought on by temporal displacement – in the first two, something is happening too early; in the last, something is not happening at all – we either have to produce a coherent narrative before we are ready or wait endlessly for the final narrative. Through this displacement, these examples reveal the dynamic of incompleteness or completeness in the construction of discourse about archaeological work. These tensions may be unusual, or they may be far more common than we like to admit – either way, I highlight them because I think they express anxieties around the process of textualization.

Implicit in this conceptual structure, though, is also a politics of representation or vocality in the discipline of archaeology. To be a 'proper' or 'full' archaeologist, you need to be producing complete discourses – you need to be writing for publication. When one looks at representability in archaeology, there is an obvious correlation between power and authorship; the archaeologist who writes and publishes is more visible than the one who does not. In terms of fieldwork and project monographs or papers, authorship is often on a scale of vocality or presence, which reflects a valuation ascribed to the work directly related to the completeness of the discourse. Thus, at the bottom of this scale is the excavator, and his or her presence in the text is almost always excluded or at most relegated to the acknowledgments, even though the excavator is often the primary producer of the archive; but then this is exactly the point – the excavator is aligned with an incomplete or marginalized discursivity, whereas the director, as author, is usually the centre of the discourse. Specialists who produce reports on aspects of the site occupy a middle ground – they produce final texts, because they produce final or definitive discourses on parts of the site. Some archaeologists are trying to move towards a more democratic vocality in texts – for example, following the convention in the natural experimental sciences in which texts are multiauthored. Another option is taken up with the Ludlow Collective, a group of North American archaeologists who worked on an early twentieth-century site of class struggle. But these exceptions only prove the rule that the extent of vocality and representation in archaeology is directly linked to a measure of discursivity and the extent of its completeness.

However, much recent thought has been arguing precisely for a more open and incomplete discourse; most typically expressed, it is the move away from grand narratives, but on a more specific level, it is also about new forms of discourse which incorporate incompleteness by design (e.g. Web-based and hypertext productions). What we have is a dynamic text. In a way, such dynamic texts are very much like field archives, for – at least in principle – an archive is always dynamic and capable of being worked on or added to. What is interesting about such dynamic texts, though, is that they throw up problems of referability; when you reference a Web site, you need to mention the date, because it can, and probably will, change. A similar issue arises with editions of printed works, albeit on a slower pace. This issue of referability has even more important consequences in relation to the production of knowledge. As Latour has suggested, one of the ways in which new facts become established is the degree of citation in the literature, as this is a reflection of the extent to which others give credence to scientific statements. Such a 'proof race' is all about gaining allies and gathering adherents to a claim so that the claim is gradually converted to a fact (Latour 1987, 1990). We can all appreciate the idea that the more an article or book is cited, the more prominence it has in discourse and is thus a reflection of its importance. However, it is the long-term continuity of citation that really counts – contentious knowledge may unleash a flurry of publications citing an original paper, but the true test of value is when that paper is still regularly cited years later or enters textbooks. Such citation acts to stabilize an interpretation and convert it into a fact.

Latour's observations on the importance of citation in the natural and/or experimental sciences are revealing, but it is questionable how applicable they are to a science like archaeology. Statements in the archaeological literature tend to be either already presented as facts, as in site reports or artifactual analyses, or offered as interpretations which tend to remain cited only as long as their theoretical basis is in vogue. It is as if the proof race simply did not exist in archaeology – although of course it may be equally true of most experimental science papers, insofar as few engender any debate. Nonetheless, the issue is how statements stabilize to become facts, whereby a fact is simply an accepted and noncontentious statement about the nature of reality. In reports on experiments, all kinds of statements are made – some are already facts (usually the conditions of the experiment), and others are offered in the hope of attaining that status (usually the results of the experiment). In reports of archaeological fieldwork, however, it is rare for any statements of results not to be given or treated as already factual; even statements tentatively expressed to draw attention to their equivocal nature can tacitly slip into a more certain mode in subsequent citations. Unlike experimental scientists, archaeologists appear much less equivocal over the results of fieldwork – why is this?

If one compares the literary products of experimental science and archaeology, the answer should be fairly obvious; experimental science reports are often brief, highly condensed texts in which a lot of data and lab work are distilled down to a regular or recurrent phenomenon. It is not each individual event or particular that is important but rather the general pattern that emerges; the pattern is what is offered as a candidate for a fact. This, however, is an historical development; early experimental science reports were highly detailed, with a strong concern for particulars (Dear 1985); in part, this is also related to the initial interest in the oddities of nature (Daston 1998). Indeed, one of the points about experimental science is that it often produces phenomena not ordinarily observed in nature (Hacking 1983: 220–32). In archaeological fieldwork, in contrast, it is precisely the particular that matters, which is why such texts are often hundreds of pages long. The presentation of every find and layer is considered essential, even if only in minimal form; indeed, the problem facing most archaeologists who wish to publish fieldwork results is how to balance the need for an acceptable level of detail with keeping the text to a readable and cost-effective size – even if new digital and Web-based media make the presentation of such details more versatile. The differences in the literary products of experimental sciences and archaeology are thus quite central to the nature of knowledge production and facts in each case. Yet at the same time as archaeological fieldwork reports present hundreds and thousands of new facts every year, other archaeological texts which draw on this literature and combine it with historical or ethnographic texts to create interpretive narratives of the past produce no facts at all. Either they attempt to propose statements as facts, offering generalizations in the mode of the experimental sciences, or they simply offer stories, which may also incorporate generalizations but with no commitment to being factual. In few cases (if at all) does one see such interpretive statements ever elevated to the status of fact in the same sense as statements given in a site report.

This suggests that we are dealing with very different forms of knowledge and facts in archaeology than in the experimental sciences; I would not suggest that this reflects some kind of distinction between the natural and social sciences, or even strictly speaking between a science concerned with particulars versus one concerned with generalities. Invoking Windleband's old distinction between nomothetic and ideographic sciences is not very helpful (see e.g. Lyman & O'Brien 2004); the issue is not about an opposition between particulars and generalities but about degrees of generality and particularity. It is helpful to think of this in terms of the common idea of excavation as the unrepeatable experiment; Edgeworth has suggested that repeatable experiments are not only possible but also common on excavations, in which the interpretation of a feature can be tested by repeating the excavation on a similar feature or on a different part of the same feature (e.g. segments along an enclosure ditch; Edgeworth 2003). Conversely, it has been argued that few experiments are really repeated, as in experimental science, each experiment usually makes modifications to the previous one to resolve problems or achieve an anticipated outcome (Knorr-Cetina 1999). Indeed, repeating someone else's experiment is often a difficult and contentious task (Collins 1985). Repeatability in a sense encapsulates what I mean by degrees of generality or particularity insofar as it rests on the distinction between recurrent and unique phenomena. What counts as a recurrent and/or unique phenomenon is itself an interpretation and varies according to the context and questions being posed.

However, the key issue here is perhaps to link these degrees of particularity and generality to the extent of their citation – or, using Latour's terminology, to their mobility. For example, a site report makes a certain number of statements about what was found at a particular locale – structures, pottery, animal bones. When another archaeologist excavating a different site finds a similar range of features with similar characteristics, he or she would conventionally cite this earlier report. The statements about certain objects from the original site are juxtaposed to ones from the new site and establish a connection; as other sites are excavated with similar features, so the chain extends. Such citations are very typical in traditional European finds reports and underlie important archaeological methods such as typological dating, in which more often than not the chain recedes into the background and becomes black boxed. For example, when I was studying Romano-British pottery, I used date ranges for certain wares or vessel forms from various general texts or even other site reports, but the date ranges were always based on some earlier association between a certain type and some dated object, usually a coin from a key site. Often the key site was excavated decades, if not a century, earlier, and although the chain can usually be followed, more often than not it isn't. Of course, sometimes these original associations need revising, but because they are being tested each time someone studies an assemblage and compares pottery whose typological dates may derive from multiple different sources, the original association is usually only strengthened and further black boxed.

Such effects work not only on things like dates but also on the definition of types. Indeed, a site on which a lot of original associations and definitions were first characterized often becomes known as the type site – its particular features travel or move across to other sites, and the further they move, the more they become generalized and less particular. For example, consider how the site of La Tène in Switzerland, discovered in 1857, swiftly became the type site for the La Tène period in late Iron Age Europe from the 1870s and 1880s with Hans Hildebrand's and later Otto Tischler's chronologies. Such naming of periods or cultures after sites was a common practice in the early decades of European prehistoric archaeology and expresses the way objects and sites are mobilized, even if the site itself is today not as important as it once was for understanding or defining the period or culture in question. However, in archaeology it is clear that in most cases such mobility is restricted; you might find Beaker or Beaker-type pottery throughout Western Europe on late Neolithic and early Bronze Age sites, but you won't find it in the Americas or the Near East during any period. The only way to make archaeological entities more mobile is to simplify their attributes; for example, as soon as one talks about pottery in the generic, one can then start to make connections all over the world – for example, between pottery production and sedentism or farming, both equally generic terms, it should be noted. The problem is that although such generalizations do work to varying extents, they are inevitably few and far between. But then most archaeologists are not that concerned with mobilizing their entities on a global scale. However, all this ignores another set of entities which archaeologists regularly use, yet are not, strictly speaking, archaeological: entities such as chiefdoms and states or persons and cultures. These are the big concepts in archaeology, those which are global and can be mobilized on a Bronze Age site in the south of England as easily as on thirteenth- and fourteenth-century sites in the U.S. Midwest. These kinds of entities I largely ignored in the previous chapter, even though they form a key part of the archaeological literature. Why are these concepts so mobile?

In the first place, their mobility is wider than archaeology; indeed, in most cases they derive from related disciplines, especially social anthropology and history. When an archaeologist claims that his or her site exhibits features characteristic of a chiefdom, there is a double mobilization going on; on the one hand, the archaeologist is simplifying certain features of the archaeology such as uneven distribution of valuable artifacts or the presence of monumental architecture to make them more mobile; on the other hand, he or she borrows the concept of chiefdom from an ethnographic context, which itself has been simplified from the particular context (e.g. a Polynesian society) to make it mobile. These two simplifications thus easily conjoin, as they have few facets. Exactly the same process is going on when archaeologists discuss personhood; using fragmentation as a simplification from the archaeological record and linking it to generalized features of fractal or individual persons from the ethnographic literature. Such mobilizations are common across the theoretical spectrum. For some archaeologists, some of the time, such mobilizations or generalizations work; in that sense, such entities can be considered real. However, there is no general consensus on these matters, and although this in itself is not necessarily problematic, we might want to consider how much archaeology actually gains by such mobilization. What I mean is, when we simplify so much, do we actually learn anything from such mobilizations?

This brings us back to the interpretive dilemma with which I opened the book; for on the one hand, if our entities become too mobile, they risk becoming vacuous, simply because they can fit with almost any configuration of archaeological evidence. On the other hand, because so many of the entities derive from empirical contexts which are non-archaeological, no amount of simplification will make them fit our data. This is why I have suggested that we need to remain as close to our empirical roots as possible and critically reflect on the specific nature of the archaeological record – as materiality, as a process, and as an intervention. I am not arguing against an active and healthy dialogue with other disciplines, or against travelling concepts (see e.g. Bal 2002). However, I do think that we need to take our own discipline more seriously, which means attending to the particular ways in which archaeologists engage in the material world and the nature of that world.

⋯7⋯

A 'New' Social Archaeology?

I
N THE PREVIOUS TWO CHAPTERS, I have attempted to try to reforge
some connections between the increasingly fragmented discourses
that have developed around the concept of the archaeological
record. In Chapter 5, I addressed the relations between materiality and
formation theory through the processes of materialization and dematerialization, exploring objects and events in terms of assemblages and
exploring residues in terms of the irreversibility of assemblages. The
very tension between the processes of materialization and dematerialization was ultimately interpreted in terms of memory through the
processes of inscription and erasure and led to the idea of the archaeological record as an autoarchive. The archaeological intervention, as
discussed in Chapter 6, can be considered simply a continuation of this
process, albeit in a radical way; as such, the archaeological operation
itself is a form of rematerialization, constructing new assemblages and
objects by combining old parts (e.g. potsherds, stone tools, soils) and
new products (e.g. photographs, drawings, texts). But it is not simply
rematerialization, it is also, often at least, simultaneously a dematerialization. Consider an excavation trench; often excavation is called
destruction (see Chapter 2), and certainly in a material sense, it acts
to erase all material memories of the past within its confines. What
is left, literally and figuratively, is a hole in the ground. For what the
trench itself tells us about the archaeological act that occurred there

is often very little; materially speaking, it can look no different from if we had dug it all out in one scoop with a machine, except perhaps tidier. So where is the real material trace of our excavation? It has been transferred into new forms – paper records, photographs, bags of finds, and samples. The archive of an excavation is thus simultaneously the archive of the excavation process and the site itself. From an operational or materializing perspective, the archaeological record is thus both given and created, simultaneously across all its elements.

There is an important symmetry between the nature of archaeological entities and the nature of archaeological intervention; both should be understood in terms of the assembling and disassembling of various elements; both should be understood as forms of archive and memory work. I think it is critical that we use the same language and approach for understanding the past as we do for understanding our understanding of the past – not only symmetry, though, but also continuity. An archaeological site can be seen in terms of assemblages, in a double sense – the residues of past assemblages and the creation of new assemblages, incorporating those residues. Thus, it is through the concept of (de)materialization as a process of (dis)assembly that we can begin to reconnect these different facets of the archaeological record and, in doing so, fight against the fragmentation of archaeological discourse. It is important to stress, though, that in using the term 'materialization', I wish to avoid any connotation of the immaterial as a separate ontological realm, such as the mental. The tension implied in the concept of materialization is that between the potential (or virtual, to use Deleuzian-Whiteheadean terms) and the actual, not the mental and the material, as discussed at the end of Chapter 4. Materialization is about the actualization of new combinations or assemblages from the rich potentialities which inhere in already existing entities. Entities always hold something back, hold more than we can see at any one time, and that is how novelty is possible.

However, there remains in my mind one major issue which needs tackling, namely the unease (or lack of unease) many feel with regard to the posthumanocentrism that seems to accompany the kind of approach I have been advocating in this book. For many, if not most, archaeologists, archaeology is fundamentally about humans; indeed, much of the feminist-inspired critique of processualism was centred on rehumanizing the past, putting faces to the blobs of prehistory (Tring-ham 1991). Does not this call for a defence of things, for a symmetrical archaeology, directly fly in the face of such a vision of archaeology? (Johnson 2010: 226). Posthumanocentrism is a complex issue, and one has to be careful to disentangle various positions. On the one hand, it is clear that adopting the approaches of actor-network theory (ANT) or object-oriented ontology (OOO) requires that we displace the human subject from the centre of our understanding of the 'social' or reality in general. When it comes to explaining the archaeological record, we ought to assume symmetry of treatment between humans and non-humans. On the other hand, we clearly cannot even talk about the archaeological record without presupposing some kind of privileging of the human; the presence of humans is what defines the archaeological and separates it from, say, the geological or palaeontological record. But such a presence should not be read in terms of providing a central point to the discipline; rather, the human simply defines its limits. Of course this is a construction that reflects a deeper belief in the special-ness of the human; for example, no other species has its own material or fossil record singled out, but rather they all are lumped together under palaeontology – even if individual scientists devote their careers to a particular species. Moreover, the geological record contains traces of human presence, just as the archaeological record is replete with the remains of other species and geological processes. Yet even if we admit that reality is more hybrid than our labels suggest, humans are still real entities like fruit flies and electrons, and there is no reason they should not form the focus of special study any less than fruit flies or electrons. Any less? No, but then the issue is rather, Any more? Well, surely as humans ourselves, why wouldn't we be especially interested in this species above all others, and privilege it within our division of sciences?

For me, the question here is how we understand this notion of priv-ileging; the critiques offered by ANT and OOO largely revolve around how the human subject is privileged in explanations of the world, whether through the Kantian notion of the transcendental subject or the Durkheimian notion of society. They do not – as far as I read them – reject the privileging of the human as an object of study in itself. Nonetheless, the absent presence of the human subject in many ANT approaches in places where it is not acknowledged is something that needs further consideration (see e.g. Fowles 2010). As such, I think archaeology always will and should be, first and foremost, about people, not things. The more relevant question is how people are treated in archaeological narratives vis-à-vis other things. This is particularly important in connection to my discussion in Chapter 5 about archaeological entities and new kinds of beings. Let me explore this question with a brief dialogue about humans and other objects between two hypothetical protagonists.

CHAIR: Think about the book you are reading now; how do we explain it?

HUMANIST: Surely it is the product of a human mind, whether we are talking about the content (author) or its physical form (e.g. cover designer, layout person, print operator)?

POSTHUMANIST: No, this is to forget all those other actors involved, such as printing machines, buildings, computers, trucks, and so on. The book cannot be distilled down to its human essence as if this were all that mattered. It is the residue of an assemblage of multiple agents, humans and nonhumans.

HUMANIST: Well, yes, but let us just take one aspect, that of authorship; of course, for the book to be written, it needed the computer (or typewriter, or pen and paper) as well as the human author, but only one of these 'agents' could have 'mobilized' (to use your terminology!) all the others towards this end. The human intention is what counts!

POSTHUMANIST: Humans can intend all they like, but if the computer (or other objects of inscription) does not exist, then that intention can never be realized; in fact one could suggest that the intention to inscribe and the objects which perform the inscription coemerge. Do you think a Palaeolithic person ever had an intention to write a book? The very idea is nonsensical.

HUMANIST: Of course it is, but that only reinforces my point – who made the computer or typewriters or pens and paper? Humans!

POSTHUMANIST: Actually computers are made by other computers, as well as by other machines and humans of course; the same goes for any other object you choose to name. Here you are just repeating the error of your first comment about who made the book – choosing to ignore other agents.

HUMANIST: Yes, but it is humans who come up with the ideas, who design these things. They would not have existed without humans.

POSTHUMANIST: Or without other tools which equally design the object in terms of the affordances they offer. You have to think only about the different types of stone tool you can make when you only have a cobble on the one hand or a hammer and bone point on the other; whatever idea or design the human has, it is limited or enabled by the other tools used. I go back to my question – pick any object you like, and you will find it is very rare that only human hands were involved in its production. Even the most primordial hominid tool of a stone chopper needed another stone to bash against to create its cutting edge.

HUMANIST: Even if I grant you that, two stones together will never create a hand axe; the one indispensable agent is the human. I take up your challenge and throw it back; pick up any object you like, and although you can substitute any of the agents involved in its production, you will get only material culture if one of the agents remains constant: humans. Take away the human, and you no longer have material culture. This is what makes material culture distinct from other things – this is why we can do archaeology. Because we recognize the human in objects.

Although contrived, this dialogue sums up some of the issues and problems around the relation between people and things. On the one hand, there is a gut feeling that the human agent somehow is more important than all the other things in the question of material culture, but on the other hand, no matter how long we play the game of causation, humans will always be closely shadowed by other things. They will not be shaken off, whether we seek the origins of material culture in history (the evolution of technology) or practice (the externalization of intention). Most objects always involve other objects in their production, whereas the intention to make an object cannot really precede the affordances of objects – both come into being together. So how do we resolve this deadlock? How can we talk about material culture as a human phenomenon, about archaeology as a science of the human past, if we cannot privilege humans in any way?

The answer, I believe, lies in shifting the whole debate away from conventional ideas of causation. The problem is, in defining explanation in terms of simple causation, we are also implicitly retaining a prior and posterior relation (i.e. cause and effect) in the explanandum. One thing has to be the cause of another; one thing has to be reduced to another; one thing has to be the origin. The protagonist who was arguing for privileging the human was taking the wrong tack – he or she was trying to argue in terms of principal causation. Only in the protagonist's last point is there a glimmer of an alternative argument. There, humans are described as indispensable, as nonsubstitutable; any item of material culture probably has nonhuman agents implicated in its existence, but any item of material culture also always has to have a human implicated. The error lies in reading this necessary condition in terms of privileged status in explanation. Humans are necessary to explain material culture, but not sufficient, and not even always central. Humans act as a connective tissue rather than as some originary explanans. This leads to a very different view of human history, one which looks at it in terms of colonization rather than origins – about how humans facilitate and mobilize connections rather than from where, when, or how things ultimately came.

Clive Gamble has talked about this in terms of our narratives of human evolution, how it has been dominated by origins research and agendas; he argues for an approach which focuses rather on how humans have spread out and colonized the planet (Gamble 1993). We can take Gamble's point, which refers to what one might call extensive colonization, and apply it more generally to ask about how humans have colonized the immediate environment, that is, the material world around them; let us call this intensive colonization. I see such intensive colonization in terms of what Renfrew has called material entanglement. Renfrew discusses the concept of material entanglement in relation to what he calls the sapient paradox (Renfrew 2001). Why did it take so long – about thirty thousand years after the appearance of biologically modern humans – for complex societies to emerge? (but see McBrearty & Brooks 2000 and Renfrew & Morley 2009 for more recent and varied discussion of this complex issue). What made the difference? Put simply, the answer is human entanglement with material culture. It is interesting to see the idea of material entanglement taken up by Hodder in his discussion of neo-thingness (Hodder 2004; also see Hodder 2011) or a similar perspective espoused by Bjørnar Olsen, who captures the idea here very well:

If there is one history running all the way down from Olduvai Gorge to Post-Modernia, it must be one of increasing materiality – and that more and more tasks are delegated to non-human actors: more and more actions mediated by things.

(Olsen 2003: 88)

The link between history and material entanglement – or as Latour would put it, the delegation of tasks to nonhuman actors – is highly significant, especially because of its evolutionary undertones. For the implication is that these material entanglements create gravitational forces, which have an impact upon the nature of historical change. Significantly, Hodder remarks that with this increase in entanglement, one would expect more inertia, yet as he points out, the opposite is the case. Referring back to Renfrew's sapient paradox, it is only with the proliferation of material culture and increase in entanglement that human history really starts to get going (Hodder 2004: 50). I have also linked this issue of entanglement to Marx's concept of the burden of history and how we need to be sensitive to historical gravity and how this is itself historically contingent (Lucas 2007a). Most of prehistory (i.e. before Renfrew's 'creative explosion') might be characterized by an unbearable lightness, because the weight of the past is much less, precisely because material entanglement is also much less.

The ideas of material entanglement and what I have called intensive colonization evoke a very different metaphor for the historical process; instead of the linear path of evolutionism and origins research, the idea of an expanding sphere is more apt. History does not trace out a path in time or act out on a given ground; it carries time (and space) with it; it alters the world as it moves. So where does all this leave us with regard to a posthumanocentric archaeology? To return to the basic point: archaeology is defined by its interest in the human, which provides the very parameters of its study. Even though archaeologists study all kinds of entities, from insects to swords, humans provide the connective tissue, the thread that links those entities together. An insect with no human connection would be of no interest to an archaeologist, except as a methodological tool. At the same time, the purely human is not what should interest us as archaeologists either, but new entities, new worlds which have emerged as humans have colonized their environment – extensively or intensively. In a sense, we have always had a word for this: 'society' or 'the social'. As I argued in Chapter 5, the problem with the social is that it got reified into an abstraction, a quasi-transcendent entity, rather than an immanent process of aggregation. My concepts of containment and enchainment, drawing on Deleuze's and DeLanda's concepts of territorialization and coding, were attempts to keep the social grounded in material practices. As I see it, archaeology is a science of new entities, new assemblages, which we can call social insofar as the human component acts as the connective tissue. Societies are real, material assemblages composed of people, stones, plates, and horses; they are not transcendent entities which only exist through human individuals (e.g. as rules, beliefs, dispositions, structures). In this sense, archaeology is, then, about the social more than it is about the human; we can call it posthumanocentric if we like, posthuman even, but only in the sense that we are studying a world after humans have entered into it. The social *is* the posthuman in this sense.

REFERENCES

Åberg, N., 1929. Typologie (Typologische Methode), in *Reallexikon der Vorgeschichte* (vol. 13), ed. M. Ebert, Berlin: Walter De Gruyter, 508–16.

Adkins, L., & R. Adkins, 1989. *Archaeological Illustration*, Cambridge: Cambridge University Press.

Allen, S. H., 1995. 'Finding the Walls of Troy': Frank Calvert, Excavator. *American Journal of Archaeology*, 99(3), 379–407.

Allen, S. H., 1999. *Finding the Walls of Troy. Frank Calvert & Heinrich Schliemann at Hisarlik*, Berkeley: University of California Press.

Allison, P. M., 1992. Artefact Assemblages: Not 'the Pompeii Premise', in *Papers of the Fourth Conference of Italian Archaeology*, ed. E. Herring, R. Whitehouse, & J. Wilkins, London: Accordia Research Centre, 49–56.

Almgren, B., 1995. The Development of the Typological Theory in Connection with the Exhibition in the Museum of National Antiquities in Stockholm, in *Oscar Montelius. 150 years*, ed. P. Åström, Stockholm: Kungl Vitterhets Historie och Antikvilets Akademien, 23–39.

Alpers, S., 1989. *The Art of Describing. Dutch Art in the Seventeenth Century*, Harmondsworth: Penguin.

Altekamp, S., 2004. The Resistance of Classical Archaeology against Stratigraphic Excavation, in *Digging in the Dirt. Excavation in a New Millennium*, ed. G. Carver, Oxford: Archaeopress, 143–9.

Ammerman, A. J., & M. W. Feldman, 1974. On the 'Making' of an Assemblage of Stone Tools. *American Antiquity*, 39(4), 610–16.

Andrén, A., 1985. *Den urbana scenen. Städer och samhälle i det medeltida Danmark*, Malmö, Sweden: Liber.

Andrén, A., 1998. *Between Artifacts and Texts. Historical Archaeology in Global Perspective*, New York: Plenum Press.

Andrews, G., J. Barrett, & J. S. C. Lewis, 2000. Interpretation Not Record: The Practice of Archaeology. *Antiquity*, 74, 525–30.

Appadurai, A. (ed.), 1986. *The Social Life of Things. Commodities in Cultural Perspective*, Cambridge: Cambridge University Press.

Ascher, R., 1961. Analogy in Archaeological Interpretation. *Southwestern Journal of Anthropology*, 17, 317–25.

Ascher, R., 1968. Time's Arrow and the Archaeology of a Contemporary Community, in *Settlement Archaeology*, ed. K. C. Change, Palo Alto, CA: National Press Books, 43–52.

Atkinson, R. J. C., 1946. *Field Archaeology*, London: Methuen.

Atkinson, R. J. C., 1956. *Stonehenge*, Harmondsworth: Penguin.

Atkinson, R. J. C., 1957. Worms and Weathering. *Antiquity*, 31, 219–33.

Audouze, F., 2002. Leroi-Gourhan, a Philosopher of Technique and Evolution. *Journal of Archaeological Research*, 10(4), 277–306.

Auslander, L., A. Bentley, L. Halevi, H. O. Sibum, & C. Witmore, 2009. AHR Conversation: Historians and the Study of Material Culture. *American Historical Review*, 114(5), 1355–404.

Babington, C., 1865. *Introductory Lecture on Archaeology*, Cambridge: Deighton, Bell.

Bailey, D. W., 2001. Review of J. Chapman (2000) *Fragmentation in Archaeology*. *American Anthropologist*, 103(4), 1181–2.

Bailey, G. N., 1981. Concepts, Time-Scales and Explanation in Economic Prehistory, in *Economic Archaeology*, ed. A. Sheridan & G. N. Bailey, Oxford: British Archaeological Reports International Series 96, 97–117.

Bailey, G. N., 1987. Breaking the Time Barrier. *Archaeological Review from Cambridge*, 6, 5–20.

Bailey, G. N., 2007. Time Perspectives, Palimpsests and the Archaeology of Time. *Journal of Anthropological Archaeology*, 26, 198–223.

Bailey, G. N., 2008. Time Perspectivism: Origins and Consequences, in *Time in Archaeology. Time Perspectivism Revisited*, ed. S. Holdaway & L. Wandsnider, Salt Lake City: University of Utah Press, 13–30.

Baird, D., 2004. *Thing Knowledge. A Philosophy of Scientific Instruments*, Berkeley: University of California Press.

Bal, M., 2002. *Travelling Concepts in the Humanities. A Rough Guide*, Toronto: University of Toronto Press.

Bapty, I., & T. Yates (eds.), 1990. *Archaeology after Structuralism*, London: Routledge.

Barad, K., 1998. Getting Real: Technoscientific Practices and the Materialization of Reality. *Differences. A Journal of Feminist Cultural Studies*, 10(2), 87–126.

Barad, K., 2003. Posthumanist Performativity: Toward an Understanding of How Matter Comes to Matter. *Signs*, 28(3), 801–31.

Barad, K., 2007. *Meeting the Universe Halfway. Quantum Physics and the Entanglement of Matter and Meaning*, Durham, NC: Duke University Press.

Barker, P., 1980. Rabies Archaeologorum: A Reply. *Antiquity*, 54, 19–20.

Barker, P., 1982. *Techniques of Archaeological Excavation*, London: Batsford.

Barrett, J., 1988. Fields of Discourse. Reconstituting a Social Archaeology. *Critique of Anthropology*, 7(3), 5–16.

Barrett, J., 2006. Archaeology as the Investigation of the Contexts of Humanity, in *Deconstructing Context. A Critical Approach to Archaeological Practice*, ed. D. Papaconstantinou, Oxford: Oxbow Books, 194–211.

Barry, A., & N. Thrift, 2007. Gabriel Tarde: Imitation, Invention and Economy. *Economy and Society*, 36(4), 509–25.

Baudou, E., 1985. Archaeological Source Criticism and the History of Modern Cultivation in Denmark, in *Archaeological Formation Processes*, ed. K. Kristiansen, Copenhagen: National Museum, 63–80.

Beck, R., D. Bolender, J. Brown, & T. Earle, 2007. Eventful Archaeology: The Place of Space in Structural Transformation. *Current Anthropology*, 48(6), 833–60.

Bell, M., P. J. Fowler & S. W. Hillson 1996. *The Experimental Earthwork Project 1960–1992*. York: Council for British Archaeology (CBA Research Report 100).

Bender, B., S. Hamilton, & C. Tilley, 1997. Leskernick: Stone Worlds, Alternative Narratives, Nested Landscapes. *Proceedings of the Prehistoric Society*, 63, 147–78.

Bender, B., S. Hamilton, & C. Tilley, 2007. *Stone Worlds. Narrative and Reflexivity in Landscape Archaeology*, Walnut Creek, CA: Left Coast Press.

Benjamin, W., 1992. *Illuminations*, London: Fontana.

Bennett, J., 2010. *Vibrant Matter. A Political Ecology of Things*, Durham, NC: Duke University Press.

Bennett, J. W., 1943. Recent Developments in the Functional Interpretation of Archaeological Data. *American Antiquity*, 9(2), 206–19.

Berggren, A., 2001. Swedish Archaeology in Perspective and the Possibility of Reflexivity. *Current Swedish Archaeology*, 9, 9–23.

Bergson, H., 1991. *Matter and Memory*, New York: Zone Books.

Bernheim, E., 1889. *Lehrbuch der historischen Methode*, Leipzig: Verlag von Duncker and Humblot.

Berr, H., & L. Febvre, 1957. History, in *Encyclopedia of the Social Sciences*, ed. E. Seligman & A. Johnson, New York: Macmillan, 357–68.

Bhaskar, R., 1975. *A Realist Theory of Science*, Brighton: Harvester.

Bhaskar, R., 1979. *The Possibility of Naturalism. A Philosophical Critique of the Human Sciences*, New York: Humanities Press.

Biddle, M., 1994. *What Future for British Archaeology?*, Oxford: Oxbow Books.

Bille, M., F. Hastrup, & T. F. Sørensen (eds.), 2010. *An Anthropology of Absence. Materializations of Transcendence and Loss*, New York: Springer.

Binford, L., 1962. Archaeology as Anthropology. *American Antiquity*, 28(2), 217–25.

Binford, L., 1964. A Consideration of Archaeological Research Design. *American Antiquity*, 29, 425–41.

Binford, L., 1965. Archaeological Systematics and the Study of Culture Process. *American Antiquity*, 31(2), 203–10.

Binford, L., 1968a. Archaeological Perspectives, in *New Perspectives in Archaeology*, ed. L. Binford, Chicago: Aldine Publishing, 5–32.

Binford, L., 1968b. Review of 'A Guide to Field Methods in Archaeology: Approaches to the Anthropology of the Dead' by Robert F. Heizer and John A. Graham. *American Anthropologist*, 70, 806–8.

Binford, L., 1968c. Some Comments on Historical versus Processual Archaeology. *Southwestern Journal of Anthropology*, 24, 267–75.

Binford, L., 1975. Sampling, Judgement, and the Archaeological Record, in *Sampling in Archaeology*, ed. J. Mueller, Tucson: University of Arizona Press, 251–7.

Binford, L., 1977. General Introduction, in *For Theory Building in Archaeology. Essays on Faunal Remains, Aquatic Resources, Spatial Analysis, and Systematic Modelling*, ed. L. Binford, New York: Academic Press, 1–13.

Binford, L., 1979. Organization and Formation Processes: Looking at Curated Technologies. *Journal of Anthropological Research*, 35, 255–73.

Binford, L., 1981. Behavioural Archaeology and the 'Pompeii Premise'. *Journal of Anthropological Research*, 37, 195–208.

Binford, L., 1982a. Meaning, Inference and the Material Record, in *Ranking, Resource and Exchange*, ed. C. Renfrew & S. Shennan, Cambridge: Cambridge University Press, 160–3.

Binford, L., 1982b. Objectivity – Explanation – Archaeology, in *Theory and Explanation in Archaeology*, ed. C. Renfrew, M. J. Rowlands, & B. A. Segraves, London: Academic Press, 125–38.

Binford, L., 1983. *Working at Archaeology*, New York: Academic Press.

Binford, L., 1989. *Debating Archaeology*, New York: Academic Press.

Blench, R., 2006. Archaeology and Language: Methods and Issues, in *Companion to Archaeology*, ed. J. Bintliff, Oxford: Blackwell, 52–74.

Bloch, M., 1954. *The Historian's Craft*, Manchester: Manchester University Press.

Bloor, D., 1976. *Knowledge and Social Imagery*, Chicago: University of Chicago Press.

Boast, R., 1997. A Small Company of Actors: A Critique of Style. *Journal of Material Culture*, 2(2), 173–98.

Boivin, N., 2008. *Material Cultures, Material Minds. The Impact of Things on Human Thought, Society and Evolution.* Cambridge: Cambridge University Press.

Bolender, D. (ed.), 2010. *Eventful Archaeologies. New Approaches to Social Transformation in the Archaeological Record*, Albany: State University of New York Press.

Bon, S. E., 1997. A City Frozen in Time or a Site in Perpetual Motion? Formation Processes at Pompeii, in *Sequence and Space in Pompeii*, ed. S. E. Bon & R. Jones, Oxford: Oxbow Books, 7–12.

Borch, C., 2005. Urban Imitations: Tarde's Sociology Revisited. *Theory, Culture and Society*, 22(3), 81–100.

Boric, D. (ed.), 2009. *Archaeology and Memory*, Oxford: Oxbow Books.

Bourdieu, P., 1977. *Outline of a Theory of Practice*, Cambridge: Cambridge University Press.

Bourne, H. 1725. *Antiquitates Vulgares, or the Antiquities of the Common People.* Newcastle: J. White.

Bowden, M., 1991. *Pitt Rivers*, Cambridge: Cambridge University Press.

Bowden, M., 2001. Mapping the Past: O. G. S. Crawford and the Development of Landscape Studies. *Landscapes*, 2, 29–45.

Bowker, G. C., 2006. *Memory Practices in the Sciences*, Cambridge: Massachusetts Institute of Technology Press.

Bradley, R. (ed.), 1998. The Past in the Past: The Re-use of Ancient Monuments. *World Archaeology* 30(1).

Bradley, R., 2002. *The Past in Prehistoric Societies*, London: Routledge.

Bradley, R., 2003. Seeing Things: Perception, Experience and the Constraints of Excavation. *Journal of Social Archaeology*, 3(2), 151–68.

Bradley, R., 2006. Bridging the Two Cultures: Commercial Archaeology and the Study of Prehistoric Britain. *Antiquaries Journal*, 86, 1–13.

Braidwood, R., 1958. J. Vere Gordon Childe 1892–1957. *American Anthropologist*, 60, 733–6.

Brain, C. K., 1967. Bone Weathering and the Problem of Bone Pseudo-Tools. *South African Journal of Science*, 63, 97–9.

Brand, J., 1777. *Observations on Popular Antiquities*. Newcastle upon Tyne: T. Saint.

Braudel, F., 1980. *On History*, Chicago: University of Chicago Press.

Brew, J. O., 1946. *The Archaeology of Alkali Ridge, Southeastern Utah*. Cambridge, MA: Peabody Museum of American Archeology and Ethnology.

Brittain, M., & O. Harris, 2010. Enchaining Arguments and Fragmenting Assumptions: Reconsidering the Fragmentation Debate in Archaeology. *World Archaeology*, 42(4), 581–94.

Brooks, R., 1982. Events in the Archaeological Context and Archaeological Explanation. *Current Anthropology*, 23(1), 67–75.

Brown, M. R., & E. Harris, 1993. Interfaces in Archaeological Stratigraphy, in *Practices of Archaeological Stratigraphy*, ed. E. Harris, London: Academic Press, 7–20.

Brück, J., 1999. Ritual and Rationality: Some Problems of Interpretation in European Archaeology. *European Journal of Archaeology*, 2(3), 313–44.

Brudenell, M., & A. Cooper, 2008. Post-Middenism: Depositional Histories on Later Bronze Age Settlements at Broom, Bedfordshire. *Oxford Journal of Archaeology*, 27(1), 15–36.

Brundage, A., 2008. *Going to the Sources. A Guide to Historical Research and Writing*, Wheeling, IL: Harlan Davidson.

Bryant, L., N. Srnicek, & G. Harman (eds.), 2011. *The Speculative Turn. Continental Materialism and Realism*, Melbourne: re.press.

Buchli, V., 1995. Interpreting Material Culture: The Trouble with Text, in *Interpreting Archaeology. Finding Meaning in the Past*, ed. I. Hodder, M. Shanks, A. Alexandri, V. Buchli, J. Carman, J. Last, & G. Lucas, London: Routledge, 181–93.

Buchli, V., 2002. Introduction, in *The Material Culture Reader*, ed. V. Buchli, Oxford: Berg, 1–22.

Buchli, V., 2004. Material Culture: Current Problems, in *A Companion to Social Archaeology*, ed. L. Meskell & R. Preucel, Oxford: Blackwell, 179–94.

Buchli, V., 2010. Presencing the Im-Material, in *An Anthropology of Absence. Materializations of Transcendence and Loss*, ed. M. Bille, F. Hastrup, & T. F. Sørensen, New York: Springer, 185–203.

Butler, J., 1993. *Bodies That Matter. On the Discursive Limits of 'Sex'*, London: Routledge.

Butzer, K., 1982. *Archaeology as Human Ecology. Method and Theory for a Contextual Approach*, Cambridge: Cambridge University Press.

Callon, M., & J. Law, 1997. After the Individual in Society: Lessons on Collectivity from Science, Technology and Society. *Canadian Journal of Sociology*, 22(2), 165–82.

Cameron, C. M., & S. A. Tomka (eds.), 1993. *Abandonment of Settlements and Regions. Ethnoarchaeological and Archaeological Approaches*, Cambridge: Cambridge University Press.

Candea, M. (ed.), 2010. *The Social after Gabriel Tarde. Debates and Assessments*, London: Routledge.

Carr, C., 1987. Dissecting Intrasite Artefact Palimpsests Using Fourier Methods, in *Method and Theory for Activity Area Research*, ed. S. Kent, New York: Columbia University Press, 236–91.

Carr, D., 1986. Narrative and the Real World: An Argument for Continuity. *History and Theory*, 25(2), 117–31.

Carr, D., 1991. *Time, Narrative and History*, Bloomington: Indiana University Press.

Carver, M., 1989. Digging for Ideas. *Antiquity*, 63, 666–74.

Carver, M., 1990. Digging for Data: Archaeological Approaches to Data Definition, Acquisition and Analysis, in *Lo scavo archeologico. Dalla diagnosi all'edizione*, ed. R. Francovich & D. Manacorda, Florence, Italy: All'Insegna del Giglio SAS, 45–120.

Carver, M., 2009. *Archaeological Investigation*, London: Routledge.

Casati, R., & A. Varzi, 2008. Event Concepts, in *Understanding Events. From Perception to Action*, ed. T. F. Shipley & J. M. Zacks, Oxford: Oxford University Press, 31–53.

Cerquiglini, B., 1999. *In Praise of the Variant. A Critical History of Philology*, Baltimore: John Hopkins University Press.

Chadha, A., 2002. Visions of a Discipline: Sir Mortimer Wheeler and the Archaeological Method in India (1944–1948). *Journal of Social Archaeology*, 2(3), 378–401.

Chadwick, A., 2003. Post-Processualism, Professionalization and Archaeological Methodologies: Towards Reflective and Radical Practice. *Archaeological Dialogues*, 10(1), 97–117.

Chang, K. C., 1967. *Rethinking Archaeology*, New York: Random House.

Chapman, J., 2000. *Fragmentation in Archaeology. People, Places and Broken Objects in the Prehistory of South Eastern Europe*, London: Routledge.

Chapman, J., & B. Gaydarska, 2007. *Parts and Wholes. Fragmentation in Prehistoric Context*, Oxford: Oxbow Books.

Charest, M., 2009. Thinking through Living: Experience and the Production of Archaeological Knowledge. *Archaeologies*, 5(3), 416–45.

Chenhall, R. G., 1971. Positivism and the Collection of Data. *American Antiquity*, 36(3), 372–3.

Cherry, J., C. Gamble, & S. Shennan, 1978. General Introduction: Attitudes to Sampling in British Archaeology, in *Sampling in Contemporary British Archaeology*, ed. J. Cherry, C. Gamble, & S. Shennan, Oxford: British Archaeological Reports 50, 1–8.

Childe, V. G., 1935. Changing Methods and Aims in Prehistory. *Proceedings of the Prehistoric Society*, 1, 1–15.

Childe, V. G., 1951. *Social Evolution*, London: Watts and Co.

Childe, V. G., 1956a. *Piecing Together the Past. The Interpretation of Archaeological Data*, London: Routledge and Kegan Paul.

Childe, V. G., 1956b. *A Short Introduction to Archaeology*, London: Frederick Muller.

Clark, G., 1957. *Archaeology and Society. Reconstructing the Prehistoric Past*, London: Methuen and Co.

Clarke, A., 2003. *Natural-Born Cyborgs. Minds, Technologies and the Future of Human Intelligence*, Oxford: Oxford University Press.

Clarke, D. L., 1972. Models and Paradigms in Contemporary Archaeology, in *Models in Archaeology*, ed. D. L. Clarke, London: Methuen and Co., 1–60.

Clarke, D. L., 1973. Archaeology: The Loss of Innocence. *Antiquity*, 47, 6–18.

Clarke, D. L., 1978. *Analytical Archaeology*, London: Methuen and Co.

Classen, C., 1993. *Worlds of Sense. Exploring the Senses in History and across Cultures*, London: Routledge.

Cleere, H. F. (ed.), 1984. *Approaches to the Archaeological Heritage*, Cambridge: Cambridge University Press.

Cleuziou, S., A. Coudart, J.-P. Demoule, & A. Schnapp, 1991. The Use of Theory in French Archaeology, in *Archaeological Theory in Europe. The Last Three Decades*, ed. I. Hodder, London: Routledge, 91–128.

Cochrane, A., & I. Russell, 2007. Visualizing Archaeologies: A Manifesto. *Cambridge Archaeological Journal*, 17(1), 3–19.

Cole, S., 1955. *Counterfeit*, London: John Murray.

Coles, B., & J. Coles, 1989. *People of the Wetlands. Bogs, Bodies and Lake-Dwellers*, London: Guild Publishing.

Coles, J., 1972. *Field Archaeology in Britain*, London: Methuen and Co.

Coles, J., 1973. *Archaeology by Experiment*, London: Hutchinson.

Coles, J., 1979. *Experimental Archaeology*, London: Academic Press.

Coles, J., & B. Coles, 1996. *Enlarging the Past. The Contribution of Wetland Archaeology*, Edinburgh: Society of Antiquaries of Scotland.

Collier, A., 1994. *Critical Realism: An Introduction to Roy Bhaskar's Philosophy*. London: Verso.

Collingwood, R. G., 1944. *An Autobiography*, Harmondsworth: Penguin.

Collingwood, R. G., 1946. *The Idea of History*, Oxford: Clarendon Press.

Collins, H. M., 1985. *Changing Order. Replication and Induction in Scientific Practice*, London: Sage.

Collins, M. B., 1975. Sources of Bias in Processual Data: An Appraisal, in *Sampling in Archaeology*, ed. J. Mueller, Tucson: University of Arizona Press, 26–32.

Collins, R., 1981. On the Microfoundations of Macrosociology. *American Journal of Sociology*, 86(5), 984–1014.

Corfield, M., P. Hinton, T. Nixon, & M. Pollard (eds.), 1998. *Preserving Archaeological Remains in Situ. Proceedings of the Conference 1st–3rd April 1996*, London: Museum of London Archaeology Service.

Cornwall, I., 1958. *Soils for the Archaeologist*, London: Phoenix House.

Coupaye, L., 2009. Ways of Enchanting: *Chaînes opératoires* and Yam Cultivation in Nyamikum Village, Maprik, Papua New Guinea. *Journal of Material Culture*, 14(4), 433–58.

Coupaye, L., & L. Douny, 2009. Dans la trajectoire des choses. Comparaison des approches francophones et anglophones contemporained en anthropologie des techniques. *Techniques et Culture*, 52–53, 12–39.

Courbin, P., 1988. *What Is Archaeology? An Essay on the Nature of Archaeological Research*, Chicago: University of Chicago Press.

Couse, G. S., 1990. Collingwood's Detective Image of the Historian and the Study of Hadrian's Wall. *History and Theory*, 29(4), 57–77.

Cowgill, G. L., 1970. Some Sampling and Reliability Problems in Archaeology, in *Archeologie et calculateurs. Problèmes sémiologiques et mathématiques* Paris: Editions du Centre National de la Recherche Scientifique, 161–75.

Crary, J., 1992. *Techniques of the Observer. On Vision and Modernity in the Nineteenth Century*, Cambridge: Massachusetts Institute of Technology Press.

Crawford, O. G. S., 1921. *Man and His Past*, Oxford: Oxford University Press.

Crawford, O. G. S., 1953. *Archaeology in the Field*, London: Phoenix House.

Criado, F., 1995. The Visibility of the Archaeological Record and the Interpretation of Social Reality, in *Interpreting Archaeology. Finding Meaning in the Past*, ed. I. Hodder, M. Shanks, A. Alexandri, V. Buchli, J. Carman, J. Last, & G. Lucas, London: Routledge, 194–204.

Daniel, G., 1975. *A Hundred and Fifty Years of Archaeology*, London: Duckworth.

Daniels, S. G. H., 1972. Research Design Models, in *Models in Archaeology*, ed. D. L. Clarke, London: Methuen and Co., 201–30.

Darvill, T., 2004. Public Archaeology: A European Perspective, in *A Companion to Archaeology*, ed. J. Bintliff, Oxford: Blackwell, 409–34.

Darwin, C., 1968. *The Origin of Species*, Harmondsworth: Penguin.

Daston, L., 1998. The Language of Strange Facts in Early Modern Science, in *Inscribing Science. Scientific Texts and the Materiality of Communication*, ed. T. Lenoir, Stanford, CA: Stanford University Press, 20–38.

Daston, L., & P. Galison, 1992. The Image of Objectivity. *Representations*, 40, 81–128.

Daston, L., & P. Galison, 1997. *Objectivity*, New York: Zone Books.

David, N., 1972. On the Life Span of Pottery, Type Frequencies and Archaeological Inference. *American Antiquity*, 37, 141–2.

David, N., & C. Kramer, 2001. *Ethnoarchaeology in Action*, Cambridge: Cambridge University Press.

Davidson, D., 1969. The Individuation of Events, in *Essays in Honour of Carl G. Hempel*, ed. N. Rescher, Dordrecht, Germany: Reidel, 216–34.

Davidson, D., & M. Shackley (eds.), 1976. *Geoarchaeology. Earth Science and the Past*, Boulder, CO: Westview Press.

Dawdy, S. L. 2006. The Taphonomy of Disaster and the (Re)Formation of New Orleans. *American Anthropologist* 108(4): 719–30.

de Certeau, M., 1988. *The Writing of History*, New York: Columbia University Press.

de Lange, J., 2008. Time Perspectivism and the Structure of Archaeological Records: A Case Study, in *Time and Archaeology. Time Perspectivism Revisited*, ed. S. Holdaway & L. Wandsnider, Salt Lake City: University of Utah Press, 149–60.

Dear, P., 1985. Totius in Verba: Rhetoric and Authority in the Early Royal Society. *Isis*, 76(2), 145–61.

DeBoer, W. R., 1974. Ceramic Longevity and Archaeological Interpretation: An Example from the Upper Ucayali, Peru. *American Antiquity*, 39, 335–43.

DeBoer, W. R., 1983. The Archaeological Record as Preserved Death Assemblage, in *Archaeological Hammers and Theories*, ed. J. A. Moore & A. S. Keene, New York: Academic Press, 19–36.

DeBoer, W. R., & D. W. Lathrap, 1979. The Making and Breaking of Shipibo-Conibo Ceramics, in *Ethnoarchaeology. Implications of Ethnography for Archaeology*, ed. C. Kramer, New York: Columbia University Press, 102–38.

Déchelette, J.,1908–1914. *Manuel d'archéologie préhistorique, celtique et gallo-romaine* (4 vols.), Paris: Picard.

Deetz, J., 1988. History and Archaeological Theory: Walter Taylor Revisited. *American Antiquity*, 53(1), 13–22.

DeLanda, M., 1997. Immanence and Transcendence in the Genesis of Form. *South Atlantic Quarterly*, 96(3), 499–514.

DeLanda, M., 2006. *A New Philosophy of Society. Assemblage Theory and Social Complexity*, London: Continuum.

DeMarrais, E., C. Gosden, & C. Renfrew (eds.), 2004. *Rethinking Materiality. The Engagement of Mind with the Material World*, Cambridge: McDonald Institute for Archaeological Research.

Department for Communities and Local Government, 2010. *Planning Policy Statement 5. Planning for the Historic Environment*, London: The Stationary Office.

Derrida, J., 1996. *Archive Fever. A Freudian Impression*, Chicago: Chicago University Press.

Dobres, M.-A., 2000. *Technology and Social Agency. Outlining a Practice Framework for Archaeology*. Oxford: Blackwell.

Dobres, M.-A., & J. Robb (eds.), 2000. *Agency in Archaeology*, London: Routledge.

Dolwick, J., 2008. In Search of the Social: Steamboats, Square Wheels, Reindeer and Other Things. *Journal of Maritime Archaeology*, 3, 15–41.

Domanska, E., 2006a. The Return to Things. *Archaeologia Polona*, 44, 171–85.

Domanska, E., 2006b. The Material Presence of the Past. *History and Theory*, 45, 337–48.

Doyle, P., & M. Bennett (eds.), 1998. *Unlocking the Stratigraphical Record*, Chichester: John Wiley and Sons.

Doyle, P., M. Bennett, & A. Baxter, 1994. *The Key to Earth History. An Introduction to Stratigraphy*, Chichester: John Wiley and Sons.

Dretske, F., 1967. Can Events Move? *Mind*, 76, 479–92.

Droop, J. P., 1915. *Archaeological Excavation*, Cambridge: Cambridge University Press.

Droysen, J. G., 1897. *Outline of the Principles of History*, Boston: Ginn and Co.

Dunnell, R. C., 1986. Methodological Issues in Americanist Artifact Classification. *Advances in Archaeological Method and Theory*, 9, 149–207.

Durkheim, E., 1953. Individual and Collective Representations, in *Sociology and Philosophy*, ed. E. Durkheim, London: Cohen and West, 1–34.

Durkheim, E., 1964. *The Rules of Sociological Method*, New York: Free Press.

Dymond, D. P., 1974. *Archaeology and History. A Plea for Reconciliation*, London: Thames and Hudson.

Edensor, T., 2011. Entangled Agencies, Material Networks and Repair in a Building Assemblage: The Mutable Stone of St. Ann's Church, Manchester. *Transactions of the Institute of British Geographers* 36(2): 238–52.

Edgeworth, M., 2003. *Acts of Discovery. An Ethnography of Archaeological Practice*, Oxford: Archaeopress.

Edgeworth, M. (ed.), 2006. *Ethnographies of Archaeological Practice. Cultural Encounters, Material Transformations*, Lanham, MD: AltaMira Press.

Edwards, E., 2001. *Raw Histories. Photographs, Anthropology and Museums*, Oxford: Berg.

Edwards, E., C. Gosden, & R. Phillips (eds.), 2006. *Sensible Objects. Colonialism, Museums and Material Culture*, Oxford: Berg.

Eggers, H. J., 1950. Das Problem der ethnischen Deutung in der Frühgeschichte, in *Ur- und Frühgeschichte als historische Wissenschaft. Wahle Festschrift*, ed. H. Kirchner, Heidelberg, Germany: Carl Winter University Press, 49–59.

Eggers, H. J., 1986. *Einführung in die Vorgeschichte* Munich: Piper.

Eggert, M. K. H., 2001. *Prähistorische Archäologie. Konzepte und Methoden*, Tübingen, Germany: A. Francke Verlag.

Elton, G., 1967. *Practice of History*, London: Fontana Press.

Evans, C., 1989a. Perishables and Worldly Goods – Artefact Decoration and Classification in the Light of Wetlands Research. *Oxford Journal of Archaeology*, 8(2), 179–201.

Evans, C., 1989b. Archaeology and Modern Times: Bersu's Woodbury 1938 & 1939. *Antiquity*, 63, 436–50.

Everill, P., 2007. A Day in the Life of a Training Excavation: Teaching Archaeological Fieldwork in the UK. *World Archaeology*, 39(4), 483–98.

Flannery, K., 1967. Culture History v. Culture Process: A Debate in American Archaeology. *Scientific American*, 217, 119–22.

Foley, R. A., 1981. A Model of Regional Archaeological Structure. *Proceedings of the Prehistoric Society*, 47, 1–17.

Ford, J., 1954. The Type Concept Revisited. *American Anthropologist*, 56, 42–53.

Forslund, P., 2004. MRT Confidential, in *Material Culture and Other Things*, ed. F. Fahlander & T. Oestigaard, Gothenburg, Sweden: University of Gothenburg, 213–58.

Foucault, M., 2002. *The Archaeology of Knowledge*, London: Routledge.

Fowler, C., 2004. *The Archaeology of Personhood. An Anthropological Approach*, London: Routledge.

Fowles, S., 2010. People without Things, in *An Anthropology of Absence. Materializations of Transcendence and Loss*, ed. M. Bille, F. Hastrup, & T. F. Sørensen, New York: Springer, 23–41.

Franken, H. J., 1984. The Lithology and Stratigraphy of Archaeological Sites. *Stratigraphica Archaeologica*, 1, 16–23.

Franklin, J., 1977. *Jean Bodin and the Sixteenth Century Revolution in the Methodology of Law and History*, Westport, CT: Greenwood Press.

French, C., 2003. *Geoarchaeology in Action. Studies in Soil Micromorphology and Landscape Evolution*, London: Routledge.

Freud, S., 1957. A Note upon the 'Mystic Writing-Pad', in *The Standard Edition of the Complete Psychological Works of Sigmund Freud (Vol. XIX, 1923–5). The Ego and the Id and Other Works*, London: Hogarth Press, 225–32.

Friedman, J., 1974. Marxism, Structuralism and Vulgar Materialism. *Man*, 9(3), 444–69.

Fritz, J. M., 1972. Archaeological Systems for Indirect Observation, in *Contemporary Archaeology. A Guide to Theory and Contributions*, ed. M. P. Leone, Carbondale: Southern Illinois University Press, 135–57.

Fritz, J. M., & F. T. Plog, 1970. The Nature of Archaeological Explanation. *American Antiquity*, 35(4), 405–12.

Gallay, A., 1989. Logicism: A French View of Archaeological Theory Founded in Computational Perspective. *Antiquity*, 63, 27–39.

Gamble, C., 1993. *Timewalkers. The Prehistory of Global Colonization*, Stroud: Sutton Publishing.

Gardin, J.-C., 1979. *Archaeological Constructs. An Aspect of Theoretical Archaeology*, Cambridge: Cambridge University Press.

Gasche, H., & O. Tunca, 1983. Guide to Archaeostratigraphic Classification and Terminology: Definitions and Principles. *Journal of Field Archaeology*, 10(3), 325–35.

Gell, A., 1998. *Art and Agency*, Oxford: Oxford University Press.

Gerhard, E., 2004. Archaeological Theses. *Modernism/Modernity*, 11(1), 173–7.

Gero, J., 1985. Socio-Politics and the Woman-at-Home Ideology. *American Antiquity*, 50, 342–50.

Gero, J., 1995. Railroading Epistemology: Palaeoindians and Women, in *Interpreting Archaeology*, ed. I. Hodder, M. Shanks, A. Alexandri, V. Buchli, J. Carman, J. Last, & G. Lucas, London: Routledge, 175–8.

Gero, J., 1996. Archaeological Practice and Gendered Encounters with Field Data, in *Gender and Archaeology*, ed. R. P. Wright, Philadelphia: University of Pennsylvania Press, 251–80.

Gero, J., 2007. Honoring Ambiguity/Problematizing Certitude. *Journal of Archaeological Method and Theory*, 14, 311–27.

Gibbon, G., 1989. *Explanation in Archaeology*, Oxford: Blackwell.

Giddens, A., 1984. *The Constitution of Society*, Cambridge: Polity Press.

Gifford, D., 1981. Taphonomy and Paleoecology: A Critical Review of Archaeology's Sister Disciplines. *Advances in Archaeological Method and Theory*, 4, 365–438.

Ginsberg, R., 2004. *The Aesthetics of Ruins*, Amsterdam: Rodopi.

Ginzburg, C., 1990. Clues: Roots of an Evidential Paradigm, in *Myths, Emblems, Clues*, ed. C. Ginzburg, London: Hutchinson Radius, 96–125.

Gladfelter, B. G., 1977. Geoarchaeology: The Geomorphologist and Archaeology. *American Antiquity*, 42(4), 519–38.

Gladfelter, B. G., 1981. Developments and Directions in Geoarchaeology. *Advances in Archaeological Method and Theory*, 4, 343–64.

Goldberg, P., & R. Macphail, 2006. *Practical and Theoretical Geoarchaeology*, Oxford: Blackwell.

Golinski, J., 1998. *Making Natural Knowledge. Constructivism and the History of Science*, Cambridge: Cambridge University Press.

Gooding, D., 1990. *Experiment and the Making of Meaning. Human Agency in Scientific Observation and Experiment*, Dordrecht, Germany: Kluwer.

Goodwin, C., 1994. Professional Vision. *American Anthropologist*, 96(3), 606–33.

Goodwin, C., 2000. Practices of Color Classification. *Mind, Culture and Activity*, 7(1–2), 19–36.

Gorecki, P., 1985. Ethno-Archaeology: The Need for a Post-Mortem Enquiry. *World Archaeology*, 17(2), 175–91.

Gorodzov, V. A., 1933. The Typological Method in Archaeology. *American Anthropologist*, 35(1), 95–102.

Gosden, C., 1994. *Social Being and Time*, Oxford: Blackwell.

Gould, S. J., 1981. *The Mismeasure of Man*, Harmondsworth: Penguin.

Gräslund, B., 1976. Dating Methods in Scandinavian Archaeology. *Norwegian Archaeological Review*, 9(2), 69–83.

Gräslund, B., 1987. *The Birth of Prehistoric Chronology. Dating Methods and Dating Systems in Nineteenth-Century Scandinavian Archaeology*, Cambridge: Cambridge University Press.

Graves-Brown, P. (ed.), 2000. *Matter, Materiality and Modern Culture*, London: Routledge.

Grayson, D. K., 1983. *The Establishment of Human Antiquity*, New York: Academic Press.

Grayson, D. K., 1986. Eoliths, Archaeological Ambiguity and the Generation of 'Middle-Range' Research, in *American Archaeology. Past and Future. A Celebration of the Society of American Archaeology*, ed. D. J. Meltzer, D. D. Fowler, & J. A. Sabloff, Washington, DC: Smithsonian Institution Press, 77–133.

Greenwell, W., 1865. Notices of the Examination of Ancient Grave-Hills in the North Riding of Yorkshire. *Archaeological Journal*, 22, 97–117, 241–68.

Griffin, L. J., 1993. Narrative, Event-Structure Analysis, and Causal Interpretation in Historical Sociology. *American Journal of Sociology*, 98(5), 1094–133.

Gross, N., 2006. Comment on Searle. *Anthropological Theory*, 6(1), 45–56.

Hacker, P., 1982. Events and Objects in Space and Time. *Mind*, 91, 1–19.

Hacking, I., 1983. *Representing and Intervening. Introductory Topics in the Philosophy of Natural Science*, Cambridge: Cambridge University Press.

Halbwachs, M., 1980. *The Collective Memory*, New York: Harper and Row.

Halbwachs, M., 1992. *On Collective Memory*, Chicago: University of Chicago Press.

Hamilton, S., & R. Whitehouse, 2006. Phenomenology in Practice: Towards a Methodology for a 'Subjective' Approach. *European Journal of Archaeology*, 9(1), 31–71.

Haraway, D., 1991. *Simians, Cyborgs and Women. The Reinvention of Nature*, London: Routledge.

Harding, A. F. (ed.), 1999. *Experiment and Design in Archaeology. Papers in Honour of John Coles*, Oxford: Oxbow.

Harding, J., 2005. Rethinking the Great Divide: Long-Term Structural History and the Temporality of the Event. *Norwegian Archaeological Review*, 38(2), 88–101.

Härke, H., 1991. All Quiet on the Western Front? Paradigms, Methods and Approaches in West German Archaeology, in *Archaeological Theory in Europe. The Last Three Decades*, ed. I. Hodder, London: Routledge, 187–222.

Härke, H., 1993. Intentionale und funktionale Daten: Ein Beitrag zur Theorie und Methodik der Gräberarchäologie. *Archäologisches Korrespondenzblatt*, 23(1), 141–6.

Härke, H., 1997. The Nature of Burial Data, in *Burial and Society. The Chronological and Social Analysis of Archaeological Burial Data*, ed. C. K. Jensen & K. H. Nielsen, Aarhus, Denmark: Aarhus University Press, 19–27.

Härke, H. (ed.), 2002. *Archaeology, Ideology and Society. The German Experience*, Frankfurt: Peter Lang.

Harman, G., 2002. *Tool-Being. Heidegger and the Metaphysics of Objects*, Chicago: Open Court.

Harman, G., 2005. *Guerrilla Metaphysics. Phenomenology and the Carpentry of Things*, Chicago: Open Court.

Harris, E., 1977. Units of Archaeological Stratification. *Norwegian Archaeological Review*, 10, 84–94.

Harris, E., 1979. *Principles of Archaeological Stratigraphy*, London: Academic Press.

Harris, E., 1989. *Principles of Archaeological Stratigraphy* (2nd ed.), London: Academic Press.

Harris, M., 1974. *Cows, Pigs, Wars and Witches. The Riddles of Culture*, New York: Vintage Books.

Harvey, K. (ed.), 2009. *History and Material Culture. A Student's Guide to Approaching Alternative Sources*, London: Routledge.

Hassan, F., 1979. Geoarchaeology: The Geologist and Archaeology. *American Antiquity*, 44, 267–70.

Hawkes, C., 1954. Archaeological Theory and Method: Some Suggestions from the Old World. *American Anthropologist*, 56(2), 155–68.

Hawkes, J., 1968. The Proper Study of Mankind. *Antiquity*, 42, 255–62.

Hayden, B., & A. Cannon, 1983. Where the Garbage Goes: Refuse Disposal in the Maya Highlands. *Journal of Anthropological Archaeology*, 2, 117–63.

Hegel, G. W. F., 1977. *Phenomenology of Spirit*, Oxford: Oxford University Press.

Heidegger, M., 1970. *What is a Thing?* Chicago: Regnery and Gateway Publishers.

Heizer, R. F., 1949. *A Manual of Archaeological Field Methods*, Milbrae, CA: National Press.

Heizer, R. F., & J. A. Graham, 1968. *A Guide to Field Methods in Archaeology*, Berkeley: University of California.

Henare, A., M. Holbraad, & S. Wastell (eds.), 2007. *Thinking through Things. Theorising Artefacts Ethnographically*, London: Routledge.

Hester, T., H. Shafer, & K. Feder, 1997. *Field Methods in Archaeology*, Mountain View, CA: Mayfield Publishing.

Hicks, D., 2007. From Material Culture to Material Life. *Journal of Iberian Archaeology*, 9–10, 245–55.

Hill, G. B., & L. F. Powell (eds.), 1934. *Boswell's Life of Johnson*, Oxford: Clarendon Press.

Hill, J. D., 1995. *Ritual and Rubbish in the Iron Age of Wessex. A Study of the Formation of a Specific Archaeological Record*, Oxford: British Archaeological Reports.

Historic Buildings and Monuments Commission, 1991. *Planning Policy Guidance 16*, London: Historic Buildings and Monuments Commission.

Hodder, I., 1982a. *Symbols in Action. Ethnoarchaeological Studies of Material Culture*, Cambridge: Cambridge University Press.

Hodder, I., 1982b. Theoretical Archaeology: A Reactionary View, in *Symbolic and Structural Archaeology*, ed. I. Hodder, Cambridge: Cambridge University Press, 1–16.

Hodder, I., 1984. Archaeology in 1984. *Antiquity*, 58, 25–32.

Hodder, I., 1986. *Reading the Past. Current Approaches to Interpretation in Archaeology*, Cambridge: Cambridge University Press.

Hodder, I., 1987. The Contribution of the Long Term, in *Archaeology as Long-Term History*, ed. I. Hodder, Cambridge: Cambridge University Press, 1–8.

Hodder, I., 1989a. This Is Not an Article about Material Culture as Text. *Journal of Anthropological Archaeology*, 8, 250–69.

Hodder, I., 1989b. Writing Archaeology: Site Reports in Context. *Antiquity*, 63, 268–74.

Hodder, I., 1992. *Theory and Practice in Archaeology*, London: Routledge.

Hodder, I., 1993. The Narrative and Rhetoric of Material Culture Sequences. *World Archaeology*, 25, 268–82.

Hodder, I., 1995. Material Culture in Time, in *Interpreting Archaeology. Finding Meaning in the Past*, ed. I. Hodder, M. Shanks, A. Alexandri, V. Buchli, J. Carman, J. Last, & G. Lucas, London: Routledge, 164–8.

Hodder, I., 1997. 'Always Momentary, Fluid and Flexible': Towards a Reflexive Excavation Methodology. *Antiquity*, 71, 691–700.

Hodder, I., 1999. *The Archaeological Process*, Oxford: Blackwell.

Hodder, I. (ed.), 2000. *Towards Reflexive Method in Archaeology. The Example at Çatalhöyük*, Cambridge: McDonald Institute for Archaeological Research.

Hodder, I., 2004. Neo-Thingness, in *Explaining Social Change. Studies in Honour of Colin Renfrew*, ed. J. Cherry, C. Scarre, & S. Shennan, Cambridge: McDonald Institute for Archaeological Research, 45–52.

Hodder, I., 2011. Human-Thing Entanglement: Towards an Integrated Archaeological Perspective. *Journal of the Royal Anthropological Institute*, 17: 154–77.

Hodder, I., & S. Hutson, 2003. *Reading the Past. Current Approaches to Interpretation in Archaeology*, Cambridge: Cambridge University Press.

Hodder, I., & P. McAnany, 2009. Thinking about Stratigraphic Sequences in Social Terms. *Archaeological Dialogues*, 16(1), 1–22.

Hodgen, M. T., 1931. The Doctrine of Survivals: The History of an Idea. *American Anthropologist*, 33(3), 307–24.

Hogarth, A. C., 1972. Common Sense in Archaeology. *Antiquity*, 46, 301–4.

Holdaway, S., & L. Wandsnider (eds.), 2008. *Time in Archaeology. Time Perspectivism Revisited*, Salt Lake City: University of Utah Press.

Holtorf, C., 2005. *From Stonehenge to Las Vegas. Archaeology as Popular Culture*, Walnut Creek, CA: AltaMira Press.

Holtorf, C., 2007. *Archaeology Is a Brand! The Meaning of Archaeology in Contemporary Popular Culture*, Oxford: Archaeopress.

Holz, M., & M. Simões, 2005. Taphonomy – Overview of Main Concepts and Applications to Sequence Stratigraphic Analysis. *Applied Stratigraphy*, 23(3), 249–78.

Howes, D. (ed.), 2004. *Empire of the Senses. The Sensual Culture Reader*, Oxford: Berg.

Hunter, J., & I. Ralston (eds.), 2006. *Archaeological Resource Management in the UK. An Introduction*, Stroud: Sutton Publishing.

Hurcombe, L., 2007. A Sense of Materials and the Sensory Perception in Concepts of Materiality. *World Archaeology*, 39(4), 532–45.

Husserl, E., 1966. *The Phenomenology of Internal Time-Consciousness*, Bloomington: Indiana University Press.

Iggers, G., 1997. *Historiography in the Twentieth Century. From Scientific Objectivity to the Postmodern Challenge*, Middletown, CT: Wesleyan University Press.

Ingersoll, D., J. Yellen, & W. MacDonald (eds.), 1977. *Experimental Archaeology*, New York: Columbia University Press.

Ingold, T., 2005. Making Culture and Weaving the World, in *Matter, Materiality and Modern Culture*, ed. P. Graves-Brown, London: Routledge, 50–71.

Ingold, T., 2007. Materials against Materiality. *Archaeological Dialogues*, 14(1), 1–16.

Ingold, T., 2008. Anthropology Is Not Ethnography. *Proceedings of the British Academy*, 154, 69–92.

Ingold, T., 2010. The Textility of Making. *Cambridge Journal of Economics*, 34, 91–102.

Isaac, G., 1967. Towards the Interpretation of Occupation Debris: Some Experiments and Observations. *Kroeber Anthropological Society Papers*, 37, 37–57.

Jakobson, R. 1959. On Linguistic Aspects of Translation, in *On Translation*, ed. R. A. Brower, Cambridge, MA: Harvard University Press, 232–9.

Jarvis, W. E., 2003. *Time Capsules. A Cultural History*, Jefferson, NC: McFarland and Co.

Jay, M., 1993. *Downcast Eyes. The Denigration of Vision in Twentieth Century French Thought*, Berkeley: University of California Press.

Jewell, P. A., 1963. *The Experimental Earthwork at Overton Down, Wiltshire 1960*, London: British Association for the Advancement of Science.

Jewell, P. A., & G. W. Dimbleby, 1966. The Experimental Earthwork on Overton Down, Wiltshire, England: The First Four Years. *Proceedings of the Prehistoric Society*, 32, 313–42.

Joerges, B., 1999a. Do Politics Have Artifacts? *Social Studies of Science*, 29(3), 411–31.

Joerges, B., 1999b. Scams Cannot Be Busted. *Social Studies of Science*, 29(3), 450–7.

Johansen, A. B., 1982. Arkeologiens teori og data. *Fornvännen*, 77, 212–25.

Johnson, M., 2006. On the Nature of Theoretical Archaeology and Archaeological Theory. *Archaeological Dialogues*, 13(2), 117–32.

Johnson, M., 2007. *The Ideas of Landscape*, Oxford: Blackwell Publishing.

Johnson, M., 2010. *Archaeological Theory. An Introduction* (2nd ed.), Oxford: Wiley-Blackwell.

Johnson, R. W., & M. G. Schene (eds.), 1987. *Cultural Resources Management*, Malabar, FL.: Krieger Publishing.

Jones, A., 2002. *Archaeological Theory and Scientific Practice*, Cambridge: Cambridge University Press.

Jones, A., 2004. Archaeometry and Materiality: Materials-Based Analysis in Theory and Practice. *Archaeometry*, 46(3), 327–38.

Jones, A., 2005. Lives in Fragments? Personhood and the European Neolithic. *Journal of Social Archaeology*, 5(2), 193–224.

Jones, A., 2007. *Memory and Material Culture*, Cambridge: Cambridge University Press.

Joukowsky, M., 1980. *A Complete Manual of Field Archaeology*, Englewood Cliffs, NJ: Prentice-Hall.

Joyce, R. & J. Pollard 2010. Archaeological Assemblages and Practices of Deposition, in *The Oxford Handbook of Material Culture Studies*, eds. D. Hicks & M. Beaudry, Oxford: Oxford University Press, 291–309.

Keane, W., 2005. Signs are Not the Garb of Meaning: On the Social Analysis of Material Things, in *Materiality*, ed. D. Miller, Durham, NC: Duke University Press, 182–205.

Keller, F., 1866. *The Lake Dwellings of Switzerland and Other Parts of Europe*, London: Longmans, Green and Co.

Kelley, J., & M. Hanen, 1988. *Archaeology and the Methodology of Science*, Albuquerque: University of New Mexico Press.

Kenyon, K., 1952. *Beginning in Archaeology*, London: Phoenix House.

Kenyon, K., 1964. *Beginning in Archaeology* (2nd ed.), London: J. M. Dent.

Kinnunen, J., 1996. Gabriel Tarde as a Founding Father of Innovation Diffusion Research. *Acta Sociologica*, 39(4), 431–42.

Kintigh, K., 2006. The Promise and Challenge of Archaeological Data Integration. *American Antiquity*, 71(3), 567–78.

Klejn, L. S., 1994. Childe and Soviet Archaeology: A Romance, in *The Archaeology of V. Gordon Childe*, ed. D. Harris, Melbourne: Melbourne University Press, 75–99.

Klindt-Jensen, O., 1975. *A History of Scandinavian Archaeology*, London: Thames and Hudson.

Knappett, C., 2002. Photographs, Skeuomorphs and Marionettes. Some Thoughts on Mind, Agency and Object. *Journal of Material Culture*, 7(1), 97–117.

Knappett, C., 2005. *Thinking through Material Culture*, Philadelphia: University of Pennsylvania Press.

Knappett, C., 2007. Materials with Materiality? Response to Ingold 'Materials against Materiality'. *Archaeological Dialogues*, 14(1), 20–3.

Knappett, C., & L. Malafouris (eds.), 2008. *Material Agency. Towards a Nonanthropocentric Approach*, New York: Springer.

Knorr, K., 1981. *The Manufacture of Knowledge. An Essay on the Constructivist and Contextual Nature of Science*, Oxford: Pergamon Press.

Knorr-Cetina, K., 1999. *Epistemic Cultures. How the Sciences Make Knowledge*, Cambridge, MA: Harvard University Press.

Kohl, P., & C. Fawcett (eds.), 1995. *Nationalism, Politics and the Practice of Archaeology*, Cambridge: Cambridge University Press.

Kohl, P., & J. A. Pérez Gollán, 2002. Religion, Politics, and Prehistory. *Current Anthropology*, 43(4), 561–86.

Kosso, P., 1992. Observation of the Past. *History and Theory*, 31, 21–36.

Kosso, P., 2001. *Knowing the Past. Philosophical Issues of History and Archaeology*, New York: Humanity Books.

Koutsoukos, E., 2005. Stratigraphy: Evolution of a Concept, in *Applied Stratigraphy*, ed. E. Koutsoukos, Dordrecht, Germany: Springer, 3–19.

Kristiansen, K., 1978. The Application of Source Criticism to Archaeology. *Norwegian Archaeological Review*, 11(1), 1–5.

Kristiansen, K. (ed.), 1985. *Archaeological Formation Processes. The Representativity of Archaeological Remains from Danish Prehistory*, Copenhagen: National Museum.

Kristiansen, K., 2002. The Birth of Ecological Archaeology in Denmark: History and Research Environments 1850–2000, in *The Neolithisation of Denmark. 150 Years of Debate*, ed. A. Fischer & K. Kristiansen, Sheffield: J. R. Collis Publications, 11–31.

Kroeber, A., & C. Kluckhohn, 1952. *Culture. A Critical Review of Concepts and Definitions*, Cambridge, MA: Harvard University.

Kuhn, T., 1962. *The Structure of Scientific Revolutions*, Chicago: University of Chicago Press.

Kuna, M., & D. Dreslerová, 2007. Landscape Archaeology and 'Community Areas' in the Archaeology of Central Europe, in *Envisioning Landscape. Situations and Standpoints in Archaeology and Heritage*, ed. D. Hicks, L. McAtackney, & G. Fairclough, Walnut Creek, CA: Left Coast Press, 146–71.

LaMotta, V. M., & M. B. Schiffer, 2001. Behavioural Archaeology: Toward a New Synthesis, in *Archaeological Theory Today*, ed. I. Hodder, Oxford: Polity, 14–64.

Langlois, C. V., & C. Seignobos, 1925. *Introduction to the Study of History*, London: Duckworth.

Last, J., 1995. The Nature of History, in *Interpreting Archaeology. Finding Meaning in the Past*, ed. I. Hodder, M. Shanks, A. Alexandri, V. Buchli, J. Carman, J. Last, & G. Lucas, London: Routledge, 141–57.

Last, J., 2007. Review of Parts and Wholes: Fragmentation in Prehistoric Context, by J. Chapman & B. Gaydarska, *Prehistoric Society Book Reviews* (http://www.ucl.ac.uk/prehistoric/reviews/07_05_chapman.htm).

Latour, B., 1987. *Science in Action*, Cambridge, MA: Harvard University Press.

Latour, B., 1990. Drawing Things Together, in *Representation in Scientific Practice*, ed. M. Lynch & S. Woolgar, Cambridge: Massachusetts Institute of Technology Press, 19–68.

Latour, B., 1992. Where Are the Missing Masses? The Sociology of a Few Mundane Artifacts, in *Shaping Technology/Building Society. Studies in Sociotechnical Change*, ed. W. E. Bijker & J. Law, Cambridge: Massachusetts Institute of Technology Press, 225–58.

Latour, B., 1993. *We Have Never Been Modern*, Cambridge, MA: Harvard University Press.

Latour, B., 1994. Pragmatogonies. A Mythical Account of How Humans and Non-humans Swap Properties. *American Behavioural Scientist*, 37(6), 791–808.

Latour, B., 1999. Circulating Reference: Sampling the Soil in the Amazon Forest, in *Pandora's Hope. Essays on the Reality of Science Studies*, ed. B. Latour, Cambridge, MA: Harvard University Press, 24–79.

Latour, B., 2002a. Gabriel Tarde and the End of the Social, in *The Social in Question. New Bearings in History and the Social Sciences*, ed. P. Joyce, London: Routledge, 117–32.

Latour, B., 2002b. Morality and Technology. The End of Means. *Theory, Culture & Society*, 19(5/6): 247–60.

Latour, B., 2003. The Promises of Constructivism, in *Chasing Technoscience. Matrix for Materiality*, ed. D. Ihde & E. Selinger, Bloomington: Indiana University Press, 27–46.

Latour, B., 2005. *Reassembling the Social*, Oxford: Oxford University Press.

Latour, B., 2010. Tarde's Idea of Quantification, in *The Social after Gabriel Tarde. Debates and Assessments*, ed. M. Candea, London: Routledge, 145–62.

Latour, B., & S. Woolgar, 1986. *Laboratory Life. The Construction of Scientific Facts*, Princeton, NJ: Princeton University Press.

Lawson, C., J. Latsis, & N. Martins (eds.), 2007. *Contributions to Social Ontology*, London: Routledge.

Lefèvre, W. (ed.), 2004. *Picturing Machines 1400–1700*, Cambridge: Massachusetts Institute of Technology Press.

Lemonnier, P., 1993a. Introduction, in *Technological Choices. Transformation in Material Cultures since the Neolithic*, ed. P. Lemonnier, London: Routledge, 1–35.

Lemonnier, P. (ed.), 1993b. *Technological Choices. Transformation in Material Culture since the Neolithic*, London: Routledge.

Leroi-Gourhan, A., 1943. *Evolution et techniques. L'Homme et la matière*, Paris: Albin Michel.

Leroi-Gourhan, A., 1945. *Evolution et techniques. Milieu et techniques*, Paris: Albin Michel.

Leroi-Gourhan, A., 1950. *Les Fouilles préhistoriques (techniques et méthodes)*, Paris: A. & J. Picard.

Leroi-Gourhan, A., 1964. *Le geste et parole*. Paris: Albin Michel.

Leroi-Gourhan, A., 1993. *Gesture and Speech*, Cambridge: Massachusetts Institute of Technology Press (October Books).

Levine, P., 1986. *The Amateur and the Professional. Antiquarians, Historians and Archaeologists in Victorian England 1838–1886*, Cambridge: Cambridge University Press.

Leys, R., 1993. Mead's Voices: Imitation as Foundation, or, the Struggle against Mimesis. *Critical Inquiry*, 19(2), 277–307.

Lightfoot, R. R., 1993. Abandonment Processes in Prehistoric Pueblos, in *The Abandonment of Settlements and Regions. Ethnoarchaeological and Archaeological Approaches*, ed. C. M. Cameron & S. A. Tonka, Cambridge: Cambridge University Press, 165–77.

Linse, A. R., & J. K. Stein, 1997. Review of *Stratigraphica Archaeologica*, Vol. 1 (1984) and Vol. 2 (1987), Publication of the Workshop for Archaeostratigraphic Classification and Terminology. *Geoarchaeology*, 5(3), 292–5.

Lowie, R. H., 1918. Survivals and the Historical Method. *American Journal of Sociology*, 23(4), 529–35.

Lucas, G., 2001a. *Critical Approaches to Fieldwork. Contemporary and Historical Archaeological Practice*, London: Routledge.

Lucas, G., 2001b. Destruction and the Rhetoric of Excavation. *Norwegian Archaeological Review*, 34(1), 35–46.

Lucas, G., 2004. Modern Disturbances: On the Ambiguities of Archaeology. *Modernism/Modernity*, 11(1), 109–20.

Lucas, G., 2005. *The Archaeology of Time*, London: Routledge.

Lucas, G., 2007a. The Unbearable Lightness of Prehistory: Archaeological Reflections on Material Culture and Time. *Journal of Iberian Archaeology*, 9–10, 25–37.

Lucas, G., 2007b. Visions of Archaeology. An Interview with Tim Murray. *Archaeological Dialogues*, 14(2), 155–77.

Lucas, G., 2008. Time and the Archaeological Event. *Cambridge Archaeological Journal*, 18(1), 59–65.

Lucas, G., 2010a. Fieldwork and Collecting, in *Oxford Handbook of Material Culture Studies*, ed. D. Hicks & M. C. Beaudry, Oxford: Oxford University Press, 227–43.

Lucas, G., 2010b. Time and the Archaeological Archive. *Rethinking History*, 14(3), 343–59.

Lucas, G., 2010c. Triangulating Absence: Exploring the Fault-Lines between Archaeology and Anthropology, in *Archaeology and Anthropology. Understanding Similarity, Exploring Difference*, ed. D. Garrow & T. Yarrow, Oxford: Oxbow Books, 28–39.

Lukes, S., 2006. Searle and His Critics. *Anthropological Theory*, 6(1), 5–11.

Lyell, C., 1833. *Principles of Geology* (vol. 3). London: John Murray.

Lyman, R. L., 1994. *Vertebrate Taphonomy*, Cambridge: Cambridge University Press.

Lyman, R. L., & M. J. O'Brien, 2004. Nomothetic Science and Idiographic History in Twentieth Century Americanist Anthropology. *Journal of the History of the Behavioural Sciences*, 40(1), 77–96.

Lyman, R. L., & M. J. O'Brien, 2006. *Measuring Time with Artifacts. A History of Methods in American Archaeology*, Lincoln: University of Nebraska Press.

Lynch, M., 1985. *Art and Artifact in Laboratory Science. A Study of Shop Work and Shop Talk in a Research Laboratory*, London: Routledge and Kegan Paul.

Lynch, M., & S. Woolgar, 1990. Introduction: Sociological Orientations to Representational Practice in Science, in *Representation in Scientific Practice*, ed. M. Lynch & S. Woolgar, Cambridge: Massachusetts Institute of Technology Press, 1–17.

Lynch, M., & S. Woolgar (eds.), 1990. *Representation in Scientific Practice*, Cambridge: Massachusetts Institute of Technology Press.

Mackay, R., 2007. Editorial Introduction. *Collapse*, 2, 3–13.

MacWhite, E., 1956. On the Interpretation of Archaeological Evidence in Historical and Sociological Terms. *American Anthropologist*, 58(1), 3–25.

Mahoney, J., 2000. Path Dependence in Historical Sociology. *Theory and Society*, 29, 507–48.

Maitland, F. W., 1897. *Domesday Book and Beyond. Three Essays in the Early History of England*, Cambridge: Cambridge University Press.

Malina, J., & Z. Vašiček, 1990. *Archaeology Yesterday and Today. The Development of Archaeology in the Sciences and Humanities*, Cambridge: Cambridge University Press.

Malmer, M. P., 1976. Comments on Relative Chronology. *Norwegian Archaeological Review*, 9(2), 97–104.

Malmer, M. P., 1984. Arkeologisk positivism. *Fornvännen*, 79, 260–8.

Marchand, S. L., 1996. *Down from Olympus. Archaeology and Philhellenism in Germany, 1750–1970*, Princeton, NJ: Princeton University Press.

Marx, K., 1975. Economic and Philosophical Manuscripts, in *Early Writings*, ed. Q. Hoare, Harmondsworth: Penguin, 279–400.

Marx, K., 1976. *Capital* (vol. 1), Harmondsworth: Penguin.

Mason, O. T., 1902. *The Origins of Invention. A Study of Industry among Primitive Peoples*, London: W. Scott.

Mathieu, J. R. (ed.), 2002. *Experimental Archaeology, Replicating Past Objects, Behaviors and Processes*, Oxford: British Archaeological Reports International Series 1035.

Matthews, W., C. French, T. Lawrence, D. Cutter, & M. Jones, 1997. Microstratigraphic Traces of Site Formation Processes and Human Activities. *World Archaeology*, 29, 281–308.

Mauss, M., 1973. Techniques of the Body. *Economy and Society*, 2, 70–88.

Maxwell, G., 1962. The Ontological Status of Theoretical Entities, in *Minnesota Studies in the Philosophy of Science* (vol. 3), ed. H. Feigl & G. Maxwell, Minneapolis: University of Minnesota Press, 3–27.

Mayo, B., 1961. Objects, Events and Complementarity. *The Philosophical Review*, 70(3): 340–61.

McBrearty, S., & A. Brooks, 2000. The Revolution That Wasn't: A New Interpretation of the Origin of Modern Human Behavior. *Journal of Human Evolution*, 39, 453–563.

McGann, J. J., 1983. *A Critique of Modern Textual Criticism*, Chicago: University of Chicago Press.

McIntosh, R. J., 1974. Archaeology and Mud Wall Decay in a West African Village. *World Archaeology*, 6(2), 154–71.

Meskell, L., 2004. *Object Worlds in Ancient Egypt. Material Biographies Past and Present*, Oxford: Berg.

Meskell, L. (ed.), 2005. *Archaeologies of Materiality*, Oxford: Blackwell.

Micale, M. G., & D. Nadali, 2008. 'Layer by Layer . . . ' of Digging and Drawing: The Genealogy of an Idea, in *Proceedings of the 51st Rencontre Assyriologique Internationale, Held at the Oriental Institute of the University of Chicago, July 18–22, 2005*, ed. R. D. Biggs, J. Myers, & M. T. Roth, Chicago: Oriental Institute of the University of Chicago, 405–14.

Miller, D., 1987. *Material Culture and Mass Consumption*, Oxford: Blackwell.

Miller, D. (ed.), 1998. *Material Cultures. Why Some Things Matter*, London: University College of London Press.

Miller, D. (ed.), 2005. *Materiality*, Durham, NC: Duke University Press.

Miller, D., 2007. Stone Age or Plastic Age? Response to Ingold 'Materials against Materiality'. *Archaeological Dialogues*, 14(1), 23–7.

Miller, D., & C. Tilley, 1996. Editorial. *Journal of Material Culture*, 1, 5–14.

Mills, B. J., 1989. Integrating functional analyses of vessels and sherds through models of ceramic assemblage formation. *World Archaeology* 21(1): 133–47.

Mills, B. J., & W. H. Walker (eds.), 2008. *Memory Work. Archaeologies of Material Practices*, Santa Fe, NM: School for Advanced Research Press.

Mills, C. W., 1970. *The Sociological Imagination*, Harmondsworth: Penguin.

Moberg, C.-A., 1981. Similar Finds? – Similar Interpretations?, in *Similar Finds? Similar Interpretations?*, ed. C.-A. Moberg, Gothenburg: University of Gothenburg, 1–17.

Momigliano, A., 1950. Ancient History and the Antiquarian. *Journal of the Warburg and Courtauld Institutes*, 13(3–4), 285–315.

Montelius, O., 1903. *Die älteren Kulturperioden im Orient und in Europa, I. Die Methode*, Stockholm: Selbstverlag.

Moore, J. A., & A. S. Keene (eds.), 1983. *Archaeological Hammers and Theories*, New York: Academic Press.

Moreland, J., 2001. *Archaeology and Text*, London: Duckworth.

Morgan, C. L., 2009. (Re)building Çatalhöyük: Changing Virtual Reality in Archaeology. *Archaeologies*, 5(3), 468–87.

Moser, S., 2007. On Disciplinary Culture: Archaeology as Fieldwork and Its Gendered Associations. *Journal of Archaeological Method and Theory*, 14: 235–63.

Mueller, J. (ed.), 1975. *Sampling in Archaeology*, Tucson: University of Arizona.

Müller, S.,1888–1895. *Ordning af Danmarks Oldsager*, Copenhagen: C. A. Reitzel.

Munro, R., 1890. *The Lake Dwellings of Europe*, London: Cassell and Co.

Munro, R., 1905. *Archaeology and False Antiquities*, London: Methuen and Co.

Murray, T., 1997. Dynamic Modeling and the New Social Theory of the Mid- to Long-Term, in *Time, Process and Structured Transformation in Archaeology*, ed. S. E. v. d. Leeuw & J. McGlade, London: Routledge, 449–63.

Murray, T., 1999. A Return to the 'Pompeii Premise', in *Time and Archaeology*, ed. T. Murray, London: Routledge, 8–27.

Murray, T., 2008. Paradigms and Metaphysics, or, 'Is This the End of Archaeology as We Know It?' in *Time and Archaeology. Time Perspectivism Revisited*, ed. S. Holdaway & L. Wandsnider, Salt Lake City: University of Utah Press, 170–80.

Myhre, B., 1991. Theory in Scandinavian Archaeology since 1960: A View from Norway, in *Archaeological Theory in Europe. The Last Three Decades*, ed. I. Hodder, London: Routledge, 161–86.

Naji, M., & L. Douny, 2009. Editorial. *Journal of Material Culture*, 14(4), 411–32.

Neustupný, E., 1993. *Archaeological Method*, Cambridge: Cambridge University Press.

Newton, C., 1851. On the Study of Archaeology. *Archaeological Journal*, 8, 1–26.

Nietzsche, F., 1957. *The Use and Abuse of History*, Indianapolis: Bobbs-Merrill Co.

Nora, P., 1989. Between Memory and History: *Les lieux de mémoire*. *Representations*, 26, 7–24.

Normark, N., 2010. Involutions of Materiality. Operationalizing a Neo-Materialist Perspective through the Causeways at Ichmul and Yo'okop. *Journal of Archaeological Method and Theory*, 17, 132–73.

O'Connor, A., 2007. *Finding Time for the Old Stone Age. A History of Palaeolithic Archaeology and Quaternary Geology in Britain, 1860–1960*, Oxford: Oxford University Press.

Olivier, L., 1999. The Hochdorf 'Princely' Grave and the Question of the Nature of Archaeological Funerary Assemblages, in *Time and Archaeology*, ed. T. Murray, London: Routledge, 109–38.

Olivier, L., 2001. Duration, Memory and the Nature of the Archaeological Record, in *It's about Time. The Concept of Time in Archaeology*, ed. H. Karlsson, Gothenburg, Sweden: Bricoleur Press, 61–70.

Olivier, L., 2008. *Le sombre abîme du temps. Mémoire et archéologie*, Paris: Seuil.

Olsen, B., 2003. Material Culture after Text: Remembering Things. *Norwegian Archaeological Review*, 36(2), 87–104.

Olsen, B., 2006. Scenes from a Troubled Engagement. Post-Structuralism and Material Culture Studies, in *Handbook of Material Culture*, ed. C. Tilley, W. Keane, S. Kuchler, M. Rowlands, & P. Spyer, London: Sage, 85–103.

Olsen, B., 2007. Keeping Things at Arm's Length: A Genealogy of Asymmetry. *World Archaeology*, 39(4), 579–88.

Olsen, B., 2010. *In Defense of Things. Archaeology and the Ontology of Objects*, Walnut Creek, CA: AltaMira Press.

Olsen, O., 1980. Rabies Archaeologorum. *Antiquity*, 54, 15–9.

Ortman, S. G., 2000. Conceptual Metaphor in the Archaeological Record: Methods and an Example from the American Southwest. *American Antiquity*, 65(4), 613–45.

Orton, C., 2000. *Sampling in Archaeology*, Cambridge: Cambridge University Press.

Outram, A. (ed.), 2008. *Experimental Archaeology. World Archaeology* 40(1).

Pálsson, G., 1996. Human-Environmental Relations: Orientalism, Paternalism and Communalism, in *Nature and Society. Anthropological Perspectives*, ed. P. Descola & G. Pálsson, London: Routledge, 63–81.

Papaconstantinou, D., 2006. Archaeological Context as a Unifying Process: An Introduction, in *Deconstructing Context. A Critical Approach to Archaeological Practice*, ed. D. Papaconstantinou, Oxford: Oxbow Books, 1–21.

Parslow, C., 1995. *Rediscovering Antiquity. Karl Weber and the Excavation of Herculaneum, Pompeii, and Stabiae*, Cambridge: Cambridge University Press.

Passmore, J., 1987. Narratives and Events. *History and Theory*, 26(4), 68–74.

Patrik, L., 1985. Is There an Archaeological Record? *Advances in Archaeological Method and Theory*, 8, 27–62.

Patrik, L., 1986. The Aesthetic Experience of Ruins. *Husserl Studies*, 3, 31–55.

Pauketat, T., & S. Alt, 2005. Agency in a Postmold? Physicality and the Archaeology of Culture-Making. *Journal of Archaeological Method and Theory*, 12, 213–36.

Pearson, M., & M. Shanks, 2001. *Theatre/Archaeology*, London: Routledge.

Perry, S., 2009. Fractured Media: Challenging the Dimensions of Archaeology's Typical Visual Modes of Engagement. *Archaeologies*, 5(3), 389–415.

Petrie, F., 1904. *Methods and Aims in Archaeology*, London: Macmillan and Co.

Petrie, F., 1906. Archaeological Evidence, in *Lectures on the Methods of Science*, ed. T. B. Strong, Oxford: Clarendon Press, 218–30.

Pettigrew, T. J., 1850. On the Study of Archaeology, and the Objects of the British Archaeological Association. *Journal of the British Archaeological Association*, 6, 163–77.

Phillips, P., J. Ford, & J. B. Griffin, 1951. *Archaeological Survey in the Lower Mississippi Alluvial Valley 1940–1947*, Cambridge, MA: Peabody Museum.

Phillips, P., & G. Willey, 1953. Method and Theory in American Archaeology: An Operational Basis for Culture-Historical Integration. *American Anthropologist*, 55(5), 615–33.

Pickles, J., 2003. *A History of Spaces. Cartographic Reason, Mapping and the Geo-Coded World*, London: Routledge.

Pictet, A., 1859–63. *Les origines de Indo-européennes ou les Aryas primitif. Essai de paléontologie linguistique*, Paris: J. Cherbuliez.

Piggott, S., 1966. *Approach to Archaeology*, Harmondsworth: Penguin.

Pinch, T., 1985. Towards an Analysis of Scientific Observation: The Externality and Evidential Significance of Observational Reports in Physics. *Social Studies of Science*, 15(1), 3–36.

Pitt Rivers, A. H. L. F., 1887. *Excavations in Cranbourne Chase*, London: Privately Printed.

Pitt Rivers, A. H. L. F., 1906. *The Evolution of Culture and Other Essays*, Oxford: Clarendon Press.

Politis, G., 2001. On Archaeological Praxis, Gender Bias and Indigenous Peoples of South America. *Journal of Social Archaeology*, 1(1), 90–107.

Pollard, J., 2001. The Aesthetics of Depositional Practice. *World Archaeology*, 33, 315–33.

Pollard, J., 2008. Deposition and Material Agency in the Early Neolithic of Southern Britain, in *Memory Work. Archaeologies of Material Practices*, ed. B. J. Mills & W. H. Walker, Santa Fe, NM: School for Advanced Research Press, 41–60.

Porpora, D. V., 1989. Four Concepts of Social Structure. *Journal for the Theory of Social Behaviour*, 19(2), 195–211.

Preucel, R., 2006. *Archaeological Semiotics*, Oxford: Blackwell.

Preucel, R., & A. Bauer, 2001. Archaeological Pragmatics. *Norwegian Archaeological Review*, 34(2), 85–96.

Price, B. J., 1982. Cultural Materialism: A Theoretical Review. *American Antiquity*, 47(4), 709–41.

Pyddoke, E., 1961. *Stratification for the Archaeologist*, London: Phoenix House.

Quine, W. V. O., 1960. *Word and Object*, Cambridge: Massachusetts Institute of Technology Press.

Quine, W. V. O., 1970. *Philosophy of Logic*, Englewood Cliffs, NJ: Prentice-Hall.

Quinton, A., 1979. Objects and Events. *Mind*, 88, 197–214.

Randall, H. J., 1934. History in the Open Air. *Antiquity*, 8, 5–23.

Randall-MacIver, D., 1933. Archaeology as a Science. *Antiquity*, 7, 5–20.

Rapp, G., 1987. Geoarchaeology. *Annual Review of Earth Planet Science*, 15, 97–113.

Rapp, G., R. Bullard, & A. A. Albritton, 1970. Geoarchaeology? *Geologist: Newsletter of the Geological Society of America*, 9(1): 1.

Rapp, G., & C. Hill, 2006. *Geoarchaeology. The Earth Science Approach to Archaeological Interpretation*, New Haven, CT: Yale University Press.

Rathje, W., & C. Murphy, 2001. *Rubbish! The Archaeology of Garbage*, Tucson: University of Arizona Press.

Reid, J. J., M. Schiffer, & W. Rathje, 1975. Behavioural Archaeology: Four Strategies. *American Anthropologist*, 77, 864–9.

Renfrew, C., 1987. *Archaeology and Language. The Puzzle of Indo-European Origins*, Harmondsworth: Penguin.

Renfrew, C., 2001. Symbol before Concept: Material Engagement and the Early Development of Society, in *Archaeological Theory Today*, ed. I. Hodder, Oxford: Polity, 122–40.

Renfrew, C., 2003. *Figuring It Out*, London: Thames and Hudson.

Renfrew, C., & P. Bahn, 1996. *Archaeology. Theories, Methods and Practice*, London: Thames and Hudson.

Renfrew, C., & I. Morley (eds.), 2009. *Becoming Human. Innovation in Prehistoric Material and Spiritual Culture*, Cambridge: Cambridge University Press.

Reynolds, N., & J. Barber, 1984. Analytical Excavation. *Antiquity*, 58, 95–102.

Richards, C., 1995. Knowing the Past, in *Interpreting Archaeology. Finding Meaning in the Past*, ed. I. Hodder, M. Shanks, A. Alexandri, V. Buchli, J. Carman, J. Last, & G. lucas, London: Routledge, 216–19.

Richards, C., & J. Thomas, 1984. Ritual Activity and Structured Deposition in Later Neolithic Wessex, in *Neolithic Studies. A Review of Current Research*, ed. R. Bradley & J. Gardiner, Oxford, 189–218.

Richards, J., 2002. Digital Preservation and Access. *European Journal of Archaeology*, 5(3), 343–67.

Richards, J., 2008. Managing Digital Preservation and Access: The Archaeology Data Service, in *Managing Archaeological Resources. Global Context, National Programs, Local Actions*, ed. F. P. McManamon, A. Stout, & J. A. Barnes, Walnut Creek, CA: Left Coast Press, 173–94.

Ricoeur, P., 2004. *Memory, History, Forgetting*, Chicago: University of Chicago Press.

Rieth, A., 1967. *Archaeological Fakes*, New York: Praeger Publishers.

Rivers, W. H. R., 1913. Survival in Sociology. *Sociological Review*, 6, 293–305.

Roskams, S., 2001. *Excavation*, Cambridge: Cambridge University Press.

Rossignol, J., & L. Wandsnider (eds.), 1992. *Space, Time and Archaeological Landscapes*, New York: Plenum Press.

Rouse, I., 1939. *Prehistory in Haiti. A Study in Method*, New Haven, CT: Yale University Press.

Rouse, I., 1960. The Classification of Artifacts in Archaeology. *American Antiquity*, 25, 313–23.

Rowe, J. H., 1962. Worsaae's Law and the Use of Grave Lots for Archaeological Dating. *American Antiquity*, 28(2), 129–37.

Ryzewski, K., 2009. Seven Interventions with the Flatlands: Archaeology and Its Modes of Engagement. Contributions from the WAC-6 Session, 'Experience, Modes of Engagement, Archaeology'. *Archaeologies*, 5(3), 361–88.

Schiffer, M. B., 1972. Archaeological Context and Systemic Context. *American Antiquity*, 37(2), 156–65.

Schiffer, M. B., 1975. Archaeology as Behavioural Science. *American Anthropologist*, 77, 836–48.

Schiffer, M. B., 1976. *Behavioural Archaeology*, New York: Academic Press.

Schiffer, M. B., 1983. Toward the Identification of Formation Processes. *American Antiquity*, 48(4), 675–706.

Schiffer, M. B., 1985. Is There a 'Pompeii Premise' in Archaeology? *Journal of Anthropological Research*, 41, 18–41.

Schiffer, M. B., 1987. *Formation Processes of the Archaeological Record*, Salt Lake City: University of Utah Press.

Schiffer, M. B., 1988. The Structure of Archaeological Theory. *American Antiquity*, 53(3), 461–85.

Schiffer, M. B., & A. Miller, 1999. *The Material Life of Human Beings. Artifacts, Behaviour, and Communication*, London: Routledge.

Schlanger, S. H., 1992. Recognizing Persistent Places in Anasazi Settlement Systems, in *Space, Time, and Archaeological Landscapes*, ed. J. Rossignol & L. Wandsnider, New York: Plenum, 91–112.

Schliemann, H., 1880. *Ilios. The City and Country of the Trojans*, London: John Murray.

Schmidt, D., 2002. Refuse Archaeology: Virchow – Schliemann – Freud. *Perspectives on Science*, 9(2), 210–32.

Schnapp, A., 1996. *The Discovery of the Past*, London: British Museum Press.

Schnapp, A., 2004. Eduard Gerhard: Founder of Classical Archaeology? *Modernism/Modernity*, 11(1), 169–71.

Searle, J., 1995. *The Construction of Social Reality*, Harmondsworth: Penguin.

Searle, J., 2006. Social Ontology: Some Basic Principles. *Anthropological Theory*, 6(1), 12–29.

Shanks, M., 1990. Conclusion – Reading the Signs: Responses to Archaeology after Structuralism, in *Archaeology after Structuralism. Post-structuralism and the Practice of Archaeology*, ed. I. Bapty & T. Yates, London: Routledge, 294–310.

Shanks, M., 1992. *Experiencing the Past. On the Character of Archaeology*, London: Routledge.

Shanks, M., 1998. The Life of an Artifact. *Fennoscandia Archaeologia*, 15, 15–42.

Shanks, M., 2004. Three Rooms: Archaeology and Performance. *Journal of Social Archaeology*, 4(2), 147–80.

Shanks, M., 2007. Symmetrical Archaeology. *World Archaeology*, 39(4), 589–96.

Shanks, M., 2009. Engagement: Archaeological Design and Engineering. *Archaeologies*, 5(3), 546–56.

Shanks, M., & R. McGuire, 1996. The Craft of Archaeology. *American Antiquity*, 61, 75–88.

Shanks, M., & C. Tilley, 1987. *Social Theory and Archaeology*, Oxford: Polity.

Shanks, M., & T. Webmoor, 2010. A Political Economy of Visual Media in Archaeology, in *Re-presenting the Past. Archaeology through Image and Text*, ed. S. Bonde & S. Houston, Providence, RI: Brown University Press, 87–110.

Shapin, S., 1982. History of Science and Its Sociological Reconstructions. *History of Science*, 20, 157–211.

Shapin, S., 1984. Pump and Circumstance: Boyle's Literary Technology. *Social Studies of Science*, 14(4), 481–520.

Shapin, S., 1988. The House of Experiment in Seventeenth-Century England. *Isis*, 79(3), 373–404.

Shapin, S., 1995. Here and Everywhere: Sociology of Scientific Knowledge. *Annual Review of Sociology*, 21, 289–321.

Shapin, S., & S. Schaffer, 1985. *Leviathan and the Air Pump. Hobbes, Boyle and the Experimental Life*, Princeton, NJ: Princeton University Press.

Shennan, S., 1993. After Social Evolution: A New Archaeological Agenda, in *Archaeological Theory. Who Sets the Agenda?*, ed. N. Yoffee & A. Sherratt, Cambridge: Cambridge University Press, 53–9.

Shipley, T. F., 2008. An Invitation to an Event, in *Understanding Events. From Perception to Action*, ed. T. F. Shipley & J. M. Zacks, Oxford: Oxford University Press, 3–30.

Shott, M. J., 1989. On Tool-Class Use Lives and the Formation of Archaeological Assemblages. *American Antiquity*, 54(1), 9–30.

Shott, M. J., 1996a. Mortal Pots: On Use Life and Vessel Size in the Formation of Ceramic Assemblages. *American Antiquity*, 61(3), 463–82.

Shott, M. J., 1996b. An Exegesis of the Curation Concept. *Journal of Anthropological Research*, 52(3), 259–80.

Shott, M. J., 1998. Status and Role of Formation Theory in Contemporary Archaeological Practice. *Journal of Archaeological Research*, 6(4), 299–329.

Shott, M. J., 2005. Two Cultures: Thought and Practice in British and North American Archaeology. *World Archaeology*, 37(1), 1–10.

Shott, M. J., 2008. Lower Palaeolithic Industries, Time and the Meaning of Assemblage Variation, in *Time and Archaeology. Time Perspectivism Revisited*, ed. S. Holdaway & L. Wandsnider, Salt Lake City: University of Utah Press, 46–60.

Skibo, J., & M. Schiffer, 2008. *People and Things. A Behavioural Approach to Material Culture*, New York: Springer.

Skibo, J., W. H. Walker, & A. E. Nielsen (eds.), 1995. *Expanding Archaeology*, Salt Lake City: University of Utah Press.

Sklenář, K., 1983. *Archaeology in Central Europe. The First 500 Years*, Leicester: Leicester University Press.

Smith, H., 1911. Archaeological Evidence as Determined by Method and Selection. *American Anthropologist*, 13(3), 445–8.

Smith, M., 1955. The Limitations of Inference in Archaeology. *Archaeological Newsletter*, 6(1), 3–7.

Sollas, W. J., 1911. *Ancient Hunters and Their Modern Representatives*, London: Macmillan and Co.

Spaulding, A. C., 1953. Statistical Techniques for the Discovery of Artifact Types. *American Antiquity*, 18, 305–13.

Sperber, D., 1992. Culture and Matter, in *Representations in Archaeology*, ed. J.-C. Gardin & C. Peebles, Bloomington: Indiana University Press, 56–65.

Staski, E., & L. D. Sutro (eds.), 1991. *The Ethnoarchaeology of Refuse Disposal*, Tucson: Arizona State University.

Stein, J. K., 2000. Stratigraphy and Archaeological Dating, in *It's about Time. A History of Archaeological Dating in North America*, ed. S. Nash, Salt Lake City: University of Utah Press, 14–40.

Stein, J. K., 2001. Archaeological Sediments in Cultural Environments, in *Sediments in Archaeological Context*, ed. J. K. Stein & W. R. Farrand, Salt Lake City: University of Utah Press, 1–28.

Steno, N., 1962. The Prodromus of Nicolaus Steno's Dissertation Concerning a Solid Body Enclosed by Process of Nature within a Solid, in *Man's Discovery of His Past. Literary Landmarks in Archaeology*, ed. R. F. Heizer, Englewood Cliffs, NJ: Prentice-Hall, 5–10.

Stern, N., 1993. The Structure of the Lower Pleistocene Archaeological Record. *Current Anthropology*, 34(3), 201–25.

Stern, N., 1994. The Implications of Time-Averaging for Reconstructing the Land-Use Patterns of Early Tool-Using Hominids. *Journal of Human Evolution*, 27, 89–105.

Stern, N., 2008. Time Averaging and the Structure of Late Pleistocene Archaeological Deposits in Southwest Tasmania, in *Time and Archaeology. Time Perspectivism Revisited*, ed. S. Holdaway & L. Wandsnider, Salt Lake City: University of Utah Press, 134–48.

Steward, J., & F. Setzler, 1938. Function and Configuration in Archaeology. *American Antiquity*, 4(1), 4–10.

Stocking, G. W., 1987. *Victorian Anthropology*, New York: Free Press.

Stone, P., & P. Planel (eds.), 1999. *The Constructed Past. Experimental Archaeology, Education and the Public*, London: Routledge.

Sullivan, A. P., 1978. Inference and Evidence in Archaeology: A Discussion of the Conceptual Problems. *Advances in Archaeological Method and Theory*, 1, 183–222.

Swartz, B. K., 1967. A Logical Sequence of Archaeological Objectives. *American Antiquity*, 32(4), 487–97.

Tainter, J. A., 2004. Persistent Dilemmas in American Cultural Resource Management, in *A Companion to Archaeology*, ed. J. Bintliff, Oxford: Blackwell, 435–53.

Tallgren, A. M., 1937. The Method of Prehistoric Archaeology. *Antiquity*, 11, 152–61.

Tarde, G., 1899. *Social Laws. An Outline of Sociology*, New York: Macmillan.

Tarde, G., 1903. *The Laws of Imitation*, New York: Henry Holt and Company.

Taussig, M., 1993. *Mimesis and Alterity. A Particular History of the Senses*, London: Routledge.

Taylor, W., 1983. *A Study of Archaeology*, Carbondale: Southern Illinois University Press.

Thomas, J., 1991. *Rethinking the Neolithic*, Cambridge: Cambridge University Press.

Thomas, J., 1996. *Time, Culture and Identity. An Interpretive Archaeology*, London: Routledge.

Thomas, J., 2000. Reconfiguring the Social, Reconfiguring the Material, in *Social Theory in Archaeology*, ed. M. Schiffer, Salt Lake City: University of Utah Press, 143–55.

Thomas, J., 2004. *Archaeology and Modernity*, London: Routledge.

Thomas, J., 2005a. Comments VIII: Between 'Material Qualities' and 'Materiality'. *Archaeometry*, 47(1), 198–201.

Thomas, J., 2005b. Materiality and the Social, in *Global Archaeological Theory. Contextual Voices and Contemporary Thoughts*, ed. P. P. Funari, A. Zarankin, & E. Stovel, New York: Kluwer Academic and Plenum Publishers, 11–18.

Thomas, J., 2006. Phenomenology and Material Culture, in *Handbook of Material Culture*, ed. C. Tilley, W. Keane, S. Kuchler, M. Rowlands, & P. Spyer, London: Sage, 43–59.

Thomas, J., 2007. The Trouble with Material Culture. *Journal of Iberian Archaeology*, 9–10, 11–23.

Thompson, R., 1956. The Subjective Element in Archaeological Inference. *Southwestern Journal of Anthropology*, 12, 327–32.

Thomson, W., 1867. Inaugural Address to the Annual Meeting of the Royal Archaeological Institute. *Archaeological Journal*, 24, 83–91.

Tilley, C., 1989. Excavation as Theatre. *Antiquity*, 63, 275–80.

Tilley, C. (ed.), 1990. *Reading Material Culture*, Oxford: Blackwell.

Tilley, C., 1991. *Material Culture and Text. The Art of Ambiguity*, London: Routledge.

Tilley, C. (ed.), 1993. *Interpretive Archaeology*, Oxford: Berg.

Tilley, C., 1994. *The Phenomenology of Landscape*, Oxford: Berg.

Tilley, C., 1999. *Metaphor and Material Culture*, Oxford: Blackwell.

Tilley, C., 2004. *The Materiality of Stone. Explorations in Landscape Phenomenology*, Oxford: Berg.

Tilley, C., 2006. Objectification, in *The Handbook of Material Culture*, ed. C. Tilley, W. Keane, S. Kuchler, M. Rowlands, & P. Spyer, London: Sage, 60–73.

Tilley, C., 2007. Materiality in Materials. Response to Ingold 'Materials against Materiality'. *Archaeological Dialogues*, 14(1), 16–20.

Toews, D., 2003. The New Tarde: Sociology after the End of the Social. *Theory, Culture and Society*, 20(5), 81–98.

Tomášková, S., 2006. On Being Heard. Theory as an Archaeological Practice. *Archaeological Dialogues*, 13(2), 163–87.

Trentmann, F., 2009. Materiality in the Future of History: Things, Practices, and Politics. *Journal of British Studies*, 48, 283–307.

Trigger, B., 1978a. Aims in Prehistoric Archaeology, in *Time and Traditions. Essays in Archaeological Interpretation*, ed. B. Trigger, Edinburgh: University of Edinburgh Press, 19–36.

Trigger, B., 1978b. The Development of the Archaeological Culture in Europe and America, in *Time and Traditions. Essays in Archaeological Interpretation*, ed. B. Trigger, Edinburgh: University of Edinburgh Press, 75–95.

Trigger, B., 1994. Childe's Relevance to the 1990s, in *The Archaeology of V. Gordon Childe*, ed. D. Harris, Melbourne: Melbourne University Press, 9–34.

Trigger, B., 2006. *A History of Archaeological Thought*, Cambridge: Cambridge University Press.

Tringham, R., 1991. Households with Faces: The Challenge of Gender in Prehistoric Architectural Remains, in *Engendering Archaeology. Women and Prehistory*, ed. J. Gero & M. W. Conkey, Oxford: Blackwell, 93–131.

Trouillot, M.-R., 1995. *Silencing the Past. Power and the Production of History*, Boston: Beacon.

Tschauner, H., 1996. Middle-Range Theory, Behavioural Archaeology and Post-Empiricist Philosophy of Science in Archaeology. *Journal of Archaeological Method and Theory*, 3, 1–30.

Turner, J., 2000. *The Extended Organism. The Physiology of Animal-Built Structures*, Cambridge, MA: Harvard University Press.

Tylor, E., 1865. *Researches into the Early History of Mankind and the Development of Civilization*, London: John Murray.

Tylor, E., 1913. *Primitive Culture*, London: John Murray.

van Dyke, R., & S. Alcock (eds.), 2003. *Archaeologies of Memory*, Oxford: Blackwell.

van Fraassen, B., 1980. *The Scientific Image*, Oxford: Clarendon Press.

van Helden, A., & T. L. Hankins (eds.), 1994. *Instruments. Osiris*, 9, 9.

van Riper, A. B., 1993. *Men among the Mammoths. Victorian Science and the Discovery of Human Prehistory*, Chicago: Chicago University Press.

Vargas, E. V., B. Latour, B. Karsenti, F. Aït-Touati, & L. Salmon, 2008. The Debate between Tarde and Durkheim. *Environment and Planning D: Society and Space*, 26, 761–77.

Varien, M. D., & B. J. Mills, 1997. Accumulations Research: Problems and Prospects for Estimating Site Occupation Span. *Journal of Archaeological Method and Theory*, 4(2), 141–91.

Varien, M. D., & S. G. Ortman, 2005. Accumulations Research in the Southwest United States: Middle-Range Theory for Big-Picture Problems. *World Archaeology*, 37(1), 132–55.

Varien, M. D., & J. B. Potter, 1997. Unpacking the Discard Equation: Simulating the Accumulation of Artifacts in the Archaeological Record. *American Antiquity*, 62(2), 194–213.

Verbeek, P.-P., 2006. Materializing Morality: Design Ethics and Technological Mediation. *Science, Technology and Human Values*, 31(3), 361–80.

Vismann, C., 2001. The Love of Ruins. *Perspectives on Science*, 9(2), 196–209.

Walker, K. R., & R. K. Bambach, 1971. The Significance of Fossil Assemblages from Fine-Grained Sediments: Time-Average Communities. *Geological Society of America Abstracts with Programs*, 3, 783–4.

Walker, W. H., 1995. Ceremonial Trash?, in *Expanding Archaeology*, ed. J. Skibo, W. H. Walker, & A. E. Nielsen, Salt Lake City: University of Utah Press, 67–79.

Walker, W. H., 2002. Stratigraphy and Practical Reason. *American Anthropologist*, 104, 159–77.

Walker, W. H., 2008. Practice and Non-human Social Actors: The Afterlife Histories of Witches and Dogs in the American Southwest, in *Memory Work. Archaeologies of Material Practices*, ed. B. J. Mills & W. H. Walker, Santa Fe, NM: School for Advanced Research Press, 137–58.

Walter, C., 2008. Towards a More 'Scientific' Archaeological Tool. The Accurate Drawing of Greek Vases between the End of the Nineteenth and the First Half of the Twentieth Centuries, in *Archives, Ancestors, Practices. Archaeology in the Light of Its History*, ed. N. Schlanger & J. Nordbladh, New York: Berghahn Books, 179–90.

Wandsnider, L., 1996. Describing and Comparing Archaeological Spatial Structures. *Journal of Archaeological Method and Theory*, 3(4), 319–84.

Warburton, D., 2003. *Archaeological Stratigraphy. A Near Eastern Approach*, Neuchâtel, Switzerland: Recherches et Publications.

Warnier, J.-P., 2001. A Praxeological Approach to Subjectivation in a Material World. *Journal of Material Culture*, 6(1), 5–24.

Warnier, J.-P., 2009. Technology as Efficacious Action on Objects . . . and Subjects. *Journal of Material Culture*, 14(4), 459–70.

Watson, P. J., 1995. Archaeology, Anthropology and the Culture Concept. *American Anthropologist*, 97, 683–94.

Watson, P. J., S. LeBlanc, & C. Redman, 1971. *Explanation in Archaeology. An Explicitly Scientific Approach*, New York: Columbia University Press.

Weber, M., 1978. *Economy and Society. An Outline of Interpretive Sociology*, Berkeley: University of California Press.

Webmoor, T., 2005. Mediational Techniques and Conceptual Frameworks in Archaeology: A Model in 'Mapwork' at Teotihuacán, Mexico. *Journal of Social Archaeology* 5(1): 52–84.

Webmoor, T., 2007. What about 'One More Turn after the Social' in Archaeological Reasoning? Taking Things Seriously. *World Archaeology*, 39(4), 563–78.

Webmoor, T., & C. Witmore, 2008. Things Are Us! A Commentary on Human/Things Relations under the Banner of a 'Social' Archaeology. *Norwegian Archaeological Review*, 41(1), 53–70.

Webster, G., 1963. *Practical Archaeology*, London: A. and C. Black.

Weissman, D., 1999. *A Social Ontology*, New Haven, CT: Yale University Press.

Western, D., 1980. Linking the Ecology of Past and Present Mammal Communities, in *Fossils in the Making*, ed. A. K. Behrensmeyer & A. Hill, Chicago: University of Chicago Press, 72–93.

Wheeler, M., 1927. History by Excavation. *Journal of the Royal Society of Arts*, 75, 812–35.

Wheeler, M., 1954. *Archaeology from the Earth*, Harmondsworth: Penguin Books.

Wheeler, M., 1966. *Alms for Oblivion. An Antiquary's Scrapbook*, London: Weidenfeld and Nicolson.

Whewell, W., 1984. The Philosophy of the Inductive Sciences, in *Selected Writings on the History of Science*, ed. Y. Elkana, Chicago: University of Chicago Press, 121–260.

White, L., 1949. *The Science of Culture. A Study of Man and Civilization*, New York: Grove Press.

White, L., 1954. Review of Kroeber & Kluckhohn's Culture: A Critical Review of Concepts and Definitions. *American Anthropologist*, 56(3), 461–8.

White, L., 1959. *The Evolution of Culture. The Development of Civilization to the Fall of Rome*, New York: McGraw-Hill.

Whitehead, A. N., 1978. *Process and Reality*, New York: Free Press.

Whitehead, A. N., 2004. *The Concept of Nature*, New York: Prometheus Books.

Wiedersheim, R., 1895. *The Structure of Man. An Index to His Past History*, London: Macmillan.

Willems, W. J. H., 1998. Heritage Management in Europe: Trends and Developments. *European Journal of Archaeology*, 1(3), 293–311.

Willey, G., & P. Phillips, 1955. Method and Theory in American Archaeology II: Historical-Developmental Interpretation. *American Anthropologist*, 57(4), 723–819.

Willey, G., & P. Phillips, 1958. *Method and Theory in American Archaeology*, Chicago: University of Chicago Press.

Wilson, M. C., 2004. Editing the Cultural Landscape: A Taphonomic Perspective on the Destruction of Aboriginal Sites on the Northwestern Plains, in *Archaeology on the Edge. New Perspectives from the Northern Plains*, ed. B. Kooyman & J. Kelley, Calgary: University of Calgary Press, 53–78.

Winner, L., 1980. Do Artifacts Have Politics? *Daedalus*, 109, 121–36.

Witmore, C., 2004. On Multiple Fields between the Material World and Media: Two Cases from the Peloponnesus, Greece. *Archaeological Dialogues*, 11(2), 133–64.

Witmore, C., 2006. Vision, Media, Noise and the Percolation of Time: Symmetrical Approaches to the Mediation of the Material World. *Journal of Material Culture*, 11(3), 267–92.

Witmore, C., 2007. Symmetrical Archaeology: Excerpts of a Manifesto. *World Archaeology*, 39(4), 546–62.

Witmore, C., 2009. Prolegomena to Open Pasts: On Archaeological Memory Practices. *Archaeologies*, 5(3), 511–45.

Woolgar, S., & G. Cooper, 1999. Do Artifacts Have Ambivalence? Moses' Bridges, Winner's Bridges and Other Urban Legends in S&TS. *Social Studies of Science*, 29(3), 433–49.

Worsaae, J. J., 1849. *The Primeval Antiquities of Denmark*, London: John Henry Parker.

Wright, T., 1861. *The Celt, the Roman and the Saxon. A History of the Early Inhabitants of Britain*, London: Arthur Hall, Virtue and Co.

Wright, T., 1866. On the Progress and Present Condition of Archaeological Science. *Journal of the British Archaeological Association*, 22, 64–84.

Wylie, A., 1985. The Reaction against Analogy. *Advances in Archaeological Method and Theory*, 8, 63–111.

Wylie, A., 1986. Arguments for Scientific Realism: The Ascending Spiral. *American Philosophical Quarterly*, 23, 287–97.

Wylie, A., 1989. The Interpretive Dilemma, in *Critical Traditions in Contemporary Archaeology. Essays in the Philosophy, History and Socio-Politics of Archaeology*, ed. V. Pinsky & A. Wylie, Cambridge: Cambridge University Press, 18–27.

Wylie, A., 1992a. The Interplay of Evidential Constraints and Political Interests: Recent Archaeological Research on Gender. *American Antiquity*, 57, 15–34.

Wylie, A., 1992b. 'On Heavily Decomposing Red Herrings': Scientific Method in Archaeology and the Ladening of Evidence with Theory, in *Metaarchaeology. Reflections by Archaeologists and Philosophers*, ed. L. Embree, Boston: Kluwer, 269–88.

Wylie, A., 1996. The Constitution of Archaeological Evidence: Gender Politics and Science, in *The Disunity of Science. Boundaries, Contexts and Power*, ed. P. Galison & D. Stump, Stanford, CA: Stanford University Press, 311–43.

Wylie, A., 2002. *Thinking from Things. Essays in the Philosophy of Archaeology*, Berkeley: University of California Press.

Wylie, A., 2008. Mapping Ignorance in Archaeology: The Advantages of Historical Hindsight, in *Agnotology. The Making and Unmaking of Ignorance*, ed. R. Proctor & L. Schiebinger, Stanford, CA: Stanford University Press, 183–208.

Yarrow, T., 2003. Artefactual Persons: The Relational Capacities of Persons and Things in the Practice of Excavation. *Norwegian Archaeological Review*, 36(1), 65–73.

Yarrow, T., 2006. Sites of Knowledge: Different Ways of Knowing an Archaeological Excavation, in *Ethnographies of Archaeological Practice*, ed. M. Edgeworth, Lanham, MD: AltaMira Press, 20–32.

Yarrow, T., 2008. In Context: Meaning, Materiality and Agency in the Process of Archaeological Recording, in *Material Agency. Towards a Nonanthropocentric Approach*, ed. C. Knappett & L. Malafouris, New York: Springer, 21–37.

Yates, T., 1990. Archaeology through the Looking-Glass, in *Archaeology after Structuralism*, ed. I. Bapty & T. Yates, London: Routledge, 154–202.

Yengoyan, A. A., 1986. Theory in Anthropology: On the Demise of the Concept of Culture. *Comparative Studies in Society and History*, 28(2), 368–74.

INDEX